BEYOND ENGLISH INC.

D1522816

BEYOND
ENGLISH
INC.

Curricular Reform in a Global Economy

Edited by
David B. Downing,
Claude Mark Hurlbert,
and Paula Mathieu

Foreword by
David Bleich

Boynton/Cook Publishers
HEINEMANN
Portsmouth, NH

Boynton/Cook Publishers, Inc.
A subsidiary of Reed Elsevier Inc.
361 Hanover Street
Portsmouth, NH 03801–3912
www.boyntoncook.com

Offices and agents throughout the world

The editors and publisher wish to thank those who have generously given permission to reprint borrowed material:

"A Blow is Like an Instrument," by Charles Bernstein, is reprinted by permission of *Daedalus,* Journal of the American Academy of Arts and Sciences, from the issue entitled, "The American Academic Professions," Fall 1997, Vol. 126, No. 4.

An earlier version of "Historical Reflections on Accountability," by Richard Ohmann, was published in the January–February 2000 issue of *Academe,* the magazine of the American Association of University Professors.

Lyrics from "Concrete Jungle" by Bob Marley. Copyright © 1972. Fifty-Six Hope Road Music Ltd. / Odnil Music Ltd. / Blue Mountain Music Ltd. (PRS). All rights controlled by Rykomusic (ASCAP). All rights reserved. Lyrics used by permission.

Library of Congress Cataloging-in-Publication Data
    Beyond English, Inc. : curricular reform in a global economy / edited by David
B. Downing, Claude Mark Hurlbert, Paula Mathieu.
      p.   cm.
    Includes bibliographical references.
    ISBN 0-86709-517-2 (alk. paper)
    1. English philology—Study and teaching (Higher)—United States. 2. Education,
Higher—Economic aspects—United States. I. Downing, David B., 1947–. II. Hurlbert, C.
Mark. III. Mathieu, Paula.

PE68.U5 B49 2002
428′.0071′173—dc21   2001051722

Editor: Jim Strickland
Production: Lynne Reed
Cover design: Darci Mehall
Typesetter: TechBooks
Manufacturing: Steve Bernier

Printed in the United States of America on acid-free paper
06 05 04 03 02 VP 1 2 3 4 5

Contents

Beyond English, Inc.

Business and education,
Business and health, another room,
Warm bodies, cold bodies,
Cradle to tomb.

      *   *   *

On the other hand,
if I build a fire in the buck stove, I can write a poem.
If I make a fire, I can read
Nature in words. Outside:
Snow-
    heavy
           pine boughs,
  tiny/maroon branch tips trying to bud,
    tamarack/blond dog barking and turning in the snowy yard, the wind
        almost still.

Walking this morning I think of my creek,
its khaki bottom glassy today,
habitat of frogs and brook trout,
the white egret with black legs
fishing there in the summer of the drought.

The water snake takes a half hour, half-under rock, to swallow fully its silvery
    lunch.

I love them all.
I believe you love them, too.

I love the boy, twenty months, who was found in Barrio Kennedy in Bogotá:
Distended belly, dirty, afraid, now unafraid and climbing
these northern Appalachian pines like a lineman,
reading line by line,
one branch at a time.
I love the laughing girl with cornrows,
reflected in the classroom window,
who says, shaking her head,
she knows he knows they know, too.

—*Maurice Kilwein Guevara*

Foreword:
It's About Time We Go "Beyond English"

I received this manuscript before 11 September 2001, but I am writing this comment afterward. The manuscript seems different to me now. From one standpoint the "Inc" part seems less of an issue. Relative to the urgency of this moment—the need to respond to a deliberate infiltration of our society by fanatic air-hijackers and biological terrorists—we may wish to suspend our attention, for the moment, to the corporatization of English. But from another standpoint, the "Inc." is more of an issue. I have been studying the history of the university in the West, from its beginnings in the twelfth century. The fact that corporations have acquired overwhelming influence in the conduct of university life is another version of how universities have functioned in society since they were founded: as an institution the university has always been protected by its benefactors. Today, Church and State influences have receded somewhat, but replacing them are the "hegemonic" powers of the present generation—corporations and their increasingly global reach. The "Inc." is more of a problem after 11 September because now our universities are in no position to claim exemption from the hostility that has put the whole society in danger. Like it or not, we who "pursue the truth" following an axiomatic sense of justice and fundamentally benign behaviors are in the same boat as our benefactors, whose behavior, as well described in this book, is harming our own lives, our classrooms, our subject matters, and our ability to teach others to become teachers and scholars.

In trying to take the measure of this problem, my focus is on the term "English." Those who converted the airliners into weapons knew English. Only a small portion of the American society that was eviscerated by the sight of people jumping one hundred stories to save their lives knows Arabic; the rest of us, for whom English is a first language and second nature, were not thinking about learning it. If the terrorists did not know English, they could not have committed this crime. While they were learning English, taking flying lessons, and studying how our airports work, we were debating "what is English." Peter Elbow's volume of that title was published by the Modern Language Association in 1990. It was as representative an event as any in our professional history. As if we did not really know what English was! Public figures and governmental leaders are taking great pains to distinguish the fight against terrorism from vigilante hostility toward Islam. But the difference between us and them is not religious, since speakers of both English and Arabic claim the support of God. The practical difference between us is that we who speak English are not quite aware of how our language is part of what we call, in self-congratulatory (and some say "imperial" [Dunn 9A]) tones, civilization; while many of us consider Arabic to be part of something else, a Third (not even a second) World, mostly uncivilized.

I think one reason we have come to this pass is that we teachers of English have not questioned the term "English." In spite of the sometimes obsessional scale reached by identity politics, we have continued to ignore our "unmarked" linguistic status and fluently claim our subject as English. We do not know why it matters that we use the term "English" instead of "language" or "first language" or "language use" to identify a subject whose scope, interest, influence, and importance is so broad and so consequential as to affect every human action in society. Moreover, we do not consider "English" as the name of our subject matter and discipline to be interchangeable with "language" or "language use." I am surprised by the strenuousness of Peter Elbow's earnest attempt to say what English is. He gives nine "definitions" of the subject and its discipline and urges us to remember that they are all part of the subject, all welcome in the discipline. Yet among those definitions I do not find the thought that English is the language we speak, the creature and instrument of our minds and social lives, the means by which we articulate our ideals, fantasies, laws, and warnings of war, exhortations to show the flag. We are accustomed to thinking that it does not matter what language carries these fundamentals of society to all of us and to those in other societies. The discussions on various e-lists are proliferating. People are speaking more and more. Why isn't this our subject? Why does it remain in "hallway" conversation and not in the curriculum? Why do we stop with the "rhetoric" of advertising instead of noticing how the words we speak daily, the sense of the right and wrong genres of address, the articulation of ambitions, are taken over from the public and private languages we meet, good or bad? Why isn't the sheer overwhelming presence of language in our lives acknowledged in our curricula? Perhaps if we did we would notice how much it matters that it is English *and* that it is language, at once, and that it is urgent to know when to teach English, when to teach the uses of language, and when to teach them as one. Those willing to die to communicate their antagonism have learned English first, before showing us that they are *beyond* language. Because we study English but not language, we could not perceive what these visitors were up to, until they stopped speaking! At the same time, as Andrea Lunsford has recently observed, because parts of our own government declined to speak to one another, we could not share information that could well have averted the catastrophe. If we studied language and not just English, we might understand that language is the basis of all human relations, and when it fails, the relationships fail, society fails.

As a constituency interested in study, teaching, and research as a fundamental path toward human survival and sustenance, we members of the university communities are trying to meet the challenge of both the corporate juggernaut and the wrath of the desperate who have grown up angry. I asked my first-year students if they would like to consider what would have to be the case to lead young men to be willing to die and to kill many benign others in the cause of communicating, of "sending a message." After a silence, one student understood: "They were raised that way." As we now see from journalistic sources, this is the truth. This means, in part, that they *spoke a language that made this action reasonable.* Their language says that in their lives, the limits of language are reached, and "death" is the only communication that will work.

Shouldn't our study of English and language teach us that the languages of some societies are so radically different from ours that catastrophic results are possible? We now sense the need to move beyond English, but not beyond language. "Beyond English" means that we English teachers acknowledge that we are, with other institutions, custodians of the language: English is viewed in the rest of the world, in this generation, as the "language of the most powerful members of the human community." As contributors to this book show, the majority of us are aware that we are, while still English teachers, language teachers and scholars. The name English, when used without understanding its reference to language and language use, may have misguided some people. But it is clear from the discussions in this book, that our subject—English and language—is urgent, not just relevant, to the welfare of our whole population.

When we discuss the changing of curriculum, some may think we are wondering about how to rearrange our courses, which certainly does happen in the many "curriculum committee" meetings whose charge is to change the curriculum. The term "curriculum" outside professional circles means "subject matter." The contributions to this book attempt to change the scope, reference, teaching, and scholarship of our subject matter, whose name, I believe, would do well to add to English the terms "language" or "language use"; that is what these essays imply to me. In this volume, the term "beyond" is addressed to those who focus on the "traditional" reference of English as meaning "grammar, writing, and literature." These essays alert us to the political and economic status of our subject; they urge us to include in our subject the fate of our departments, the processes of interaction with the university, and the need to step out and recognize, finally, that we are responsible to every walk of society. By teaching that our subject is language use, in addition to English, we may better teach how to face the behavior of those who take us to the only destination there is "beyond language": violence, silence, the end of society.

Historically, "English" is a recent (nineteenth century) term for a subject that has been in the Western university since its twelfth-century beginnings, and it is traceable back to classical Athens. The historical precursor of English has been the trivium: rhetoric, grammar, and logic. When the trivium was the principal propadeutic subject for the six centuries after the twelfth, the language was Latin, whose identity, like that of English today, was unquestioned but, unlike English today, definitely marked as an elite language. When university languages changed from Latin to the vernaculars (over a period of perhaps three centuries), writing as a propadeutic subject replaced rhetoric and included grammar. Thus, regardless of which language was the "language of knowledge," the *subject of language was always merely propadeutic:* Language, if heard in lectures before writing, had to be mastered; if needed for actual writing, it also had to be mastered. Hastings Rashdall observed that, in the thirteenth century, "after the rise of the law school at Bologna, rhetoric and grammar came to be looked upon mainly as a schoolboy preparation for the higher professional studies" (234). Understanding its roles in society was not part of the subject, as contributors to this volume suggest it has become today.

Here is a historical anecdote that represents the scope and urgency of the problems raised in this volume. My source is Walter Ruegg in the recent Cambridge multivolume history of the European university. There was Lorenzo Valla, a Professor of Rhetoric at the University of Rome in the 1450s. He is known for having challenged Church documents which purport to show that Constantine, in his will, ceded power to the Church.[1] He studied "spoken discourse" (456) and interpreted authors in terms of "his understanding of language and his situation." He was one of the earliest annotators of the New Testament. He "analyzed the Latin language as a living expression of the changing self-understanding of human beings" (457). He tried to create a logic derived from the grammar of ordinary speech. One may describe his approach as "contextualist," as he clearly responded to language as something *living* in a variety of social situations. Ruegg describes how Valla's reaching out beyond the faculty of arts "came into conflict with the other faculties." Ruegg continues:

> As a result of such expansion, Valla had to flee from his professorship in Pavia because of the physical danger arising from his violent persecution at the hands of the members of the faculty of law; in Rome he was protected from the attacks of theologians only because he enjoyed the favor of the pope. (457)

Valla was considered dangerous because his subject, rhetoric, when pursued freely, implicated other subject matters. It was as if suddenly the professor of the "schoolboy subject" was interfering with the "men's" games. This amounted to an academic heresy, an overstepping of boundaries. The momentum of the Renaissance was carried forward by the discovery of new texts and by the increasing ease of reproducing existing texts. Should a scholar of rhetoric follow the manifest implications of the subject, all texts in all subjects become eligible of study, language critique, and, in some cases, discrediting. Those scholars most comprehending of grammar, logic, rhetoric, and who had the most languages at their disposal, were in the best position to recast the received texts in new lights. Valla treated the subjects of rhetoric and grammar as "language use" insofar as his knowledge of these subjects studied texts that were considered authoritative and made his critical findings public. Recently, as the ruminations of what English is were being prepared for publication (1990), Linda Brodkey's attempts to behave at the University of Texas as Valla did in Rome, led to a result analogous to Valla's experience, if less violent: Her attempts, endorsed by her department, to teach students to examine authoritative texts (court rulings in civil rights cases), were censored by the university administration, and her position, though tenured, was no longer viable.

Language itself was never recognized as posing problems about life, the body, society, and God in the same sense, for example, as medicine, astronomy, theology, or law did. The essays in this book raise issues—corporations, unionization, service learning, technology, disciplinarity, non-English speakers—that point to how our subject can no longer be thought of as simply English, but beyond (and including along with other "mother tongues") English, to language and its fundamental presence in every part of society. These essays teach us that because English is language as much as it is English, our subject matter is moving to a place where language is a principal site of social inquiry.

—David Bleich

Note

1. Thanks to Jeff Wheeler of the UCLA Rhetoric Program for this information and for sources not found in Ruegg.

Works Cited

Dunn, Kevin. "Without Doubt, the United States Is Fighting an Imperial War Abroad." *Rochester Democrat and Chronicle.* 22 October 2001: 9A.

Elbow, Peter. *What Is English?* New York: MLA, 1990.

Lunsford, Andrea. Keynote address at "Writing as a Human Activity" conference at the University of California Santa Barbara, 5 October 2001.

Rashdall, Hastings. *The Universities of Europe in the Middle Ages,* Vol. 1 (1895). Eds. F. M. Powicke and A. B. Emden, Oxford UP, 1936.

Walter Ruegg, "The Rise of Humanism," in Hilde De Ridder-Symoens, ed., *A History of the University in Europe,* Vol. 1. Cambridge: Cambridge UP, 1992.

Acknowledgments

This collection was a collaborative project that benefited from the work of many hands. We would like to thank everyone who helped usher this project toward completion. First, to the contributors: We thank those of you who co-wrote and team-wrote these essays, even when to do so meant extra time and difficulties of coordination—as well as potentially less institutional recognition. And to all the contributors for diligently and cheerfully engaging a long process of revision and editing with us as we worked to make the book cohere as a whole.

Next we owe a deep debt of thanks to our editors at Boynton/Cook, Jim Strickland and Lynne Reed. We appreciate your care and spirit of good humor.

To Maurice Kilwein Guevara for writing the poem that begins this volume.

To Roland Hurlbert, for letting us use your iMac and for enduring a few too many boring Saturdays while we prepared the manuscript.

To David and Mark's colleagues, Susan Marguerite Comfort, Maurice Kilwein Guevara, Donald A. McAndrew, Gian S. Pagnucci, Thomas J. Slater, and Roxann Wheeler, who helped us imagine curricular alternatives as we collaboratively composed a proposal for "Teaching the Writing and Reading of Cultures."

To the memory of James A. Berlin, whose work, especially in *Rhetorics, Poetics, and Cultures* inspires and informs this volume.

Chapter One

English Incorporated
An Introduction
David B. Downing, Claude Mark Hurlbert,
and Paula Mathieu

The Classroom, the Curriculum, and
the Global Economy

In 1998, U.C. Berkeley formed a partnership with Novartis, a Swiss pharma-
ceuticals corporation that produces genetically engineered crops. Under the
agreement, Novartis gave $25 million to the Department of Plant and Microbial
Biology, and, in return, received rights to occupy two of five seats on the department's research committee and to license one-third of the department's
research discoveries. Some observers applaud this agreement for taking university and industry relationships "to a new level," allowing the university to
invest sorely needed funds into equipment and building renewal, without compromising academic freedom (Blumenstyk, "Vilified" A24–25). Critics worry
that this partnership represents unprecedented threats to "student priorities"
and "scientific openness," making the department "'captive' to the company"
(Blumenstyk, "Vilified" A24; see also Press and Washburn).

Sponsored research agreements are nothing new in the sciences. English
studies are different, you may say, because they carry fewer directly patentable
discoveries. Nevertheless, English does not escape the notice and influence of
corporations. In *English in America,* Richard Ohmann explains how English
has traditionally had the role of providing literate workers to businesses. Many
colleges look to businesses to help define at least part of their curricula. How are
such influences shaping English studies? How is English already incorporated?[1]

These are ethical and political questions; but they are also curricular questions. More than a program's course content, a curriculum is a contested representation of the public identity of an institution and a discipline—a framework

1

for a department's pedagogical possibilities such as collaboration, team teaching, or distance education. A curriculum is imbued with commercial interests, from business investments to textbook production and consumption. It is a set of legitimations for the range of practices, methodologies, and other behaviors possible in a university or college department. Curricula represent where departments spend money, how people get hired, how work is rewarded, and how working conditions transpire. It is no wonder that, as Gerald Graff argues: "The academic curriculum has become a prominent arena of cultural conflict because it is a microcosm, as it should be, of the clash of cultures and values in America as a whole" (*Beyond* 8). A curriculum can be a trigger for conflict, especially in the discipline of English.

College English has lost its referent more than, say, college mathematics or college biology. The categories of the "literary," the "textual," the "rhetorical," and the "creative" have been deeply crossed with cultural, technological, and economic change. David Damrosch contends that recent changes represent a crisis situation, causing "an insecurity of purpose [to] pervade both the humanities and the social sciences" as they "struggle for self-definition," an uncertainty that calls our missions, both as researchers and teachers, into question (1).[2]

Recent developments in cultural studies, feminism, environmentalism, multiculturalism, and postcolonialism seek to broaden the field of English to include a fuller range of issues facing students today. At the same time, economic forces pressure disciplinary borders, curricular designs, and program structures by necessitating a trimmed-down, thrifty English studies. Negotiating this complicated situation leads educators to question the mission of English studies: In the face of cultural transformations and economic cutbacks, what should we be teaching? How, as English scholars and teachers, can we act as agents to engage the economic and technological shifts our discipline faces? This book explores these questions, especially at the points of contention between curriculum and corporatization.

Much current research on reconfiguring English studies has been on the classroom, the text, or the culture as objects of study. This research implicitly or explicitly calls for new curricular visions and institutional alignments. But by focusing on classroom methods and texts, we have neglected essential connections among curricular, disciplinary, and institutional issues. For instance, in recent years we have heard calls for taking cultural studies into the classroom, which means addressing broad-scale social and economic conditions in the world, making them part of our teaching. But the reflection at the curricular level often gets neglected as cultural studies' insights get inserted into courses or subdisciplines of composition, literature, or creative writing in ways that do not fundamentally alter the curricular arrangements. Robert Yagelski writes that "our classrooms, our curricula, and the structure of our schools have remained largely unchanged for most of the past century, despite various pedagogical reform movements . . . and more theoretical arguments than we can cram into an ever-increasing number of professional journals and scholarly books" (ix).

Recent studies of disciplinarity, even when directly addressing English, have focused primarily on debating disciplinary status and research methodologies (Greenblatt and Gunn; Menand, "Demise"). Only a few studies of disciplinary conditions—such as Robert Scholes' new model of English studies, Graff's call for a teach-the-conflicts curriculum, and North's advocacy of a "fusion model" Ph.D. curriculum—discuss specific curricular designs as possible visions of what our field might look like. This is regrettable because, as Graff explains, "the curriculum is the major form of representation through which academic departments identify themselves to the world (or fail to do so)" ("Is There" 12).

In his 1996 address to the Conference on College Composition and Communication, Lester Faigley claimed that the greatest challenges facing English professors originate beyond one's department. Larger forces of change, he argued, "affect how we see ourselves and what we do" (5). He identified two shifts: the redistribution of wealth in ways disconnected from the labor that produces it, which he called the "revolution of the rich"; and the "digital revolution," which, he points out, has led to the creation of flexible forms of professional work. In some circumstances, such flexibility can provide a measure of professional adaptability to new intellectual and social contexts. In others, however, flexibility can be highly destructive of faculty well-being and job security. This book situates curricular reform in English within the social and economic conditions that have dramatically altered higher education, especially the rapid economic and technological changes that have beset the world's economies since the early 1970s.

Reporters and scholars have spent enormous amounts of ink exploring the recent economic trends using terms such as "globalization," "flexible accumulation," "transnationalism," "neoliberal market capitalism," and even "postmodernity." In *Spaces of Hope*, David Harvey describes the evolution of the term *globalization*, which came to prominence in the 1970s as American Express began proclaiming the global reach of its credit card. According to Harvey, the term "spread like wildfire" serving as a justification for deregulating financial markets, which in turn led to the "disempowerment of national and local working-class movements and trade union power" (13). By the mid-1980s, the rhetoric of globalization helped create a "heady atmosphere of entrepreneurial optimism" proclaiming the "brave new world of globalizing neoliberalism" (13). This prevalence of entrepreneurial rhetoric spread from the world of financial markets to all areas of life, even university life. In *Academic Capitalism: Politics, Policies, and the Entrepreneurial University*, Sheila Slaughter and Larry L. Leslie describe how academic work at public research universities has changed as a result of commercial interests and global economic pressures. As spending has been redirected or cut from state and land-grant university budgets, academics compete more vehemently for scarce resources, research grants, and government support, even as they claim intellectual autonomy. But autonomy can be illusory. The cost-cutting that follows conservative political agendas leads to retrenchment or freezing of positions, programs, and sometimes even departments.

"Globalization," however, is a problematic term because it has been used in many different ways to serve many ends. Giles Gunn acknowledges as much in the "Globalizing Literary Studies" issue of *PMLA:* "Globalization is fraught with so many complications and discontents that one almost wishes to substitute another term" (19). In *Millennial Dreams,* Paul Smith argues that "even while something that might be called globalization is...happening, we're in danger of letting the term become the next great shibboleth" (1). Globalization, according to Smith, is a term that signifies as a fait accompli a not-fully achieved capitalist "millennial dream," in which corporations claim to have transcended the constraints of nation-states. But such "millennial visions" do "nothing to change the fact that this is an unjust system...[the] effects [of which] are devastating for the majority, especially...those who are not managers of the military–industrial–medical–sports complexes of the North" (Smith 56). Peter Marcuse registers Smith's resistance to the obfuscating uses of the term *globalization* by claiming it does not signify an abrupt departure from the past: "Most of the phenomena that globalization refer to are not new, but are 'an expansion of capitalist relationships,' both geographically and in their penetration into more and more aspects of life.... Clarifying such concepts paves the way for an 'alternative globalization' " ("A Glance"). Because the concepts and materiality of globalization are bound up in rhetorical processes and geographic areas included in cultural study, English curricula are inevitably implicated in the struggles over the meanings and effects of globalization. A great challenge facing English educators is how to imagine and work for reformed curricula that provide alternatives to the exploiting forces of the global economy.

The power and scope of economic and technological transformations can make effective change seem impossible. Understanding these processes, however, is a first step in making and claiming spaces of agency within a framework of institutional and economic constraint. Where we live and teach is where we can begin. For this reason, we have titled our volume *Beyond English, Inc.*[3] to suggest that whatever curricular innovations we imagine, we must negotiate our visions within specific institutions and against specific constraints of powerful corporate-management models commanding our educational system. This title does not lack irony because, as business practices of accounting have become deeply inscribed within the everyday, there exists no simple "beyond" the commodified life world.

The Rise of English Incorporated

Understanding the current moment of "English Incorporated" benefits from a historical awareness that the ties between the corporate world and the university are long-standing. Even though a symbiosis between universities and commercial interests is nothing new, that relationship has taken on particular shapes throughout each historical stage of US economic development. We provide here a brief gloss on some scholarship detailing the changing relationship between business and universities during the twentieth century.

The Rise of Scientific Management

In *Universities and the Capitalist State,* Clyde Barrow details the relationship between businesses and universities in the United States from 1894 to 1928. During this period, Barrow shows, business interests influenced higher education through increased representation on university boards, advancing scientific management, and creating educational funding agencies such as the Carnegie Foundation. From 1860 to 1930, bankers, business executives, and corporate lawyers greatly increased their presence on university governing boards, gradually displacing clergy, judges, and local government officials. At public universities, for example, the percentage of trustees with business occupations increased from 20 percent in 1860 to nearly 47 percent in 1930 (37). When adding in lawyers, most of whom were corporate lawyers, the business presence on boards of public universities in 1930 amounted to 67 percent (37). Boards at private and technical institutions experienced similar trends. The effect of this leadership is significant for social and material reasons, as Barrow explains: "Modern governing boards inherited this dual responsibility for regulating the orthodoxy of academic staff and curriculum and for acting as the primary institutional mechanism through which the university lays claim to socially scarce material resources that can be converted into the material means of mental production" (Barrow 43).

Fueled by corporate regulation of academic orthodoxy, scientific management began to affect university practices (Barrow, Newfield). In 1909, Henry Pritchett, president of the Carnegie Foundation for the Advancement of Teaching (CFAT), consulted Frederick Taylor, father of scientific management, to commission "an economic study of education." Taylor recommended that his friend, Morris Cooke, "a young mechanical engineer . . . develop a calculus by which to measure the efficiency and productivity of educational institutions in a manner similar to that being employed in industrial factories" (Barrow 67). This study yielded most of the terms with which we still measure academic labor:

> The key unit of measurement in this new calculus was called the "student hour." A student hour was "one hour of lectures, of laboratory work, or recitation room work, for a single pupil." . . . The theoretical effect of this new measurement was to focus attention on professors as mental workers for the first time in their history. If the university was conceptualized as an economic unit of production, the role of the professor as its chief producer was altered as well. The religious mentality that promoted university life as a unique and special "calling"

was discarded by Cooke for an industrial conception of intellectual "labor." (Barrow 70)

The Carnegie Foundation was impressed with the possibilities of scientific-management practices and guaranteed its spread by granting access to pension funds only to universities that complied with their standards of efficiency and governance (Barrow 73–74). As a result, faculty were removed from the core of administrative work, placing university management in the hands of nonacademic supervisors. A desire to standardize and precisely evaluate the work of faculty led to the primacy of academic specialization and research: "Cooke therefore recommended greater research and teaching specialization by faculty as a condition for promoting more intensive mass production" (Barrow 72). Bureaucratic management discovered that one of the primary sources of a university's social prestige was its ability to attract specialized researchers onto the faculty. Advocates of scientific management instituted national job searches to increase the size of job pools and enhance competitiveness (71). While facing greater specialization and scientific accountability, faculty enjoyed limited forms of academic freedom, which was "confined to the teaching and publication of empirical 'facts' that were generally accepted by other experts in the field" but not freedom to "speculat[e] about untested, political, moral or social arrangements" (Barrow 195). Academics claiming and benefiting from this disciplinary view of academic freedom worked directly against collective movements that might have disrupted management's consolidating power.

Consolidating Ties in the Period of Expansion

In *The Condition of Postmodernity,* David Harvey describes the period from the late 1920s to the early 1970s as an era in which models of mechanized industrial production combined with Keynesian methods of monetary control and social investment to bring about relative economic stability. The Fordist factory model of routinized and deskilled production, the rise of massive government and military spending, and the spread of mass consumption highlight this economic period. Harvey shows that corporations, labor, and government each made concessions in return for certain gains or privileges. For example, organized labor allowed for deskilled production practices, while businesses conceded wage increases to allow workers to become part of the consuming class. Following the Depression, economist John Maynard Keynes revolutionized the economy through aggressive government intervention and investment in a wide range of private industry and public works projects ranging from Roosevelt's New Deal; the rise of the military–industrial complex; and, of course, public funding for education.

Universities benefited from the rise of public spending. During World War II, the precipitous decline in student-age populations available for higher education led the government to subsidize many postsecondary institutions. As

Christopher Lucas explains: "By 1945, upwards of half of the income supporting certain academic institutions came from the national government" (232).
This growing government funding for education continued for twenty-five years
after the war. The 1944 G.I. Bill funded the swelling college enrollments of returning veterans, and with the advent of the Cold War and the launching of
Sputnik in 1957, the government directly linked education to national security interests. The late fifties witnessed the formation of the National Science
Foundation and the National Institutes of Health and the passage of the National
Defense Education Act to provide low-cost government loans to students. Lucas
writes: "Increased federal funding for higher education in the fifties and early
sixties, at the height of the Cold War, was usually defended by the argument that
in strengthening colleges and universities, the government was bolstering the
nation's defenses and helping to advance vital national policy objectives" (233).

    Under this climate, Bill Readings argues, university disciplines in the hu-
manities functioned in part to bolster the patriotic mythos of the nation-state.[4] In
addition, English, produced an economically useful process of sorting, screen-
ing, and selecting students whose basic literacy skills could then be certified as
eligible to contribute to the ranks of the professional/managerial class. According to Evan Watkins, the specific content of work in an English class became
secondary to grades as a measure to differentiate status: "Beyond the classroom . . . few people ever have a clue about a student's expertise in reading
Romantic poetry, or even what such expertise would look like. For what is
circulated *systematically* is a grade as an index of performance whose value is
read off in relation to other grades, not to the specific qualities of work" (6).
This dual role of supporting nationalist ideals through the study of transcendent works of literature and serving the economy by identifying literate and
successful students through grading characterizes the split that has structured
English departments for much of its 125-year history. Writing instruction has
provided the most economically useful social function, while the disciplinary
content of the field has largely been based on the analysis and interpretation of
British and American literature.

    As the size of universities began swelling by the mid–twentieth century,
English departments developed graduate programs that trained students to become professors of literature, while during their time of apprenticeship they
taught writing courses for low wages. This arrangement allowed the mostly
male, white faculty to teach upper-division and graduate courses in literature
and "purchase" release time for research. Beginning in the 1960s, groups outside
this traditional university hierarchy—including women, people of color, gays
and lesbians (as well as people with interests in culture, teaching, and film)—
started pressuring the discipline of English to reform its contents. Some recep-
tive departments of English responded to such challenges by adding courses
or subdisciplines in women's studies, various ethnic literatures, as well as cultural studies, composition, creative writing, film studies, and so on. Until about
1973, this principle of disciplinary expansion worked relatively well because the

post-War economic expansion allowed new subdisciplines to be simply added on to the existing curriculum (see Bérubé, *Employment;* Graff, *Professing;* Nelson; and North).[5]

Transformations: Towards "Flexible Labor" and the "Great Contraction" after 1970

By the early 1970s, according to Harvey's analysis, the uneasy agreement among business, labor, government, and education under the Fordist/Keynesian economy was shaken by a number of crises, and new economic arrangements began to emerge:

> The sharp recession of 1973, exacerbated by the oil shock evidently shook the capitalist world out of the suffocating torpor of "stagflation" (stagnant output of goods and high inflation of prices), and set in motion a whole set of processes that undermined the Fordist compromise. The 1970s and 1980s have consequently been a troubled period of economic restructuring and social and political readjustment. In the social space created by all this flux and uncertainty, a series of novel experiments in the realms of industrial organization as well as in political and social life have begun to take shape. These experiments may represent the early stirrings of the passage to an entirely new regime of accumulation, coupled with a quite different system of political and social regulation. (Harvey, *Condition* 145)

Harvey tentatively calls this post-Fordist regime "flexible accumulation," which includes rewritten labor arrangements, increasing corporate mergers, the transfer of manufacturing to geographically peripheral locations, quick turnover of capital, increased technology, and a focus on niche marketing and new product lines. The resulting culture is marked by a reduction in the core of permanent salaried employees and an increasing reliance on part-time, temporary, or subcontracted workers. This shift further exacerbates the vulnerability of disadvantaged groups, especially women and Third World workers (*Condition* 153).

Flexible labor arrangements have had dramatic effects on hiring in higher education. The "flexible" university has witnessed a huge and expensive growth in administrative ranks designed to direct curricula, downsize or eliminate programs, plan niche marketing, carry out corporate–university partnerships, and regulate "admissions, retention, scholarships, discretionary accounts, and hirings, as well" (Martin 11). At the same time, tenured faculty lines continue to decrease while temporary, part-time, and graduate employees do the bulk of undergraduate teaching.

Downsizing and underemployment have been particularly harsh for English departments during this time North calls "The Great Contraction." We have witnessed both an undergraduate shift away from the English major, a declining job market for English Ph.D.s (often trained as literary critics), and an increasing use of temporary and part-time instructors to staff general writing courses.

This trend, according to James Engell and Anthony Dangerfield, is general for the humanities: "Since the late 1960s the humanities have been neglected, downgraded, and forced to retrench, all as other areas of higher education have grown in numbers, wealth, and influence" (quoted in Press and Washburn 52). As Press and Washburn conclude: "[In] the new 'Market-Model University,' . . . subjects that make money, study money, or attract money are given priority" (52). It is no wonder, though no less regrettable, that under such pressures, the discipline and curricula are so often adapted to market conditions, limiting course offerings, for instance, in response to administrative calls for niche programming or "targeted" excellence.

In *The University in Ruins,* Bill Readings offers a provocative articulation of how a rhetoric of excellence dominates the administrative planning and execution of post-Fordist universities. As he argues, scripts informed by the priorities of "excellence" shape institutions of higher education so that they will more efficiently serve as conduits for meeting the needs of local, national, and transnational corporate interests. Since the 1980s, according to Jan Currie and Lesley Vidovich, the boundaries that have somewhat mediated the relationship between higher education, government, and business have dramatically deteriorated, resulting in university cultural missions subordinated to the explicitly business discourse of excellence. Stanley Aronowitz explains the consequences:

> Administrations of most colleges and universities have responded to the economic and cultural uncertainties provoked by budget constraints and a volatile job market by constructing their institutions on the model of the modern corporation. Consequently, many have thrust training to the fore and called it education. Lacking a unified national culture into which to socialize students and . . . an educational philosophy capable of steering an independent course, the academic system as a whole is caught in a market logic that demands students be job-ready upon graduation. . . . [A]cademic leaders chant the mantra of "excellence" . . . [which] means . . . all parts of the university "perform" and are judged according to how well they deliver knowledge and qualified labor to the corporate economy and how well the administration fulfills the recruitment and funding goals needed to maintain the institution. (158)

The current economic climate has thus eroded the compromise between faculty and business interests that persisted in slightly different forms during the bulk of the twentieth century. Professorial privileges, such as job stability, limited academic freedom, and relative autonomy in work arrangements, have not disappeared altogether, but they are shared by fewer and fewer academic workers. Great disparities exist among university teachers with regard to pay, teaching load, benefits, and working conditions, depending on the wealth and prestige of the university, the job title, and decided star potential of the faculty member. The current picture of higher education is not the same for all academic workers, but none can fail to see the impact of economic and technological changes on today's university.

English, Inc. and Global Technology

In today's corporate university, an education is packaged and sold as a complex commodified event.[6] The consumers are, in one sense, the students who purchase their education, but in another, the consumers might be more accurately seen as the corporations who "purchase" successful college graduates as an already screened pool of literate bodies for the workforce. Student-consumers become the commodity consumed by businesses. Students are not ordinary customers in another way, in that when they "buy" a course, they receive varying levels of credentials depending on what and how well they purchase. A student buying a community college education purchases a very different set of credentials than one who buys an Ivy League event. In either case, grading still functions as a form of credentializing and sorting as it did in earlier historical periods, although poor grades from a prestigious university are likely to carry more cultural capital than straight As at a vocational, community, or regional college.

In anxious need to competitively market their universities as worthwhile credentializing events, administrators set up managerial apparatuses for producing testimony to their institutions' worth and justifying themselves to corporations, governments, and students. Because of this market focus, universities have shifted from "guardianship of knowledge and wisdom to ancillary production of knowledge for corporate capital" (Harvey, *Condition* 160). Managers concern themselves with promoting short-term, external signs of success, such as rankings, rather than with long-term educational and social value. Institutions create prestige by hiring famous-name academics or pioneering hi-tech research. The goal of prestige is to climb in public rankings, and ironically prestige and wealth are what help determine high rankings. Ohio State University, for example, has developed a model of "taxing" all departments to create a fund available only to a few, chosen departments, which can use those dollars to hire academic stars and increase their public rankings (Wilson). The increase in dollars converts directly into higher rankings, which converts back into dollars headed into the university from competitively won tuition payments, government grants, and corporate sponsorship. At Ohio State, English happens to be one of the winners, for the time being, but the College of Arts has not faired well overall. The college's dean, Judith Smith Koroscik, "wonders whether her college missed out because many of its fields, like dance, design, and art education, aren't ranked by either *U.S. News* or the National Research Council" at all (Wilson A9). Because those departments were unable to prove their competitive value in the downsizing marketplace of university departments, they lost out on the ability to access funding that would have fueled prestige and, hence, rankings.

Searching for dollars or other justifications to remain within the marketplace of education, academic departments and universities turn to corporate ventures to fuel economic and technological endeavors. In the "Homogeniza-tion of Education," Maude Barlow and Heather-Jane Robertson explain that Canadian universities follow the lead of many sponsorship practices of US institutions:

> In exchange for free merchandise, universities offer exclusive access to students for corporate sponsors. A professor's ability to attract private investment is now often more important than academic qualifications or teaching ability.... Funding-agency mandates now state clearly that grant money should benefit business.
>
> Universities now have CEOs, business-liaison officers, and cor-porate advisers. Fund-raising campaigns are increasingly, of neces-sity, the highest priority of administration, the board of governors and faculty; and in more and more universities, the arts and humanities, considered "soft" largely because they do not attract corporate spon-sorship, are being phased out. (67)

In May 2000, Nike CEO Phil Knight announced that he would halt Nike's charitable contributions to his alma mater, the University of Oregon, when that university announced it would join the Worker Rights Consortium—a group of colleges and universities devoted to ensuring living wages and reasonable work-ing conditions for manufacturers of university products (Lively). By February 2001, however, the Oregon State Board of Higher Education blocked the uni-versity's action to join the consortium, claiming that it contradicted the state's fair-trade business policy (Van der Werf). The university's right to association ended when it conflicted with commercial interests.

Nowhere, it seems, are commercial interests in higher education more immediately detectable than in the areas of technology, online partnerships, and distance education. *The Chronicle of Higher Education* has reported about the institution of private online or "virtual" universities such as the University of Phoenix and Western Governors University.[7] Billionaire Rupert Murdoch and John Saylor, the CEO of software company MicroStrategy, have each an-nounced plans for online universities, as has the Harcourt publishing company (Blumenstyk, "Harcourt's"). Established universities, Columbia University for one (Kiernan), as well as many community colleges (Lords), have entered for-profit distance-education consortiums to offer online classes and degrees. Some colleges have sold courses to private companies that package them into certificate and degree programs. The US Army has even instituted on-line courses for service men and women (Carr). The British government has announced the institution of a government–education venture, the e-university, with start-up expenditures "estimated at $190-million over two years" (Walker). There are, in other words, many students being educated without ever walking into a college classroom or meeting any part-time, let alone tenure-track, faculty.

Businesses interest in education seldom comes without a cost. Distance ed-ucation often packages poorly designed pedagogy and depends on overworked and underpaid workers (see Neff and Comfort in this book). In exchange for advertizing space on university web pages that tie the name of the university with pitches for credit cards or athletic shoes, corporations supply universities with website portals and financial supports (see DeVoss et al.). Many university administrators are willing, according to Wayne Ross, to "sell their institutions' reputations in exchange for the resources to mount online programs" ("A Glance").

Any online initiative takes place in a deeply inscribed and contested cultural domain.[8] Cultural theorist Saskia Sassen argues that cyberspace is shaped by "power, concentration and contestation as well as by openness and decentralization" (177). Technology has opened up new spaces for activist groups and e-commerce alike through the World Wide Web, yet it "has emerged not simply as a means for transmitting information, but as a major new theater for capital accumulation and the operations of global capital" (Sassen 190). Technology is tied in complex ways to the uses and abuses of power in our society. As Gail Hawisher and Cynthia Selfe argue, the terrain of technology is crucial to the future of education:

> The electronic territory . . . is one of the most important educational landscapes we have available for our profession to explore. With it, we will face, for the next decade, the challenges associated with global literacy; the problems associated with the nature of education as a complex set of cultural processes . . . and the historical, unsolved challenges of students marginalized or silenced within our schools due to race, age, ethnicity, sexual orientation, gender, or handicap. (*Literacy*, ix)

While technology is and will continue to represent a key arena for the battles of education and economic justice, it is not necessarily a force only aligned with capital. Paul Smith reminds us that "technology is . . . not in itself a cause of anything, and the propensity even of commentators on the left to buy into or assume such a teleological function for technology inhibits an understanding not just of the current conjuncture, but equally of the whole history and workings of capital" (23). Rather than seeking to escape the reach of technology or corporatization, the challenge facing English educators is to find ways of tactically engaging and resisting this terrain.[9]

In "The Corporate University," Cary Nelson and Stephen Watt write that "corporatization is here to stay. It cannot be stopped, but it can be shaped and, where appropriate, resisted. At its worst, corporatization strips faculty of its intellectual independence, impoverishes the teaching staff and diminishes its intellectual freedom, deprives students of appropriate intellectual challenges" (94).[10] Under these conditions, we may need to resist the corporatized university's exclusive use of short-term cost accounting administered by vertical, undemocratic management practices. As Christopher Newfield argues: "We should go beyond critique to achieving real managerial power for the nonprofit approaches to human development that drew many of us into higher education in the first place" (71). Financial accounting based exclusively on short-term economic gain loses sight of the public realm in which both employees and administrators live. A culture will ultimately impoverish itself, both economically and socially, if it doesn't invest for a well-educated citizenry where critical thinking, imagination, creativity, and independence provide resources for a better world. Indeed, these are important, marketable skills that businesses and the public deserve in abundance.[11]

Reforming the Public Function of English Studies

Working in large institutions and confronted by massive economic transformations, one can feel overwhelmed, hopeless, or lose a sense of purpose. The first step in reforming English studies is to reform ourselves to believe in our power as workers, teachers, and writers capable of imagining new ways of interacting in universities and acting on our desires. We can find power in our local affiliations, or we can cling to the vestiges of individual privilege from the historical past. We can engage the work to reinvigorate English studies, or we can passively hope that things will change—or stay the same. In the realms of education and social transformation, one cannot easily account for how persuasive or effective one's efforts have been. Work, which at the time seemed a failure, may be more than we imagine.

Paul Loeb, in *Soul of a Citizen,* claims that any process of social transformation is a mysterious one, and it is difficult to know when you have been effective or how social movements grow. By example, Loeb relates the story of Dr. Benjamin Spock, famed baby doctor, who was driving through Washington, DC, one rainy, miserable day. As his car passed the Capitol, he saw a small group of women huddled with their children under umbrellas, holding handmade protest signs, smeared and wet due to the rain. He slowed his car to see what issue kept these mothers out with their kids in such horrible weather. The women never saw him, but he read their antinuclear signs. He was so moved by their resolve, he began to research nuclear disarmament and became one of the country's most well-known leaders of the antinuclear movement, arguing that reducing the nuclear threat was a vitally important children's health issue. Loeb's argument is that we can and do change lives through ordinary actions, but change is an unreliable process. When taking collective action, moments that feel like failure may have future effects we cannot know or imagine. For example, if a group plans an ambitious new curriculum and it fails to be implemented, that process might have succeeded in other ways: bringing people together to highlight tacit departmental divisions, educating broader audiences about literacy and literary goals, or setting the stage for future change.

To design curricula that are ethical and publicly accountable, we can start by recognizing that not all academic experiences are subsumed by financial accounting management models. There exists limited spaces and moments that are unaccounted for within the strict economic determinism prevailing in higher education.[12] Many teachers and scholars have availed themselves of these limited freedoms to create and sustain meaningful learning experiences. As Lisa Delpit, Mike Rose, Mary Rose O'Reilly, Michael Blitz and C. Mark Hurlbert, Jonathan Kozol, Stanley Aronowitz, and others have argued, relevant, life-affirming teaching happens despite corporate management of education. *Beyond English, Inc.* is devoted not to these individual spaces of creativity, but to the socialized, collaborative, and curricular possibilities for imagining new ways to work as professional educators in English studies. Many contributors to this book present curricular experiments that meet the educational needs of students and faculty in the face of corporate models of efficiency and expediency.

In *The Employment of English,* Michael Bérubé argues that English professionals must publicly defend what we do from claims of irrelevancy, a task whose importance increases as university-wide competition for funding increases. We need to articulate a rationale not only for ourselves but to the university and the public. We are not powerless in this role. Cathy Davidson reminds us: "English departments do have power within today's universities. Our numbers may be diminishing and our proportion of the total resources of the university shrinking, but to simply lament our situation is to underestimate the source of our strength" (99). And it's not through what Davidson calls "minute tinkerings" with the curriculum that we will convince others of the importance of what we do. We need innovative, visionary, and collectively imagined possibilities for a vital English studies in a technological, global economy.

English educators will have to work harder at justifying our needs. The general way of adapting to new disciplinary interests and pressures is no longer working. The method of accretion and addition—by which programs add a theorist, a multiculturalist, a women's studies component, and so on—has reached a saturation point. Rethinking any one theoretical or practical domain of our work in the discipline now virtually means that it will be felt as a pressure throughout the curriculum.

Beyond English, Inc. addresses the problems and possibilities we face as we try to imagine how we might inhabit the university in the twenty-first century. The contributors to this book offer a range of answers to several questions:

- What should our profession look like now that, for a growing number of teachers and scholars, most of the traditional rationales and mission statements for English departments no longer seem germane to what we actually do in our teaching and research?

- How and why will we reconstruct English studies so that our profession can be accountable to public concerns, student needs, and faculty interests?

- How can we create a space for imagining new kinds of institutional relations, disciplinary practices, and curricular designs that accommodate innovation as well as honor the cultural past?

- How can reimagining disciplinary boundaries respond to the complexities of our multicultural worlds, our changing demographics, the painful splits between literature and writing, our shift to electronic environments, and the corporate management of academic concerns?

In short, this book's contributors articulate both practical and theoretical explorations of these questions within the context of the increasing pressure to model and adapt postsecondary education to business interests and corporate needs. As Judith Fetterly explains, when we design any curricular innovation, "we are inevitably engaged in dreaming the future of our field, for that future lies in the hands of those we teach, and the vision that drives the design of our program is our vision of what we want the field to become" (703). *Beyond English, Inc.* is intended to foster visions of what the contributors want our field to become, even as managerialism reaches deeply into our academic lives.

Beyond English, Inc. contains four sections investigating areas of concern that will determine disciplinary and curricular possibilities for the coming generation.

1. Theorizing Disciplinary Revision and Curricular Reform for the Twenty-first Century

Essays in this section address theoretical and historical questions about the relationships among disciplinarity, corporate management, and curricular change. David Downing argues that refining curricular content without challenging the orthodoxy of disciplinarity will result in curricular reform that fails to reach its own aims. Poet Charles Bernstein addresses the tensions among the various subdisciplines of English by foregrounding the poetic imaginary and arguing that universities have an obligation to provide a sanctuary for experimental, noncommodified forms of imaginative work. Deborah Holdstein argues that textbook companies and online textbook enhancements must be examined for the ways they inscribe commercial interests and traditional notions of the discipline. Richard Ohmann addresses the accountability movement in higher education by historicizing how accountability discourse has served conservative interests by appearing to increase "standards."

2. The Curricular Politics of Local, Regional, and National Differences

This section explores how the broad-ranging economic, managerial, and technological effects discussed in this introduction play out in the specific local contexts of the writers' home institutions. The writers offer tactics and responses given local possibilities and constraints. Bruce Horner, Kelly Latchaw, Joseph Lenz, Jody Swilky, and David Wolf, from the Department of English at Drake University, tell a sobering tale of departmental downsizing in the face of institutional revision. Writing from the perspectives of the department chair, tenured faculty, and visiting and adjunct faculty, they discuss the material implications of curricular choices and self-definition. Pancho Savery writes that the required classics humanities curriculum at Reed, a liberal arts college in Portland, Oregon, allows for a rigorous educational experience for students but hinders racial integration at the school. Savery shows that democratic departmental and institutional processes, not always external corporate pressures, can lead to tokenizing faculty of color and marginalizing priorities for racial diversity. The collaboration of David Stacey, Rob Pope, and Claire Woods extends across three continents—North America, Europe, and Australia—to address curricular designs with an eye toward a global study of English. Derek Owens provides an ambitious, yet grounded, vision for English studies dedicated to environmental sustainability. Owens argues that implicit within many English departments are the resources and courses that can be recycled to yield a curriculum that foregrounds responsibility toward future generations.

3. Places of Writing in the English Curriculum

Composition's place within English departments has been and continues to be contested. Economic pressures pushing for more writing and less literature intensify these debates, leading to various proposals for either integrating writing throughout the English curriculum or forming new departments of writing separate from English. The essays in this section detail ways that writing has been "renegotiated" at specific institutions. Amy Goodburn and Deborah Minter examine the process of creating an undergraduate concentration in writing and rhetoric at the University of Nebraska by exploring the interpersonal, departmental, and institutional dynamics of curricular reform in order to make more explicit the process of curricular revision itself. James Seitz, writing about graduate curricular reform at the University of Pittsburgh, focuses on collaboration and the processes of departmental change open to faculty in an urban state university. James Zebroski concludes this section with a narrative analysis of a nationally influential curricular experiment—the Writing Program for Composition and Cultural Rhetoric at Syracuse University. Zebroski offers a cautionary tale about working in institutions during post-Fordist regimes of capital but nevertheless remains optimistic about the possibilities of teaching and social change.

4. New Missions: The Impact of Technology, Service, and the Vocationalizing of Higher Education

The essays in the final section investigate the missions of English studies as they incorporate changes such as distance and online learning initiatives, service-learning projects, and vocational programs in higher education. Although these trends have arisen, in part, from the desire to make universities more marketable, the contributors seek ways to define the new missions in ethical and publicly accountable ways. Joyce Neff and Juanita Comfort, writing about distance education from positions as researcher and teacher, respectively, in English distance-education courses, discuss issues of imbalance and accountability for teachers of distance courses. Online initiatives, which are designed to meet administrative aims, often signal larger class sizes, inhospitable pedagogical spaces, and punitive forms of evaluative criteria for faculty running distance courses. Daniel Collins writes about the day representatives of General Electric arrived at his community college, seeking to discuss how the school curricula could better meet the corporation's desire for vocationally trained employees. Collins redefines vocationalism not to lose sight of students' desires for marketable skills nor to let such skills subsume the entire curriculum. Ellen Cushman advocates moving service-learning initiatives out of the periphery of composition studies into the center of English. Connecting to local communities would help reinvigorate literary, not just writing, studies and provide an organizing mission to English. James Sosnoski, Patricia Harkin, and Ann Feldman advocate developing collaborative learning networks as humane technological efforts to link people and communities.

This collection adds to the ongoing dialogue about what can or might be done with English studies within the climate of technological, economic, and bureaucratic constraint that constitutes postsecondary education today.

Notes

1. The subject of the corporate university has yielded critique and activist response. See, for example, "From 'Radical University' to Handmaiden of the Corporate State" (Sakolsky and Fox); Cary Nelson's "What Hath English Wrought: The Corporate University's Fast-Food Discipline" (in *Workplace,* 4:1, "Composition in the Managed University"); Janice Newton's "The Corporate-Linked University: From Social Project to Market Force"; and David McNalley's "Welcome to the Corporate University." For student activism, see Liza Featherstone's "The New Student Movement: Protests Rock the Corporate University" and the "Corporate University," sponsored by Students for Environmental Action at Stanford.

2. See also Moran 202.

3. Our title, in part, echoes North's *Refiguring the Ph.D. in English Studies.* North uses "College English Teaching, Inc." to characterize the way the profession has produced Ph.D.s in the traditional "magisterial" model of the literary critic: English professors' course loads and release time are dependent on the use of graduate teaching assistants and part-time faculty to teach writing courses. Our use of "English, Inc." refers to this but also to the incorporation of English studies by bureaucratic management.

4. Working to indirectly bolster nationalist ideals, according to Readings, is the key concession academics in the humanities made to business and government during this period. In return, professors enjoyed limited academic freedom and job security.

5. This claim is not intended to disregard the considerable social struggle that led to the opening of canons or adding of programs that realign English studies; however, only in a time of greater funding could the discipline capitulate in relatively painless ways by adding content areas without cutting existing ones.

6. Harvey notes that post-Fordism has led to a consumer market marked by post-modern aesthetics. Consumption has expanded into the commodification of experience and events, like a university experience. Smith, following Martin Aglietta, describes this as an "increase in the modes of consumption" (see 47–48).

7. An education is a commodity, and for-profit initiatives have opened to try to offer courses of study more cheaply and efficiently. The results have been profitable; for example, the founders of the University of Phoenix landed in the *Forbes 400* list of wealthiest Americans by 1999.

8. The Internet and World Wide Web began as Arpanet, a project of the Pentagon to allow the network of defense contractors to share data from different companies, universities, and laboratories around the world. While no one "owns" the Internet, there is a centralized backbone (see Zakon).

9. Reed Way Dasenbrook argues that "we need some 'business-mindedness' in the university at some level for us to get paid on time, receive salary increases, have money to buy books for the library, and so on" (655). While fiscal responsibility is not an inherently negative goal, problems arise when administrations cite fiscal responsi-bility to justify increasing part-time labor, cutting relevant areas of study, encourag-ing competition for scarce resources within departments, and outsourcing curricular content.

10. The term "corporate university" began among the business community in the 1980s as a way to discuss "creating a strategic umbrella for developing and educating em-ployees . . . in order to meet an organization's business strategies [and] . . . to streamline learning and development efforts" (see Minnesota State Colleges).

11. Newfield explains: "Even for free-market advocates such as [Peter F.] Drucker, the future of capitalism depends on the strength of civil society, on *cultural* forces that workforces and populations shape" (83). Curricular reform must make the case for innovation and creativity as resources for long-term social growth.

12. David Damrosch argues that while universities model businesses, they also maintain traces of ascetic and guild practices.

Works Cited

Aronowitz, Stanley. *The Knowledge Factory: Dismantling the Corporate University and Creating True Higher Learning.* Boston: Beacon P, 2000.

Barlow, Maude, and Heather-Jane Robertson. "Homogenization of Education." *The Case Against the Global Economy.* Eds. Jerry Mander and Edward Goldsmith. San Francisco: Sierra Club Books, 1996, 60–70.

Barrow, Clyde. *Universities and the Capitalist State: Corporate Liberalism and the Re-construction of American Higher Education, 1894–1928.* Madison: U of Wisconsin P, 1990.

Bérubé, Michael. *The Employment of English: Theory, Jobs, and the Future of Literary Studies.* New York: New York UP, 1998.

Blitz, Michael, and C. Mark Hurlbert. *Letters for the Living: Teaching Writing in a Violent Age.* Urbana, IL: NCTE, 1998.

Blumenstyk, Goldie. "Harcourt's Virtual University Gears Up for Marketing Effort, Courses." *The Chronicle of Higher Education* (*http://chronicle.com*), 17 August 2000.

———. "A Vilified Corporate Partnership Produces Little Change (Except Better Facilities)." *The Chronicle of Higher Education* (22 June 2001): A24–26.

Carr, Sarah. "Army Bombshell Rocks Distance Education." *The Chronicle of Higher Education* (*http://chronicle.com*), 18 August 2000.

"Corporate University." *Stanford University DisOrientation Guide* (*seas.stanford.edu/diso/corporate.html*), 15 June 2001.

Currie, Jan, and Lesley Vidovich. "The Ascent Toward Corporate Managerialism in American and Australian Universities." In Martin, *Chalk Lines,* 112–44.

Damrosch, David. *We Scholars: Changing the Culture of the University.* Cambridge: Harvard UP, 1995.

Dasenbrook, Reed Way. "A Comment on 'Brave New University' and 'Who Killed Shakespeare'?" *College English* 62.5 (May 2000): 654–58.

Davidson, Cathy N. "Them versus Us (and Which One of 'Them' Is Me?)." In *Profession 2000,* 97–108.

Delpit, Lisa. *Other People's Children: Cultural Conflict in the Classroom.* New York: New P, 1995.

DeVoss, Danielle, Dawn Hayeden, Cynthia L. Selfe, and Richard J. Selfe, Jr. "Distance Education: Political and Professional Agency for Adjunct and Part-Time Faculty, and GTAs." In Schell and Stock, *Moving a Mountain,* 261–86.

Faigley, Lester. "Literacy After the Revolution: 1996 CCCC Chair's Address." In Taylor and Ward, *Literacy Theory in the Age of the Internet,* 3–16.

Featherstone, Liza. "The New Student Movement: Protests Rock the Corporate University" (*www.commondreams.org/views/042800-104.htm*), 15 June 2001.

Fetterly, Judith. "Dreaming the Future of English," Symposium: English 1999. *College English* 61.6 (July 1999): 702–11.

"A Glance at the July/August Issue of 'Monthly Review': The Language of Globalization." *The Chronicle of Higher Education* (*http://chronicle.com*), 29 August 2000.

Graff, Gerald. *Beyond the Culture Wars: How Teaching the Conflicts Can Revitalize American Education.* New York: Norton, 1992.

———. "Is There a Conversation in This Curriculum? Or, Coherence Without Disciplinarity." In Raymond, 11–28.

———. *Professing Literature: An Institutional History.* Chicago: U of Chicago P, 1987.

Greenblatt, Stephen, and Giles Gunn, eds. *Redrawing the Boundaries: The Transformation of English and American Literary Studies.* New York: MLA, 1992.

Harvey, David. *The Condition of Postmodernity.* Oxford: Blackwell, 1989.

Gunn, Giles. "Introduction: Globalizing Literary Studies." *PMLA*. 116.1 (January 2001): 16–31.

———. *Spaces of Hope*. Berkeley: U of California P, 2000.

Hawisher, Gail, and Cynthia Selfe, eds. *Literacy, Technology, and Society: Confronting the Issues*. Upper Saddle River, NJ: Prentice Hall, 1997.

———. *Passions, Pedagogies, Technologies*. Urbana, IL: USUP/(NCTE), 1999.

Kiernan, Vincent. "A For-Profit Web Venture Seeks to Replicate the University Experience Online." *The Chronicle of Higher Education* (*http://chronicle.com*), 3 April 2000.

Kozol, Jonathan. *Amazing Grace: The Lives of Children and the Conscience of a Nation*. New York: HarperPerennial, 1995.

Lively, Kit. "Nike Chief Ends Giving to U. of Oregon to Protest Its Tie to Anti-Sweatshop Group." *The Chronicle of Higher Education* (*http://chronicle.com*), 5 May 2000.

Loeb, Paul. *Soul of a Citizen: Living with Conviction in a Cynical Time*. New York: St. Martins P, 1999.

Lords, Erik. "Pennsylvania Community Colleges Form Online Consortium." *The Chronicle of Higher Education* (*http://chronicle.com*), 20 March 2000.

Lucas, Christopher J. *American Higher Education: A History*. New York: St. Martin's P, 1994.

Martin, Randy, ed. *Chalk Lines: The Politcs of Work in the Managed University*. Durham, NC: Duke UP, 1998.

———. "Introduction." In Martin, *Chalk Lines,* 1–29.

McNalley, David. "Welcome to the Corporate University" (*www.fortunecity.com/victorian/byron/895/mcnally.html*), 15 June 2001.

Menand, Louis. "The Demise of Disciplinary Authority." In Kernan, 201–19.

———. ed. *The Future of Academic Freedom*. Chicago: U of Chicago P, 1996.

Minnesota State Colleges. "Corporate University." (*www.academicaffairs.mnscu.edu/corporateuniversity.html*), 16 April 2001.

Moran, Charles. "English and Emerging Technologies." *College English* 60.2 (1998): 202–9.

Nelson, Cary, "What Hath English Wrought: The Corporate University's Fast-Food Discipline" (*www.workplace-gsc.com/features1/nelson.html*), 15 June 2001.

Nelson, Cary, and Stephen Watt. "The Corporate University." *Academic Keywords: A Devil's Dictionary for Higher Education*. New York: Routledge, 1999, 84–98.

Newfield, Christopher. "Recapturing Academic Business." In Martin, *Chalk Lines,* 69–102.

Newton, Janice. "The Corporate-Linked University: From Social Project to Market Force." *Canadian Journal of Communications* (23.1) (*www.wlu.ca/~wwwpress/jrls/cjc/backissues/23.1/newson.html*), 15 June 2001.

North, Stephen. *Refiguring the Ph.D. in English Studies*. Urbana, IL: NCTE, 2000.

Ohmann, Richard. *English in America: A Radical View of the Profession*. New York: Oxford UP, 1976.

O'Reilley, Mary Rose. *The Peaceable Classroom*. Portsmouth, NH: Boynton/Cook, 1993.

Press, Eyal, and Jennifer Washburn. "The Kept University." *Atlantic Monthly* 285:3 (March 2000): 39–54.

Profession 2000. New York: MLA, 2000.

Raymond, James C. *English as a Discipline, or Is There a Plot in this Play?* Tuscaloosa and London: U of Alabama, 1996.

Readings, Bill. *The University in Ruins*. Cambridge: Harvard UP, 1996.

Rose, Mike. *Lives on the Boundary*. New York: Penguin Books, 1989.

Sakolsky, Ron, and Dennis Fox. "From 'Radical University' to Handmaiden of the Corporate State" (*www.uis.edu/~fox/state-agent.html*), 15 June 2001.

Sassen, Saskia. *Globalization and Its Discontents*. New York: New P, 1998.

Schell, Eileen E., and Patricia Lambert Stock. *Moving a Mountain: Transforming the Role of Contingent Faculty in Composition Studies and Higher Education*. Urbana, IL: NCTE, 2001.

Slaughter, Sheila, and Larry L. Leslie. *Academic Capitalism: Politics, Policies, and the Entrepreneurial University*. Baltimore: Johns Hopkins UP, 1997.

Smith, Paul. *Millennial Dreams: Contemporary Culture and Capital in the North*. London/New York: Verso, 1997.

Taylor, Todd, and Irene Ward, eds. *Literacy Theory in the Age of the Internet*. New York: Columbia UP, 1998.

Van der Werf, Martin. "Oregon Blocks Public Colleges From Enforcing Anti-Sweatshop Codes of Conduct." *The Chronicle of Higher Education* (*http://chronicle.com*), 27 February 2001.

Walker, David. "Britain Moves Forward with Plans for a Major E-University." *The Chronicle of Higher Education* (*http://chroniscle.com*), 2 May 2000.

Watkins, Evan. *Work Time: English Departments and the Circulation of Cultural Value*. Stanford: Stanford UP, 1989.

Wilson, Robin. "Ohio State 'Taxes' Departments to Make a Select Few Top-Notch." *Chronicle of Higher Education* (1 June 2001): A8–9.

Yagelski, Robert P. "The (Ir)relevance of English: Literacy and Instruction at the Turn of the Millennium." *The Relevance of English*. Eds. Robert P. Yagelski and Scott A. Leonard. Urbana, IL: NCTE (forthcoming), 2002.

Zakon, Robert Hobbes' "Hobbes Internet Timeline" (*www.zakon.org/robert/internet/ timeline*), 14 June 2001.

Chapter Two

Beyond Disciplinary English
*Integrating Reading and Writing
by Reforming Academic Labor*
David B. Downing

In the summer of 1996, I collaborated with a group of seven colleagues at Indiana University of Pennsylvania to investigate a possible new track for our doctoral programs in English.[1] Our intention was to create a more integrated model of graduate study called "Teaching the Writing and Reading of Cultures." We were excited about this possibility precisely because it drew on courses in our department's existing doctoral programs: Literature and Criticism, and Rhetoric and Linguistics. It required very little in the way of added funding, faculty, or departmental staff and resources. We anticipated correctly that our proposal would meet the administration's cost-effectiveness impulses since it adhered to bureaucratic imperatives to get more from less. We developed a detailed rationale, mission statement, and core curriculum based on a combination of courses drawn from the existing doctoral programs. Our goal was to open a new possibility for students to link reading and writing, literature and composition, poetics and rhetorics, teaching and research, in ways that the separate programs prohibited.

The existence of two independent, parallel doctoral programs at Indiana University of Pennsylvania, of course, reflects the long-standing divisions in English studies between literature and composition. Our initiative to provide an integrated, alternative track rested largely on assumptions that perhaps we could negotiate an effective middle ground that, on one hand, allowed for the subdisciplinary integrity of each specialty, while, on the other, opened an integrated possibility for those students interested in a generalist degree. Our group failed even to get this proposal considered by the two program committees. This fact may reflect what was our inexperience in departmental politics, but it also points to a widely shared fear of blurring disciplinary borders and losing program identities when the institution has organized programs to compete with each other for limited resources. Our experience stands in stark contrast to the extensive curricular changes Stephen North describes at SUNY/Albany where, for a period of time at least, they managed to institutionalize his version of a "fusion-based" curriculum for graduate English studies.

Although not successful, the intense summer collaboration helped our group better understand the obstacles that confront any effort to heal the split between literature and composition, poetics and rhetorics, reading and writing. The eight of us involved in this abortive curricular experiment drew somewhat different, and sometimes painful, conclusions from the events that transpired, and we also came to share a sense of key issues that transcend local politics. That's what this chapter is about, at least as told from my perspective.

For one thing, most of us abandoned our hopes that we could reach our goal through an act of disciplinary tinkering. That is, we came to believe that any successful curricular integration of reading and writing would require getting beyond the dominance of the whole disciplinary apparatus of the modern university. As ambitious as that project sounds, it helps to recognize that curricular innovations linking cultural, rhetorical, and composition studies are moving in that direction already. Unfortunately, disciplinary practices still serve to measure success and failure in our profession in ways that often prohibit or defeat the kinds of innovations toward which many of us would like to work. Although the extent of the problem varies considerably from institution to institution, this is a professionwide story about how all in English studies labor under disciplinary conditions. This chapter articulates what such disciplinary reform might call for and how we might go about making such changes.

The Split Between Reading and Writing: The Academic Disciplining of Knowledge and the Scientific Management of Labor

The relation of discipline to curricular design is complicated because a kind of endemic instability characterizes the discipline of English.[2] Indeed, making English into a respectable academic discipline that could organize a coherent curriculum has generally been a contentious project.[3] English professors have struggled, at times with success but often with great difficulty, to adapt what they do to disciplinary practices, such as identifying stable bodies of knowledge and methodically verifying truth claims, practices better-suited to the needs of scientists.[4]

Historically speaking, it wasn't always the case that disciplines served to structure curricula. Prior to the rise of what Keith Hoskin calls the "ecosystem" of disciplinarity in the late nineteenth century, curricula were determined not by disciplinary but by moral and ethical criteria. Indeed, the origins of disciplinarity in the modern sense involved a significant transformation of the meaning of the term "discipline" as it had been used in colleges prior to the Civil War. As Laurence Veysey explains, prior to the academic transformation of knowledge in the last quarter of the nineteenth century, academic "discipline" referred to moral rules of piety and conduct as in the "mental discipline" necessary to build character: "under the banner of 'mental discipline,' a phrase which referred to the sharpening of young men's faculties through enforced contact with Greek and Latin grammar and mathematics, the old-time college sought to provide a four-year regime conducive to piety and strength of character" (9). Belief in such "mental discipline was part of an interlocking set of psychological, theological, and moral convictions" (22). Since in 1870 only about 2 percent of the population in America attended college (Lucas 204), the consequences of such mental discipline served as one possible means to accrue and secure the social status of the ruling classes for those who could afford such a luxury as higher education.[5]

With the dramatic increase in scientific investigations, the traditional college curriculum based on the classics and mathematics no longer served to represent the expanding domains of knowledge. Drawing on the models of German universities that had already begun to reshape knowledge, the American universities began a process of academic reform leading up to the departmentalized, hierarchical university structure that virtually all postsecondary institutions had adopted by the early part of the twentieth century. The new curriculum replaced the moral sense of mental discipline with an institutional structure of specific fields of disciplined knowledge, based not on piety but on the "disinterested pursuit of truth" as best exemplified by scientific fields. The research ideal became the dominant model of university work. But, as Richard Ohmann points out, "the central authority behind this concerted transformation was mainly that of the unseen hand that guides a laissez faire economy" (288).

The force of the new curriculum for administering and defining separate fields of departmentalized knowledge as the distinguishing feature of postsecondary education has enabled it to persist in relatively stable form despite the otherwise dramatic shifts in higher education during the past century. As distinguished from its common use as a synonym for the field or profession, the more specialized function of the "discipline" has fundamentally shaped the divisions between literature and composition. I will focus here on just three key characteristics of the institutional mechanisms of disciplinarity: (1) a discipline is constituted by a specific body of knowledge, the *object* of the discipline; (2) the stability of that knowledge is produced, constituted, and warranted by application of specific, identifiable *methods;* (3) all methods deployed depend on prior protocols for argumentation: refutation, verification, and falsification as rhetorical acts necessary to test and delimit the claims of practitioners. In the case of English, the informal logic of these protocols derive primarily from the more formal logic of the sciences and their ability to produce reliable forms of knowledge (Sosnoski, *Modern*). This means that expository forms of argumentation take precedence over all other imaginative, narrative, figural, or textual innovations.[6]

While the strict processes of disciplining have become the quintessential measure of academic value, the institutionalized protocols for disciplinary practices often exclude or delimit a significant range of socially valuable intellectual labor.[7] This is especially the case for certain activities many English practitioners perform: research or teaching that focuses on ameliorating the local needs of specific groups of people, process-oriented work, research that does not narrowly define objects of investigation, work that engages rhetorical modes other than expository argumentation, or writing for broad audiences through publication in nonacademic magazines and books (a feather for academic celebrities, but a risk for junior faculty seeking tenure credentials). In English departments, disciplinarity both facilitates and justifies the subordination of writing to literature, even though, ironically, writing serves a fundamental role in the practices of examining and grading across all disciplines (Hoskin). The institutional principles of disciplinary knowledge produce what Messer-Davidow, Shumway, and Sylvan call "economies of value" that will always favor those domains where the objects of knowledge, such as literary texts (or, as in the disciplining of cultural studies, cultural texts), can be more successfully designated than the "processes" of composing.

The guild nature of the disciplines means that the expository arguments suitable for scholarly publication produce knowledge if those arguments can be measured or refereed by an audience of trained professionals (who might be considerably divorced from the local contexts and issues). As Ohmann puts it, disciplinary practices reenforce "loyalty to the guild rather than to the college or university" (220), or to the students or the local community or the public, for that matter (see also Larson). The disciplinary measure of success, therefore, purposefully displaces any accountability to people immediately affected by a practical innovation, such as the development of an interactive website linking local high school, community college, and university English departments in a collaborative network. Although it is no doubt possible to give credit for such work, disciplinary pressure will inevitably tend to give greater significance to the published article about the website than reward those who created it and participated in its ongoing success.

From the opposite direction, efforts to speak beyond the disciplinary guild to nonacademic audiences also run the risk of being "unscholarly," and these risks persist despite an increasing concern within the profession to gain what Bérubé calls "public access." Such instances register forms of disciplinary injustice, although in other contexts such disciplinary distancing of local interests from broader knowledge claims has tremendous value for certain kinds of work. Argument is what the academy does best, and as John Michael contends, becoming "masters of our specific disciplinary technologies" (3) is part of what it means to be a critical intellectual in the contemporary world. When claims for knowledge are in dispute, disciplines can serve as critical arbiters for equality, even though race, class, and gender differences, as well as corporate interests often compromise claims of disciplinary autonomy. Non- or postdisciplinary activities will be in tension with disciplinary forms of argumentation, so the hard work will always depend on understanding when and for whom the discipline provides a measure of justice.

The picture is especially complicated in English because of the range of professional tasks we regularly perform. However permeable they may sometimes seem, disciplinary conditions establish the parameters for narrowing that range: Academic value accrues to those practices that can more fully specify both the primary objects of study, such as literary or cultural texts, as well as the secondary critical methods for producing knowledge about those objects through expository prose. It simultaneously devalues the rhetorical practices of poetic, aesthetic, and imaginative forms of discourse and artistic production. Even though, as James Berlin argues, poetics took precedence over rhetoric, it did so not as the active creation *of* poetic texts but through the secondary activity of publishing expository arguments *about* poetic texts themselves. Consequently, the domination within institutional evaluation practices of disciplinary discourse has often meant the crippling and devaluing of some of our most crucial concrete labor practices.

By the early twentieth century, the basic disciplinary principles guided the formation of distinct academic departments, defining specialized fields and subfields according to their specific objects and methods as the distinguishing feature of the modern university. At the same time, what is perhaps most striking in the three primary characteristics of disciplines is the complete absence of any reference to business, labor, race, class, or gender differences. What has long been considered the key virtue of the disciplinary system is its resistance to market forces or the winds of cultural change. As Menand explains, many academics in the early part of the century argued that protecting the disciplines "against market forces is the only way of elevating excellence over profits in a capitalist economy" ("Demise" 203). In the late–nineteenth-century economy, which was "driven by efficiency and self-interest," the disciplines "set standards for performance that value quality over dollars" (203). And, to varying degrees, disciplines did and still do provide some measure of resistance to market forces by providing semiautonomous academic realms where some people who work in English have considerable freedom in terms of concrete labor practices.

It is also true, however, that the disciplines were deeply compromised from the beginning by the material conditions of capitalism, and, as Richard Ohmann first argued, the disciplines were adapted to serve precisely those forces they were supposed to protect against. As Mark, Paula, and I argue in this book's introduction, the disciplinary principles were exactly those that could be appropriated and best serve the principles of scientific management as developed by Frederick Taylor and Henry Ford (see Barrow). One of the most significant consequences of these academic appropriations of corporate models was that teaching became subordinated to research because it was easier to

commodify and manage by standardizing and quantifying disciplinary knowledge production than the quality of teaching.

Working under the conditions of managed disciplinarity, English departments grew dramatically in symbiosis with the tremendous growth of the university in the first half of the twentieth century. Despite the statistical successes in
rising numbers of faculty and students, English professors competed for disciplinary justifications equal to those of the sciences, even while the intellectual
tasks of English professors did not always measure up to disciplinary criteria. The most painful disciplinary squeeze happened to writing practices, even
though they were the skills most highly in demand. To identify their objects and
methods as well as literature professors, composition specialists had little choice
but to adapt accordingly. Disciplinary pressure for such specification led to the
predominance of what James Berlin has called "current-traditional" rhetoric,
with its dependence on measurable formalist skills (the methods) and quantifiable grammatical errors (the objects). Such formalist adaptations of rhetoric to
disciplinary criteria meant a noticeable reduction in the range of writing practices at all levels with, of course, dire consequences for the politics of writing
specialists within English departments (Ohmann, Scholes, Winterowd). Because "literature" had become a privileged term in cultural discourse since the
romantic period (1770–1830), it could better meet the requirements for disciplinary discourse. This was particularly the case when the corporate models of
management were tied to the political mission of the nation-states, and literature could be seen to inculcate a form of nationalist identity and cultural pride
(Readings).

The principles of scientific management had thereby adapted the disciplinary conditions for the production of knowledge. Teaching became so clearly
subordinated to research that, for instance, the MLA abandoned teaching in 1916
by revising a clause in the constitution that originally described "the object of
the Association as 'the advancement of the *study* of the Modern languages and
their literatures'" to read "the advancement of *research* in the Modern languages and their literatures" (emphasis in Graff's, *Professing* 121). With its
formation in 1911, the NCTE became the home for teaching and writing in the
profession, and the basic splits between composition and literature, teaching
and research, became solidified as prestige accrued, naturally enough, to the
more disciplinary forms of literary research.

Historical studies of the period from 1900 to 1945, such as Graff's,
Shumway's, Applebee's, Leitch's, and others, document the intellectual content of the battles to make the unruly field of the literary into a respectable
academic discipline, leading up to the rise of New Criticism after the Second
World War. What is relevant here is that the basic principles of New Criticism
gave rise to the greatest period of disciplinary stability for English departments.
They authorized English departments to develop curricula that enabled them
to define their objects and methods, the primary characteristics of disciplinary
discourse, with almost as much confidence as the sciences. Ideological claims

for the spiritual richness of the unmediated, unparaphraseable "verbal icon" of the poetic experience justified study of the "intrinsic" properties of the text as an object of knowledge, but the ideological claims mattered far less than the powerfully consistent disciplinary practices that became institutionalized in everyday use. Although the New Critics themselves evidenced a much wider range of ideological beliefs about the transcendent values of literary art than many of their critics have acknowledged, their curricular successes depended less on such literary values as on their working practices with respect to the discipline. In short, with literature as the object, close reading as the method, and expository critical writing about canonized texts as the verifiable procedure for producing knowledge, the program for an English major could now be succinctly mapped by organizing courses on the periods and genres of English and American literature.[8]

But, the categories of difference among the disciplinary objects and the workers in the profession tend to be forgotten. No one needed to pay attention to the fact that the profession of literary studies "was for all practical purposes a brotherhood based on race, citizenship, and class, bound together by what might be called, in a play on both its literal and figurative senses, the old school tie" (North, *Refiguring* 22). Indeed, as Messer-Davidow, Shumway, and Sylvan point out, "disciplines produce practitioners," and the orthodox "brotherhood" that ruled English departments in the first half of this century produced practitioners with a remarkable consistency of race, class, and gender characteristics. Such homogeneity also ensured an underlying disciplinary consistency.

With college enrollments nearly quadrupling between 1945 and 1970, the basic inequities of the disciplinary system of English could be tolerated, if not camouflaged, by the postwar economic boom in corporate America. Challenges to the system from new areas of investigation, such as women's studies and African American studies, could be addressed by adding to the existing curriculum without fundamentally changing the orthodox curriculum of literary periods and genres because there were always enough students to fill whatever classes were offered. Moreover, the corporate structuring of disciplinary hierarchy consolidated itself during the period of New Critical hegemony. North describes how undergraduate and graduate English education took the shape of what he calls "College English Teaching, Inc." In this system, tenured senior professors replicate themselves through apprenticeship programs whereby graduate students teach the composition courses while professors develop literary research in graduate seminars. The ongoing corporate need for writing skills could thus be met in a system calling for increased numbers of Ph.D.s even when graduate training itself had nothing to do with teaching or writing. In short, the discipline set the criteria by which the "less-disciplined" could be exploited, and in times of relative bounty, few complained vociferously. By the late 1970s, however, College English Teaching, Inc. began to experience deeper signs of crisis.

Privatization, Flexible Accumulation, and Professional Class Differences Between Literature and Composition

As the introduction to this book points out, David Harvey's description of the restructuring of the labor market provides a remarkably precise account of the past thirty years in English departments: a shrinking core of tenured faculty preside over an expanding array of part-time, temporary instructors, and graduate students. As Ohmann puts it in his 1995 reissuing of *English in America:* "English has, it would almost seem, served as a small laboratory for innovative uses of flexible labor" (xxxix). These flexible labor practices affect our views about potential curricular reform and the discipline of English. In times of economic contraction, budget restraint, and the exploitation of part-time labor, one can understand the drive to shore up the discipline, to make English stronger by rigorously defining its subject matter and precisely identifying its subdisciplines. Academics seek, that is, to resist administrative budget cuts and loss of tenure-track faculty by resorting to the traditional mechanism of resisting market forces: *disciplinarity*. If we just define our objects more precisely and our methods more specifically, disciplinary integrity should justify our preservation, if not expansion. If we appear less "soft" as intellectual dilettantes and more "hard" as knowledge-producing researchers, then the sharpness of our rhetoric will have more political effect in staying the course against market pressures. At least that's the hope; sometimes, in strategic places at the right time, it has the desired effect.

But here's the problem—disciplinarity works better for disciplines, especially the sciences, where specificity and rigor have direct consequences on the securing of grants and endorsements. The better the discipline, the better able it is to attract funding agencies. Administrators have not lost sight of this accounting procedure.[9] Disciplinary research in the humanities does not generally produce short-term revenues because having large numbers of full-time English researchers is costly; however, writing, the one marketable skill that everyone needs, gets staffed by less-disciplined, part-time employees. Historically devalued by disciplinary criteria favoring literature, writing is considered by market forces as a "skill" necessary for any corporate task. Flexible accumulation favors separating writing into smaller, independent units or programs so that the smaller unit can then be more quickly fine-tuned to shifting market needs, whether toward electronic forms of literacy, professional writing, technical writing, or business writing. We will be hard-pressed to argue that more disciplinary rigor and specialization will heal the wounds that our disciplinary history has in fact produced.

As composition theorists have argued for years, teaching writing and reading at any level calls for all the skills, resources, lore, and knowledge of a wide range of activities and practices, even though some forms of disciplinary criteria may not highly honor such work. These scholars call for specialists to teach, write, and research, and to develop links among those activities. As Steven

Mailloux has argued: "A multidisciplinary coalition of rhetoricians will help consolidate the work in written and spoken rhetoric, histories of literacies and communication technologies, and the cultural study of graphic, audio, visual, and digital media" (23). For such coalitions to happen, however, it will have to go beyond disciplinary specializations, not by negating them, but by recognizing that a broader spectrum of intellectual and rhetorical practices will never be fully accountable under strictly disciplinary criteria of evaluation.

There are also political and intellectual reasons that smaller disciplinary units (or writing, literature, or cultural studies) cut their group members off from the support of their peers. Of course, short-term gains to such compartmentalized subfields can accrue, as evidenced by the history of literary elitism and condescension to compositionists. The long-term consequences of this elitism will eventually cast literary separatists into what Jim Sosnoski has called the "underworld of the university system" (*Modern* 29). There is little in the long-term economic future to sustain such privileges. The aesthetic and the political, the literary and the rhetorical, the textual and the extratextual are deeply entwined, and their disciplinary separation has been costly. Administrators out to cut budgets are the only ones to gain from the internecine warfare among competing subdivisions. In the end, disciplinary isolation makes any small unit or program more vulnerable to administrative surveillance.[10]

Curricular innovations from literary scholars, even when they claim to break down the hierarchies between reading and writing, often disable the institutional force of their worthy innovations by insisting on, as Robert Scholes puts it, "making English studies more rather than less disciplined" (108). Two significant proposals for curricular reform—Scholes' own curricular model for English studies and Paul Jay's important work on globalizing literary studies—do not sufficiently alter the institutional role of the discipline of English studies. Because neither addresses disciplinarity as the precondition for curricular change, the fine changes that they do recommend will not adequately respond to the increased class differences emerging from the uses and abuses of academic labor.

Scholes' proposal for a reformed English curriculum has many attractive features, all aimed at linking reading and writing, which he calls consumption and production. He proposes a return to the classic "trivium" of grammar, dialectic, and rhetoric, and he describes an attractive array of new courses investigating these key terms. Under the new rigors of his disciplinary trivium, he proposes a "realignment" of "two types of canonicity," "between canons of texts and canons of methods" (111). It should be clear from my previous discussion of the rise of disciplinarity that realigning objects and methods will indeed alter the content of the discipline, but it will not significantly alter the conditions for disciplinary discourse since "methods" is one of the central characteristics of disciplinary discourse.[11] Scholes grants that "*discipline,* like *canon,* is a word that scarcely conceals its potential for abuses of power. We need disciplines in order to think productively. We also need to challenge them in order to think creatively" (108). This is a wise admonition even though disciplines are neither a necessary nor a sufficient prerequisite to "think productively."

Within English departments, one of the key points of contact for the exercise of disciplinary power takes place through evaluation and hiring committees and the particular criteria they deploy to make crucial personnel decisions. Disciplinary evaluation criteria become measures of competitive individualism as colleagues strive to acquire symbolic capital primarily through their publications and other forms of acceptable labor. Without significant alteration, disciplinarity both discourages and devalues the kinds of collaboration necessary for many of the diverse forms of rhetorical, political, and intellectual work that English professors actually perform. Without considerable study of how to alter our evaluation practices, disciplinary criteria reign in powerful de facto ways. Scholes' analysis focuses on curricular content and method and leaves routine disciplinary evaluation practices in place: As he puts it again, he wants to make English "more rather than less disciplinary."[12]

Although Scholes claims that "[t]he skill of a writer is a happy one because it is based upon play" (102), disciplinarity doesn't often value play unless it produces "serious" forms of knowledge in expository prose that clearly identifies its own objects and methods. Disciplinary criteria will, for example, more highly value an expository article *about* a highly playful and innovative performative literacy event such as a collaborative improvisation by students and faculty at the local writing center, but not the event itself. By not revising the basic conditions of disciplinarity, Scholes' curriculum will diminish the value of certain forms of labor that he himself says he values. That is, the power of disciplinarity is such that various kinds of textual and rhetorical innovations, multimedia studies, pedagogical experimentation, collaborative teaching and research projects, and community literacy endeavors will continue to be subordinated in value even though they may have considerable social and market value for some forms of business. And such hierarchies of value get, as it were, *naturalized* into the criteria deployed in the evaluation and hiring committees.

With respect to the wider university and public, I find Scholes' use of the "medieval trivium" of "grammar, dialectic, and rhetoric" a troublesome set of terms to "sell," which of course we must do since we need to exercise control over the commodification of our interests. Without more substantial revision of the conditions of disciplinarity accompanying Scholes' reformed curriculum, there's nothing to prevent the new organizational terms from adapting to traditional disciplinary hierarchies. Teachers engaged in various kinds of non-, extra-, or postdisciplinary forms of investigation, calling for collaboration with students to improve their learning and their contribution to local communities, will find their work diminished by strictly disciplinary criteria. Without a fair assessment of the value of these other activities as determined by nondisciplinary criteria, the disciplinary practices will ensure that a small core of highly trained faculty will have the resources to study the complicated terrain of dialectics and rhetoric, while many of the most valuable practices of most faculty will continue to be devalued or forced to adapt to back-to-the-basics forms of grammar where they can be more easily exploited in a flexible market. Nondisciplinary practices will likely remain subordinated within Scholes' model of English unless disciplinary reform accompanies the curricular remodeling.

In a recent *PMLA* essay, provocatively entitled "Beyond Discipline? Globalization and the Future of English," Paul Jay demonstrates the limits of the older, dominant "nationalist paradigm" for literary study as exemplified by Scholes' articulation of the "story of English." Like Scholes, Jay advocates the need to expand and alter the basic content of the discipline of English to reflect a new, more proper emphasis on "literature's relation to the historical processes of globalization" (33). He advances the "need to make a programmatic commitment to the study of English in a newer, global framework, one that recognizes the transnational character of English in the past and the global context in which it will be produced in the future" (46). In themselves, these are superb goals designed to stretch the borders of the discipline because, as Jay comments, without "such a commitment, we may see the discipline of English become ever more marginal, in the university of the future" (46).

However important such expanding borders must inevitably be, Jay's title is ironic to the extent that it should really read: "Beyond the Current Content of the Discipline of English Literary Studies." The changes he recommends don't get "beyond" disciplinary English at all, in the sense in which I am arguing that we must. That is, although Jay mentions that writing and composition are equally important, and that he only excludes them for purposes of space in his article, Jay does not envision any particular change in the disciplinary practices as I have outlined them in this chapter. He advocates remapping the literary terrain, in order to "develop new terms and paradigms to describe what we do" (44). But as I have argued elsewhere, paradigms themselves inevitably call for a reassertion of the hierarchy of disciplinary forms (Downing). Moreover, whether one teaches Hawthorne or Achebe will likely not matter so much in terms of public accountability if the pressing need is for literacy and rhetorical skills. As Evan Watkins puts it: "Just as a political praxis of change is not only a matter of inventing new concrete work practices, it is not a matter either of changing the texts we teach, reforming the 'canon.' Such reform can of course be made part of a 'war of position,' but the point is that it must be *made* so against the working organization of English" (17). Bracketing off the literary skills from the literacy component strikes at the core of the disciplinary problem in realigning curricula. The disciplinary presumptions of Jay lead him to focus primarily on a shifting of the objects (texts) and methods (theories) of the discipline. But the human context of many of our workplaces are now for the most part so crossed by the international and global mix of student and faculty populations that the kinds of writing tasks, narratives, stories, and investigations need to be integrated directly into the work of curricular reform at the beginning, not after the content has been shifted.

Stephen North offers one of the few models for what he has called the "fusion" option for reinvigorating English studies, and I share his assessment that without the hard work of rebuilding the subdisciplinary splits that have characterized the history of the profession, we won't even be able to "*begin* the negotiations that might result in substantive change" (*Refiguring* 237). Besides healing the disciplinary splits within the field, this kind of broader institutional reform aims not only to legitimize emergent kinds of postdisciplinary academic work, but to recognize many practices that are already taking place but that have been systematically devalued. Such practices may always be challenges to, and in tension with, strictly disciplinary forms of academic research, which is as it should be so long as disciplinary research does not continue to get preferential treatment.

Although the current crisis of English studies has been most commonly seen as evolving out of a need to expand the objects and methods of the discipline, my argument calls for the more fundamental task of altering the strictly hierarchical role of disciplinarity itself in determining the range of institutionally authorized labor practices of English professors. It will be best to see the range of tasks carried out by English professors along a horizontal spectrum from disciplinary to non- or postdisciplinary practices, with different kinds of evaluative criteria appropriate for different kinds of work. This argument raises large questions about the material processes whereby certain kinds of professorial labor get legitimized and authorized within our specific institutions. Significant curricular reform will depend on our success in altering some of the basic institutional practices that we have long taken for granted. It's time for a change at this basic level.

My more ambitious claim is that, in the case of English, we may have reached the end of the 125-year history where disciplinary criteria should continue to be the exclusive measure of academic performance and curricular design. This involves more than just expanding the borders of the canon or becoming increasingly interdisciplinary, no matter how vital such practices may be to curricular transformation. Although we cannot easily alter the market forces in the current regime of "flexible accumulation," we can design curricula that more fully integrate reading and writing practices so that we can resist the isolation and exploitation of what James Sosnoski so aptly calls "token professionals" (*Token*)—a large segment of our professional ranks whose labor never quite counts for much under strictly disciplinary criteria. The ultimate irony of such reforms might be that by making the range of our professional practices more flexible than the focus on disciplinary criteria might otherwise allow, we regain some of the autonomy that would enable us to heal the class differences within the profession. We simply don't have any choice about whether we will experience economic flexibility because that's a rapidly globalizing phenomenon of the contemporary social and cultural marketplace in which we must operate. We must draw on the spaces of relative autonomy still left to us to determine as far as possible the terms of how that flexibility will affect us. One would hope, therefore, that reformed and integrated curricula could better resist the "flexible accumulation" carried out by management practices that have used disciplinary justifications to further the exploitation of nondisciplinary peripheral labor. Of course, none of this will be easy, but that's the hard political work of disciplinary and curricular revision.

The arts and the humanities have always encompassed more than disciplinary discourse, and this imaginative and rhetorical excess accounts for the uneasy relations in the disciplinary status of English studies.[13] Given the wide-ranging economic, social, and technological changes taking place in our culture, it becomes possible to see humanistic work as engaging a spectrum of practices that take place along a horizontal continuum from disciplinary to postdisciplinary, or even antidisciplinary modes. This continuum need not be hierarchical, but differential. Obviously, hierarchies of value will continue to be exercised because the basic evaluative task of professionals is to make such judgments, but they need not emerge on the predominant disciplinary scale. Since disciplinary constraints can sometimes foster forms of social injustice, the production of knowledge may need to be subordinated to the search for justice and understanding. We need not, therefore, require that all humanistic literacy practices fit within the system of disciplinary forms of argumentation and exclusion. Fundamental to such an integrated vision of English studies will be a thorough refiguring of the role of writing in both graduate and undergraduate education.

If our concern for reforming English studies resonates with a commitment to equitable labor conditions, this chapter is a cautionary tale with a potentially happier ending. There are possibilities for retooling evaluation practices and re*visioning* humanities' labor as running across a spectrum of disciplinary and extra-, non-, or postdisciplinary activities that need not be measured according to a single disciplinary yardstick. And the human labor involved in these practices calls for revaluations throughout our professional ranks as we re*imagine* the activities of reading and writing our cultures for a better future.

Notes

1. The participants were Susan Marguerite Comfort, myself, Maurice Kilwein Guevara, Thomas J. Slater, and Roxann Wheeler from the Literature and Criticism Program; and C. Mark Hurlbert, Donald A. McAndrew, and Gian S. Pagnucci from the Rhetoric and Linguistics Program.

2. The term "discipline" is used in sometimes contradictory ways. While many people use the term as a synonym for a "field" or "profession," this general use is often confused with a narrower and research-based sense of the term as it applies to academic work. In this second sense, "discipline" refers to the specific conditions of disciplinary discourse that have evolved over roughly the past 130 years (see Hoskin). For this chapter, I use "discipline" to refer to the latter, narrower, more specific set of practices within the broader range of professional work.

3. See this book's Introduction and Bérubé, Goggin, Graff ("Is There," *Professing*), North, and Raymond.

4. See Mailloux, 14.

5. See Graff (*Professing* 21) for an important qualification of this overview.

6. For the scope of this chapter, I work with only three characteristics of a discipline. There are more. I have drawn especially on the work of Sosnoski, Shumway, Messer-Davidow, Hoskin, Toulmin, Foucault, and Bové.

7. See Messer-Davidow et al., viii.

8. Ohmann notes that, by 1970, there was considerable variation within English departments in America. Despite these variations, the curricula "have a common basis" (222)—a disciplinary basis.

9. See Lucas, 237.

10. See Bartholomae, 1954.

11. Scholes explains his goal "to reconstruct our field as a discipline," suggesting his investment in disciplinary discourse. His answer: "To put it in grossly simplified form, is to replace the canon of texts with a canon of methods—to put a modern equivalent of the medieval trivium at the center of an English education" (145).

12. It is also the case that a wide range of professional resources must be established and developed to support all the various kinds of non- and postdisciplinary activities needed for wide-scale curricular reform. These would include new kinds of journals, websites, conferences, online networks, and so on, all supporting alternative kinds of reading and writing practices.

13. Although some may lament the "demise of disciplinary authority" (Menand, "Demise"), it might be better to think of it as the demise of the exclusive reign of one form of knowledge, and thus opening university spaces for new kinds of practices that are valuable to the public in general and that are well suited to being carried out within the more broadly conceived role of the university in the contemporary world.

Works Cited

Applebee, Arthur. *Tradition and Reform in the Teaching of English: A History.* Urbana, IL: NCTE, 1974.

Barrow, Clyde. *Universities and the Capitalist State: Corporate Liberalism and the Reconstruction of American Higher Education, 1894–1928.* Madison, WI: U of Wisconsin P, 1990.

Bartholomae, David. "Composition, 1900–2000." *PMLA* 115.7 (December 2000): 1950–54.

Berlin, James A. *Rhetorics, Poetics, and Cultures.* Urbana, IL: NCTE, 1996.

Bérubé, Michael. *The Employment of English: Theory, Jobs, and the Future of Literary Studies.* New York: New York UP, 1998.

———. *Public Access: Literary Theory and American Cultural Politics.* London: Verso, 1994.

Bové, Paul. *Intellectuals in Power: A Genealogy of Critical Humanism.* New York: Columbia UP, 1986.

Downing, David B. "The 'Mop-up' Work of Theory Anthologies: Theorizing the Discipline and the Disciplining of Theory." *Symploke* 8.1–2 (2000): 96–116.

Foucault, Michel. *Discipline and Punish*. London: Allen Lane, 1977.

Goggin, Maureen Daly. "The Tangled Roots of Literature, Speech Communication, Linguistics, Rhetoric/Composition, and Creative Writing: A Selected Bibliography on the History of English Studies." *Rhetoric Society Quarterly* 29.4 (Fall 1999): 63–89.

Graff, Gerald. *Beyond the Culture Wars: How Teaching the Conflicts Can Revitalize American Education*. New York: Norton, 1992.

———. "Is There a Conversation in This Curriculum? Or, Coherence Without Disciplinarity." In Raymond, *English* . . . 11–28.

———. *Professing Literature: An Institutional History*. Chicago: U of Chicago P, 1987.

Harvey, David. *The Condition of Postmodernity*. Oxford: Blackwell, 1990.

Hoskin, Keith W. "Education and the Genesis of Disciplinarity: The Unexpected Reversal." In Messer-Davidow et al., *Knowledges,* 271–304.

Jay, Paul. "Beyond Discipline? Globalization and the Future of English." *PMLA* 116.1 (January 2001): 32–47.

Kernan, Alvin, ed. *What's Happened to the Humanities?* Princeton: Princeton UP, 1997.

Larson, Magali Sarfarti. *The Rise of Professionalism: A Sociological Analysis*. Berkeley: U of California P, 1977.

Leitch, Vincent B. *American Literary Criticism from the 30s to the 80s*. New York: Columbia UP, 1988.

Lucas, Christopher J. *American Higher Education: A History*. New York: St. Martin's P, 1994.

Mailloux, Steven. "Disciplinary Identities: On the Rhetorical Paths Between English and Communication Studies." *Rhetoric Society Quarterly* 30.2 (Spring 2000): 5–29.

Martin, Randy, ed. *Chalk Lines: The Politics of Work in the Managed University*. Durham, NC: Duke UP, 1998.

Menand, Louis. "The Demise of Disciplinary Authority." In Kernan, *What's Happened to the Humanities?*. 201–19.

———. ed. *The Future of Academic Freedom*. Chicago: U of Chicago P, 1996.

Messer-Davidow, Ellen, David R. Shumway, and David J. Sylvan, eds. *Knowledges: Historical and Critical Studies in Disciplinarity*. Charlottesville: UP of Virginia, 1993.

Michael, John. *Anxious Intellects: Academic Professionals, Public Intellectuals, and Enlightenment Values*. Durham, NC: Duke UP, 2000.

Newfield, Christopher. "Recapturing Academic Business." In Martin, *Chalk Lines,* 69–102.

North, Stephen. "On the Business of English Studies." *The Relevance of English*. Eds. Robert P. Yagelski and Scott A. Leonard. Urbana, IL: NCTE (forthcoming), 2002.

———. *Refiguring the Ph.D. in English Studies*. Urbana, IL: NCTE, 2000.

Ohmann, Richard. *English in America: A Radical View of the Profession*. New York: Oxford UP, 1976.

Raymond, James C. *English as a Discipline, or Is There a Plot in This Play?* Tuscaloosa and London: U of Alabama P, 1996.

Readings, Bill. *The University in Ruins*. Cambridge: Harvard UP, 1996.

Scholes, Robert. *The Rise and Fall of English*. New Haven: Yale UP, 1998.

Shumway, David. *Creating American Civilization: A Genealogy of American Literature as an Academic Discipline*. Minneapolis: U of Minnesota P, 1994.

Sosnoski, James J. *Modern Skeletons in Postmodern Closets: A Cultural Studies Alternative*. Charlottesville: U of Virginia P, 1995.

———. *Token Professionals and Master Critics: A Critique of Orthodoxy in Literary Studies*. Buffalo: SUNY P, 1994.

Toulmin, Stephen. *Human Understanding: The Collective Use and Evolution of Concepts*. Princeton: Princeton UP, 1972.

Veysey, Laurence. *The Emergence of the American University*. Chicago: U of Chicago P, 1965.

Watkins, Evan. *Work Time: English Departments and the Circulation of Cultural Value*. Stanford: Standord UP, 1989.

Chapter Three

"A Blow Is Like an Instrument"
The Poetic Imaginary and Curricular Practices
Charles Bernstein

There are no core subjects, no core texts in the humanities, and this is the grand democratic vista of our mutual endeavor in arts and letters, the source of our greatest anxiety and our greatest possibilities. In literary studies, it is not enough to show what has been done but also what it is possible to do. Art works are not just monuments of the past but investments in the present, investments we squander with our penurious insistence on taking such works as cultural capital rather than capital expenditure.

I often teach works that raise, for many students, some of the most basic questions about poetry: What is poetry? How can this work be a poem? How and what does it mean? These are not questions that I especially want to talk about nor ones that the works at hand continue to raise for me. Whatever questions I may have of this sort, I have either resolved or put aside as I listen for quite different, much more particular, things. My own familiarity with the poetry I teach puts me at some distance from most students, who are coming to this work for the first time. And yet, when I overcome my resistance and engage in the discussion, which I often find becomes contentious and emotional, I am reminded that when a text is dressed in the costume of poetry, that, in and of itself, is a provocation to consider these basic questions of language, meaning, and art. Inevitably, raising such questions is one of the uses of the poetry to which I am committed; that is, poetry marked by its aversion to conformity, to received ideas, to the expected or mandated or regulated form. These aversions and resistances have their history, they are never entirely novel nor free of traditions, including the traditions of the new; that history is nothing less than literary history. But the point of literary history is not just that a selected sequence of works was created nor that they are enduring or great (or deplorable and hideous) nor that they form a part of a cultural fabric of that time or a tradition that extends to the present. All that is well and good, but aesthetically secondary. The point, that is, is not *(not just)* the transcendental or cultural or historical or ideological or psychoanalytic deduction of a work of art but how that work plays itself out: its performance not (just) its interpretation. But as history is written by the victors, so art (as a matter of professional imperatives) is taught by the explainers.

It needn't be so, for we are professors not deducers: Our work is as much to promote as to dispel, to generate as much as document. I am not—I know it sounds like I am—professing the virtue of art over the deadness of criticism but rather the aversion of virtue that is a first principle of the arts and an inherent, if generally discredited, possibility for the humanities.

I suspect part of the problem may be in the way a certain idea of philosophy as critique, rather than art as practice, has been the model for the best defense of the university. I don't say critique as opposed to aesthetics but critique without aesthetics—that is, the sort of institutionalized critique that dominates the American university—is empty, a shell game of Great Books and Big Methods full of solutions and cultural capital, signifying nothing. That is, Professionalized Critique dogs every school of criticism when as a matter of routine (and perhaps against its most radical impulses), it turns art into artifact, asking not what it does but what it means; much as its own methods are, and quicker than a wink, turned from tools to artifacts.

Poetry, and the arts, are living entities in our culture. It is not enough to know the work of a particular moment in history, removed from the context of our contemporary culture; such knowledge risks being transmitted stillborn. Just as we now insist that literary works need to be read in their socio-historical context, so we must also insist that they be read into the present aesthetic context. So while I lament the lack of cultural and historical information on the part of students, I also lament the often proud illiteracy of contemporary culture on the part of the faculty.

I do not suggest that the (contemporary) practice of poetry should eclipse literary history (as, for a time, the contemporary practice of analytic philosophy eclipsed the history of philosophy). I do believe, however, that literary history or theory uninformed by the newly emerging forms of poetic practice is as problematic as literary criticism or literary history uninformed by contemporary theoretical or methodological practices. I realize that my insistence on the aesthetic function of poetry and the significance for literary studies of contemporary literature has an odd echo with some of the tenets of the New Critics. But I point this out mainly to debunk the dogma that works that "create linguistic difficulty and density and therefore make meaning problematic" have remained, or were ever, the center of attention of literary studies from the New Critics until the present, as Catherine Gallagher suggests (140).

As far as English literary studies of this century are concerned, *The Waste Land* and *Ulysses* have had to bear most of the weight of this claim. But these cease to be difficult texts insofar as they are fetishized as Arnoldian tokens of "bestness"—a process that replaces their linguistic, aesthetic, and socio-historical complexity with the very unambiguous status of cultural treasure; in any case, they have not been contemporary texts for well over half a century. Despite the homage, difficult or ambiguous literature has not, as a rule, meant teaching disorienting or unfamiliar works of literature to college students, and especially not works that challenged the professor's critical or ideological paradigms or were written in unfamiliar or disruptive dictions, dialects, or lexicons. Rather it has meant turning a narrow range of designated difficulties into puzzles resolvable by checking off the boxes on the "Understanding Poetry" worksheet, while rejecting ways of reading poetry that do not produce "understanding" but rather response, questions, disorientation, interaction, more poems. In fact, if you look at the anthologies of English and American literature that have been used in humanities classes over the past fifty years, you will see that if difficulty is a criteria at all, it is as likely to be one for the exclusion of a work as for its inclusion; a tendency that has only accelerated in recent years as accessibility and moral uplift have taken on both a political and pedagogic imperative.

In the end, despite their defense of difficulty, the New Critics were primarily responsible for defanging radical modernism and enthroning its milquetoast other, High Antimodernism (a reference to their own work certainly, but also bringing to mind the work they abjured). Moreover, as Gallagher accurately points out, and it is also a point made with synoptic brilliance by Jed Rasula in *The American Poetry Wax Museum,* the New Critics and their heirs actively discounted much of the demotic, folk, vulgar, idiosyncratic, ethnic, erotic, black, women's, and genre poetry for which its reading methods were inadequate. This is not, I would insist, because this work was not ambiguous or difficult enough but because it posed the wrong kind of difficulties and ambiguities.

The academic profession is not a unified body but a composite of many dissimilar individuals and groups pursuing projects ranging from the valiantly idiosyncratic to the proscriptively conventional. Most of the popular generalizations about what professors do or don't do are unsupported by facts; for example, it turns out that, as a whole, professors work very long hours, generally beyond anything required of them. Moreover, there is a disturbing trend to equate classroom hours with work hours, leading to a fundamental misrepresentation of the nature of academic labor. It's as if you measured the work of a lawyer only by the hours spent in her client's presence, or the work of a cook by how long it takes to eat his soufflé, or the work of a legislator by the number of pages of legislation he or she has written. Yet comparable misrepresentations of the academic profession are having dire consequences, most specifically in abetting the increase in nontenured part-time employment that is eroding not only the working conditions of the university but the quality of education that universities can provide.

Misinformation feeds on misinformation, so it is particularly unfortunate that political expediency has encouraged many of those who speak in the name of the university to abandon any vision of the radically democratic role the university can, but too often does not, play in this culture. That is to say, tenure and academic freedom are not primarily valuable because they provide job security to individual faculty members but because they serve the public good. There is no conflict between the public interest and full-time tenured employment: Short-term cost savings cannot justify the long-term economic folly of compromising one of the most substantial intellectual and cultural resources this society has created. The question is not whether our society can afford to maintain the intellectual and cultural space of the university at present levels but whether it can afford not to.

The greatest benefit of the university is not that it trains students for anything in particular, nor that it imbues in them a particular set of ideas, but that it is a place for open-ended research that can just as well lead nowhere as somewhere, that is wasteful and inefficient by short-term socioeconomic standards but is practically a steal as a long-term research and development investment in democracy, freedom, and creativity—without which we won't have much of an economic future or the one we have won't be worth the flesh it's imprinted on. At its most effective, the university is not oriented toward marketplace discipline and employment training, but rather toward maximizing the capacity for reflection and creativity. When it is most fully achieving its potential, university classes are not goal-oriented or preprofessional but self-defining and exploratory. Attempts to regulate the university according to market values only pervert what is best and least accountable about these cultural spaces. We cannot make education more efficient without making it more deficient.

My plea then is for enriched content, especially aesthetic and conceptual content, over a streamlined vocational goal orientation. There is an educational payoff but it has to do with degrees of intellectual resonance and creativity not measurable (always) in immediate job readiness (for which, as Silicon Valley has shown, college may be unnecessary). Almost everyone agrees there is a practical value in students being able to write in conventional business English but minimum standards are notoriously hard to achieve, as even those who emphasize basic skills realize. To create good writers you need to create good readers. There is no shortcut. A correction-oriented expository writing drill might produce barely competent writers (it often doesn't) but such competence may come at the cost of alienating students from their own language practices (talking and writing and reading). Taking an image from Rousseau's *Emile,* if we swaddle the young scholar in the strictures of grammatical correctness, we may induce immobility while fostering uprightness. And mobility is a practical skill for a "people in transition," to use a phrase from Langston Hughes that speaks to our American social space at the beginning of the twenty-first century. In correcting a perceived deficit, we must keep in mind that teachers, just as doctors, need to be sure to do no harm.

The university I envision is more imaginary than actual, for everywhere the tried and, sometimes, true pushes out the untried but possible.

Within the academic profession, fights are often intramural as new disciplinary and methodological projects threaten older ones—the new and old both claiming to be the victims of unprecedented dogmatism, bad faith, and lack of intellectual or cultural values. In literary studies, these conflicts tend to be among three different conceptions of the field. One group defines literary studies in terms of its traditional subject matter—that is, the literary works that have traditionally served as the principal objects of study in the field. This group maintains relative consensus among its constituents. A second group accepts the idea of the field as defined by its subject matter, but proposes a new range of subject matter—from works underrepresented in traditional literary study to works that challenge the very idea of the literary. There is consensus among the constituents of this second group on broadening the subject matter of the field but necessarily no consensus on exactly what the new subjects should be. A third group consists of those who define the field primarily in terms of a particular method of analysis, critique, or interpretation. There is little consensus among the constituents of this third group since the approaches adopted are often seen to be mutually exclusive. No doubt many in the profession are sympathetic, to varying degrees, with all three of these conceptions of the field.

The danger for the academic profession is not that one side or another will "win"—that the new barbarians will become the old boys or the traditionalists will block innovation. Rather, the problem is the idea that consensus should prevail. The manufacturing of consent always involves the devaluing or exclusion of that which doesn't fit the frame. What I value is not temperance but tolerance, for an insistence on temperance can mark an intolerance not only of the intemperate but also of unconventional—or unassimilated—forms of expression. We don't need to agree, or even converse, so long as we tolerate the possibility of radically different approaches, even to our most cherished ideas of decorum, methodology, rationality, subject matter. The university that I value leaves all of these matters open, undecided—and not just open for debate, but open for multiple practices. The point is not to replace one approach with another but to reorient ourselves toward a kind of inquiry in which there are no final solutions, no universally mandated protocols—an orientation that is fundamental to the chapters in this book. The point is not to administer culture but to participate in it.

In discussions about the state of the university, complaints about "tenured radicals" abound. I am more worried about tenured smugness and tenured burnout.

While I respect the authority of scholarship I reject the authoritativeness of any prescribed set of books, methods, experts, standards. The problem is not that there has been too much reform but that there has hardly been any at all: The content has shifted, but this reflects demographic changes more than ideological ones; the structure of authority remains the same. Given the passionate engagement with their research of most of the graduate students I know, the often-deanimating mandates of perceived professional success are the surest symptom of the problem. From the time they enter graduate school, the passions, commitments, and creativity of the young scholar are routinely reoriented toward a cynical professional wiliness that emphasizes who it is opportune to quote or what best fits market prospects rather than what the young scholar is most capable of doing or what best suits her or his passions or aesthetic proclivities. The profession, both panicked by the market and temperamentally conservative (even in its apparently nonconservative guises) seems bent on shaping young scholars in its own image rather than encouraging the production of new and unexpected images. In these circumstance, professors—sometimes unintentionally, sometimes with the best intentions—often seem less inclined to offer themselves as aids to young scholars' research than to act as living roadblocks.

Although specialization is appropriate for a scholar's own work—and there is nothing more sublime about the university than those obsessive scholars who seem to know everything about a specific subject, writer, or period— specialization is too often projected out on students at large, as the same few books get taught over and again, while the vast wealth of new books and old books remain "outside my field" (why not take a walk on the adjacent fields from time to time?). The problem may well be that many professors do not feel they have the authority to teach or supervise work in which they do not have expertise. I suppose imagining I have no expertise at all may be my greatest advantage: I can consider teaching or discussing almost anything if a student makes a compelling proposal for its necessity. My subject is contemporary poetry, but I find it stretches from there to almost anywhere. By that I mean to say that whatever time students have in the university, in college or graduate school, should be a time of indiscriminate, prodigal, voracious reading and searching: *One text must lead directly to the next.* Against the mandated hypotactic, rationalized logic of conventional syllabi, I suggest we go *avagabonding*—let our curriculums spin out into paratactic sagas. I propose we focus less on adducing the meaning of a homogenous sequence of works and more on addressing the relation of heterogeneous series of works (Li Po next to Oulipo, "Jabberwocky" with Newton's *Optics*). Nor is this another appeal to interdisciplinarity, which assumes the constituent disciplines that are already established and carefully preserves their distinctness through the process. Indeed, I've come to realize that poetry is one of the most intradisciplinary topics in the humanities, but this is because—since well before Lucretius—poetry already potentially encompasses all the disciplines of the humanities.

I realize my approach will not be to everyone's taste, nor do I wish to impose my sensibilities on the academic profession at large. What I ask for is greater tolerance for such approaches in a university that allows for the multiple and even incommensurable not just in its theories but in its practices.

It's not that I overstate my case, I am making a case for overstatement.

This wild adventure in learning is surely what inspired many of us to make the arts or humanities our calling, yet we lose the passion as we go from this adventure in texts to administering culture by teaspoon. And this is very like what we do when we imagine our graduate programs primarily in terms of vocational training in narrowly predefined fields, rather than opportunities for open-ended research, centers for the study of the arts, lavish emporiums of further thinking. Does anyone doubt that we deaden the potential of future research and future teaching with our cramped, vocational/preprofessional disciplinary fantasies? And what a travesty, in particular, this training for jobs that do not even exist— even though we must all do all we can to reverse the pernicious trend toward poorly paid adjunct work in place of full-time, tenured employment. Yet I must disagree with those who, with great probity, advise that we reduce graduate programs to make them conform more precisely to the job market so as to avoid overproduction of Ph.D.s. Rather we should welcome into our graduate programs those whose goal is not to have the same job as their teachers, but who, for a number of reasons, want to take one, two, or five years, modestly funded in exchange for some teaching, to pursue their studies, in ways they must be primarily responsible for defining.

And what of academic standards? Aren't these the dikes that protect us from the flood of unregulated thought? Or are they like the narrow Chinese shoe that deforms our thinking to fit its image of rigor? When I examine the formats and implied standards for peer-reviewed journals and academic conferences, they suggest to me a preference for a lifeless prose, bloated with the compulsory repetitive explanation of what every other "important" piece on this subject has said. Of course, many professors will insist that they do not subscribe to this, but the point is not what any one of us does but the institutional culture we accept. It seems to me that the academic culture of the humanities places more emphasis on learning its ropes, on professional conformity, than it does on any actual research, writing, thinking, or teaching of the people who make up the profession. Indeed, it doesn't really matter what constitutes this conformity— the distinction being made is in an important sense antipathetic to substance. This is the chief function of anonymous peer review: not ensuring quality or objectivity but compliance.

Anonymous peer reviewing enforces prevalent disciplinary standards, especially standards about the tone or manner of an argument, even while permitting the publication of a wide range of ideas, *as long as the ideas are expressed in the dominant style*. While it might seem that anonymous review would encourage greater textual freedom, in practice the submission of an anonymous article to multiple anonymous readers ends up favoring work that comes closest to conforming to accepted norms of argument and writing style; indeed, such a procedure is one of the best ways of determining what these norms are. Of course, it's no big surprise that institutions perpetuate their institutional styles. But perhaps what may make what I am saying sound, to some in the profession, exaggerated is that I find it deplorable that academic the profession is, well, too *academic*. Maybe this is because I am more accustomed to a form of cultural exchange and production among poets and through independently produced "small press" books and magazines that seems more vital, and more committed to the values often ascribed to the academic profession—that is, more committed to fomenting imagination than controlling imagination—than is the academic profession itself. The academic profession has a lot to learn from such communities of independent artists and scholars. I also feel that the academic profession has an obligation to provide a sanctuary for the arts, especially in a period of devastating defunding of government support.

What I object to is disciplinarity for the sake of disciplinarity and not in the service of inquiry. Too often, the procedures developed by the academic profession to ensure fairness and rigor end up creating a game that rewards routinized learning over risk. Blind peer reviewing, like its cousins—standardized testing and evaluation—is certainly an advantage when it comes to discouraging preferential treatment for individuals, but the price it often pays for this is bolstering preferential treatment for the most acceptable types of discourse and fostering the bureaucratization of knowledge production. Anonymous peer review, like standardized testing and uniform assessment, encourages blandness and conformity in the style of presentation and response, leading those whose futures are dependent on such reviews and evaluations to shy away from taking risks with their writing styles or modes of argument or ideas. The policy is to reward the best test-takers but not necessarily the most engaging or culturally significant achievements. The result is that academic prose, like the career patterns it reflects, tends to avoid animation in favor of caution and to defer exuberance in favor of interminable self-justification and self-glossing that are unrelated to the needs of documentation or communication, research or teaching. I am not saying there is no place for anonymous peer reviewing, nor that it should be abolished, but that there is far too much deference given to a system that in trying to eliminate one kind of bias actually institutes another kind. In contrast, not enough recognition is given to those activities of the members of the academic profession that question the rules of the game, that champion rather than adjudicate, that see universities as places for wild questions and not just prescribed answers.

In contrast to the sciences, in the humanities we shrink from teaching difficult or hard to grasp material in a desperate, self-defeating effort to make literature and art accessible. From an educational point of view, it might be better to insist that what is inaccessible or impossible to grasp is exactly what needs to be taught in our schools. This is why I feel that, with all the attention to radical changes in the humanities, we have not changed nearly enough. The focus on teaching representative and expressive works, where representation and expression are understood in an almost entirely unrelated sense, marks a continuity from the 1890s to the 1990s. If the earlier phase of humanism marked literature as expressive of humankind, the new humanism of identity politics condemns universalization but adopts the underlying structure: Literary works are expressive or representative not of humankind but of particular subsets of human beings (by means of which their basic humanity shines forth).

> SHORTY PETTERSTEIN INTERVIEW (Henry Jacobs and Woodrow Leifer)
> *How would you compare the kind of music you play with a, how would you compare that with art, you know, what kind of art, artistic . . . ?*
> Man like I think Art blows the most, I mean, uh, he came with the band about three years ago, man, dig, and, uh, like, he was a real uh you know small town cat—and I mean he was swinging, man, but he was a small time cat. And I mean he started to blow with us and he was real nut, you know, cool. . . .
> *What would you advise the young artist, the young musician, to do? Would you advise him to get an academic education or strive immediately for self-expression?*
> Well, man, I mean, I'm a musician, dig. And I mean to me the most important thing is that you should blow, you know. . . . If a cat wants to blow and he wants to blow, and uh then he's got to have a scene where he can blow.
> *That would apply to the artists playing horns and wind instruments, they would have to blow. What about those, for example, who are playing string instruments? Or would you say, how's the picture there?*
> Well, I mean, you know, it's, uh, pretty much all the same, man. A blow is like an instrument, you know.

The arts and sciences of this century have shown that deductive methods of argument—narrow rationalizing—hardly exhaust the full capacity of reason. Induction and discontinuity are slighted only at the cost of slighting reason itself. There is no evidence that the conventional expository prose that is the ubiquitous output of the academic profession produces more insights or better research than nonexpository modes. There is no evidence that a tone of austere probity rather than tones that are ironic or raucous furthers the value of teaching or inquiry. It may be true that standard academic prose permits dissident ideas, but ideas mean little if not embodied in material practices and, for those in the academic profession, writing is one of the most fundamental of such practices. Writing is never neutral, never an objective mechanism for the delivery of facts. Therefore the repression of writing practices is a form of suppressing dissidence—even if it is dissidence, I would add, for the sake of dissidence.

So while my attitude to the academic profession is highly critical, I want to insist that one of the primary values such a profession can have results from its constituents who challenge authority, question conventional rhetorical forms, and remain restless and quarrelsome and unsatisfied, especially with the bureaucratizing of knowledge that is the inertial force that pulls us together as a profession. Which is to say: *The profession is best when it professionalizes least.* As negative as I am about the rhetorical rigidity of the academic profession, comparison with journalism, corporate communications, or technical writing will show that these other professions police writing styles far more completely than the academic profession. That is why it is vital to raise these issues about rhetorical and pedagogic practices: because universities remain among the few cultural spaces in the United States in which there is at least a potential for critical discourse, for violation of norms and standards and protocols.

At SUNY–Buffalo (UB), I am the director of the Poetics Program, co-founded in 1991 by Robert Creeley (our first director), Susan Howe, Raymond Federman, Dennis Tedlock, and myself. The program has its roots in Albert Cook's formation of the English Department at Buffalo in the early 1960s, Cook had the idea that you could hire literary artists to teach not creative writing but literature classes, and in particular literature classes in a Ph.D. program. It was with this in mind that he hired Creeley, Charles Olson, and others; it marked a decisively other path from far more prevalent graduate (usually M.A. and M.F.A.) creative writing programs that emerged at the same time.

By formalizing this concept in the early nineties, shortly after Howe and I came to UB, we were suggesting an alternative model for poets teaching in graduate, but also undergraduate, programs. The Poetics faculty teaches in the English Department's doctoral program, supervising orals and directing scholarly/critical dissertations, even if our license to this is more poetic than formal. A frequent question I get from students applying to the program is whether they can write a creative dissertation. I always do a double take: "I hope it will be creative, but it can't be a collection of poems or a novel." For the fact is that Poetics students have the same requirements as all other graduate students and are admitted by the same departmental committee. Although we encourage active questioning of the conventions of critical and scholarly writing, we remain committed to the practice of poetics as something distinct from, even though intersecting with, the practice of poetry. The implications of this perspective are perhaps more pragmatic, not to say programmatic, than theoretical: While the "creative writing" approach at universities often debunks the significance of critical reflection, sometimes pitting creativity against conceptual thinking, the Poetics Program insists that scholarship, historical research, and critical writing are at the core of graduate education.

This is not to say that a Ph.D. program is appropriate for most poets. I tend to discourage people who ask my advice from pursuing this degree at any institution, partly to ensure that they have considered the limitations of the academic environment in terms of artistic freedom, compensation, and future employment. But if this is the choice they make, it is likely because they want to be teachers, editors, and writers and that their writing is as likely to be criticism or poetics as poetry.

The Poetics Program is fully integrated into the English Department, presenting seminars and sponsoring events within that context, even while marking such offerings as our own. We also provide modest funding to students to publish magazines and books (print and electronic) as well as to organize their own poetry readings, talks series, and conferences. Over the past decade, this has resulted in dozens of magazines, scores of books, and numerous visitors, not to mention our website, and the Electronic Poetry Center, created by Loss Pequeño Glazier (epc.buffalo.edu).

Although many doctoral programs in English expect students to choose between being poets and scholars, we suggest that the one activity may enhance the other, for those so inclined. The poets, as I've suggested, do their poetry and their editing on their own: It informs their graduate work but is never the explicit content of it. Equally significant, the Poetics graduate students form a vital community among themselves, where their shared interest in criticism and scholarship, poetry writing, and teaching make for an active bond. As it turns out, this mix seems to produce Ph.D.s who are eager and well qualified to teach literature as well as writing.

Even though Poetics suggests a long history of laws of composition, the Poetics Program stresses *poiesis*—the actual making or doing: poetry as process. Every *doing* carries the potential of something new, emergent, something not already predicated by poetics. Practice overtakes theory, practice changes theory. And not just writing practice, but performance practice, from poetry reading to talks and lectures to teaching.

UB undergraduates actively participate in the Poetics Program through numerous class visits and readings by visiting poets and writers and interactive and creative responses to assigned readings in modern and contemporary poetry and fiction. The best way I can describe how I teach is by calling it a creative reading workshop, for I am less concerned with analysis or explanation of individual poems than with finding ways to intensify the experience of poetry, of the poetic, through a consideration of how the different styles and structures and forms of contemporary poetry can affect the way we see and understand the world. No previous experience with poetry is necessary. More important is a willingness to consider the implausible—to try out alternative ways of thinking; to listen to the way language sounds before trying to figure out what it means; to lose yourself in a flurry of syllables and regain your bearings in dimensions otherwise imagined as out-of-reach; to hear how poems work to delight, inform, redress, lament, extol, oppose, renew, rhapsodize, imagine, incite; and on and on.

As an alternative to papers and tests, I ask students to do a kind of "deformative" criticism in which they alter the assigned works in various ways:

reordering, rewriting, translating, imitating, and performing. An emphasis is also placed on identifying textual features (mood, sound, rhetoric, diction, style, and device) rather than concentrating primarily on thematic or metrical analysis. After that, it remains to correlate these textual features with aesthetic values over which there will necessarily be sharp disagreement rather than attempt to reconcile differences through ideas of craft or expression.

The most salient values of the university are reflected by the fact that it is the largest and most vibrant noncommercial quasi-public space in the United States. As others in this book note, this is changing as universities are increasingly governed on output-driven, consumer-oriented business principles. Yet at its best education delivers nothing—it enables, animates; that is, the value imparted is embedded in an interaction not measurable by output alone. The bright ideas of managers and politicians to adopt commercial decision making on campus are almost always an erosion of the immutable value of the institution, destructive beyond measure. To put it more bluntly, we must move beyond what this book's editors provocatively call "English, Inc."

Yet, it is no longer taken for granted that immersion in the literature, art, and philosophy of the past and present has any practical benefit for society. This, too often, has had the perverse effect of making those who would believe otherwise respond with a narrow, and sometimes shrill, insistence on the necessity of one list or other of treasured or representative works that must be taught (because we can't ensure that they will be read or understood). The "boat" is sinking and we spend our time debating which pieces of furniture ought to go into the main dining room, instead of fixing the leaks. But, the value of the noncommercial space of the university is independent of any particular work or method, no matter how much any one of us loves the works or methods we have chosen to profess. For the values taught are reading values: critical thinking; reflection; social and bibliographic contexts of meaning; the relation of forms, styles, dictions, and genres in determining what any work has to say. For most students who come out of media-intense but breathtakingly narrow cultural confines distance learning and large lecture classes, while efficient in cost per student terms, are ineffective. Teaching in our culture at this time is more than ever a labor-intense activity. It requires prolonged engagement with individual students: gauging their reactions and responding to each one, individually. The answer is never in the technology—audiovisuals, web connections, books to include—but in how we learn to use these technologies.

My commitment is to public education: the education of the public at large and an education about the public—how it is constituted. We are, however, writing off our large public institutions of learning with the cynical assumption that graduates of such colleges have no practical need for the sort of open-ended education in the arts and sciences that most of us in the humanities support. "I never learned anything in college, so why can they." Indeed, from a corporate point of view, having too many people in the workforce who think too much may be detrimental if they end up in dead-end jobs that require little thought. Such ideas are fundamentally antidemocratic of course; they are breeding ground for a passive and malinformed citizenry that is unable to make sense of the complex issues that confront the nation. What price do we have to pay for an informed citizenry—one that can understand the complex multiplicity of American culture and read into events and not simply register them as a series of fated accomplishments? What sort of investment are we willing to make in the intellectual and cultural development of our citizens so that we can remain, as a country, innovative, vibrant, socially responsible? How can we prepare ourselves for the unexpected, the difficult, the troubling events that are sure to lie ahead for all of us? Will we spend billions for defense while begrudging any money that is spent on what we are defending? The great experiment in mass education is not even a hundred years old: It has had virtually no downside. That we teeter on abandoning this commitment now is a testament to a smallness, to a lack of generosity, and to a contempt for noncommercial values that can only make us poorer—not only culturally, but economically.

Works Cited

Gallagher, Catherine. "The History of Literary Criticism." *Deadalus* 126.1 (Winter 1997): 133–53.

Rasula, Jed. *The American Poetry Wax Museum: Reality Effects 1940–1990*. Urbana, IL: NCTE, 1996.

Chapter Four

Corporate Textbook Production, Electronic Resources, and the Responsible Curriculum

Deborah H. Holdstein

When I think about textbooks and the teaching of composition, I think of August 1973, when I, young and relentlessly enthusiastic, was about to begin the graduate program in Comparative Literature at the University of Illinois. I had been fortunate to be awarded a teaching assistantship within the English department. English became the focus of my teaching and research. Barely older than the undergraduates I would too soon teach after arriving at my standard-order, ramshackle apartment, I nervously sought any and all counsel about how to teach writing. My focus would be literature, but I would face my first class—an Engineering section of composition—in ten days.

But I was fortunate: While it would be several years before the Department instituted a professional seminar for teaching writing, the composition program had prepared a "Guide to Teaching Rhetoric 105" that featured good, general advice, information regarding policies, and template syllabi. I had been assigned a mentor—a graduate student ahead of me in the program. I was also given one copy each of the required rhetoric and reader; these books still have a special place on my bookshelf: McCrimmon's *Writing with a Purpose, Fifth Edition* (1972), and Eastenan's *The Norton Reader, Third Edition* (1973).

While the special nature of these textbooks for me has much to do with my need to honor the past, I suspect that there is something more. As far as I was concerned, *Writing with a Purpose* could just as easily have been called *How to Teach Writing and What Is Important About It*. Technologies to enhance the teaching of writing included the pen, the pencil, the (usually manual) typewriter, and the ditto master. Photocopies were expensive and therefore *verboten*.

52

Certainly no one at Illinois would have encouraged me to see textbooks in that way or to foreground the various technologies I used in teaching—the point, of course, was learning to write, not mastery of the tools I might use in teaching. Indeed, as McCrimmon himself asserts at the start of the textbook, it is written explicitly to encourage good writing and, as a post-1960s gesture, to give "greater attention to the prevailing interests and preoccupations of students today" (v). As Joseph Janangelo writes:

> My idea is that handbook authors are compelled to plot their stories of writing process and instruction as ones of directed growth—what George Lukacs calls "significant landmarks along a clearly mapped road" (81)—as a corrective of the unspeakable truth that writing instruction cannot offer definitive, or even quantifiable, proof that it always can train students to become invested in their writing or to write well. (94)

The student, in this case, however, was as much me as were my own students-to-be. Revised during this transitional period in composition's history to reflect the then-recent hotbed of composing and process, the Fifth Edition of *Writing with a Purpose* superimposes the pedagogical relief of order and formula on the necessary messiness of prewriting and rewriting. What insecure teacher could resist the chapter entitled "Patterns of Organization," with its heaven-sent, comparison–contrast essay assignment based on William Hogarth's engravings—*Beer Street* and *Gin Lane?* Or—my personal favorite, "Argument and Persuasion," in which one analyzed advertisements—who could deny that "paragraphs" are indeed "compositions in miniature"?

We seem to accept as truth the less-than-benign relationship between and among curriculum and pedagogy as theorized, practiced, and represented in and implied by composition textbooks. Even more troubling are the ways in which textbooks and their ancillaries continue to dictate policy, good pedagogy, and curricular design, and not the other way around. Composition programs are more often than not supervised by writing-program administrators making textbook decisions that they expect will support curricular theory and practice. Unfortunately, many of these curricular decisions seem dictated by textbooks—and by extension, electronic supplements—that replicate old economies that writing-program administrators otherwise claim to reject.

Not surprisingly, the ideologies and corporate interests of textbook production are complicated by newer technologies and the economic interests of publishers themselves, the latter certainly having always been the case. For instance, the back cover of this year's program for the Conference on College Composition and Communication features an advertisement for Bedford-St. Martin's that boasts, "We do new media the way we do books." Although the parenthetical tag line reads, "very carefully," the ad's visual features sample web pages and CDs that primarily place ditto-master exercises—"Exercise

Central," for example—on the web. No matter Bedford's reputation as the cream of textbook publishers: What, *really,* does it mean pedagogically, as one of these featured pages asks students, "to visit a Hacker [the noted author] Handbook Site?" Will one find examples of good teaching? Good advertising? Another ad for a web page features "Arguing a Position: Write." A banner at the top of the page, not unlike the advertising banner in the same location on any commercial site, reifies as a type of overarching mantra the kind of linear description of the writing process—Invention, Plan and Draft, Revise, Edit, and Proofread—compositionists and writing program administrators claim to have long ago reconsidered if not discredited. (At this point I am forced to confess an early software program I developed for the Apple II+—part of my *WriteWell* Series at the Illinois Institute of Technology in the *early 1980s*—that did essentially the same thing.)

If Bedford's advertisement represents the best of what publishers embrace as they incorporate technology within their products, the lot for the most part—except for databases and library searches—appears at best to transfer ditto-master exercises to the web, and at worst, to offer the illusory stardust of technology to forms of pedagogical practice we otherwise purport to have dismissed.

Despite a trove of scholarly work on textbooks—and enlightening critiques of much of that work—we have little reflection regarding the fairly recent incorporation of technological enhancements to otherwise standard composition textbooks and readers. Libby Miles' review of Gale and Gale's *(Re)Visioning Composition Textbooks: Conflicts of Culture, Ideology, and Pedagogy* offers astute scholarly counterpoint to the volume itself, documenting the wealth of scholarship beginning in the 1980s and left unaddressed—and unacknowledged—by most of the contributors to the book. Throughout the Gale and Gale volume, Miles asserts, the true actors are absent, as "books 'argue,' they 'control,' they 'fail to prepare students.' One book 'perceives,' while another 'respects,' but a third 'fails to show an awareness' " ("Disturbing" 764). Several questions, then, complicate the problematic nature of the textbook within composition studies and our collective accountability as teachers for the corporatization of these books; these complexities are deepened by the (in)corporation of websites and other Internet-related enhancements to textbook development and production. Given the corporate interests by which we live when we develop, write, and choose textbooks for courses, by what assumptions do we attach current technologies to the mix?

Economic interests dominate decisions about which textbooks are published. Despite a reviewing process that purports to receive advice from composition faculty conversant with (and often actually doing) current scholarship, we eagerly participate in perpetuating certain types of textbooks rather than others. This complicity already reveals itself in CD and web-based composition ancillaries, where the technology seems to permit, however inexplicably, our acceptance of a type of "new media"—textbook connections with ancillary forms that replicate old forms, old economies—and not necessarily *good* old economies. What are the potential pitfalls? The scholarly groundwork regarding textbooks, by extension, provides ample context for concern.

In a recent *WPA* essay that offers a thorough review of scholarship about composition textbooks, Libby Miles notes that "much excellent scholarship on composition textbooks emphasizes the normative and reproductive function circulating through both the books themselves and the pedagogical practices surrounding textbooks" ("Constructing" 29). Further, Miles emphasizes another vexing, fundamental problem with scholarship on textbooks: "[I]t too often examines the textbook as a static *product* only—an odd contradiction in a field of inquiry built on the privileging of *processes*" ("Constructing" 30). Indeed, publishers—not unlike the young, unschooled Deborah Holdstein—look to authors they have already signed, not necessarily ones who might truly write the most informed or innovative composition text.

As a recent discussion on the *WPA* listserv makes clear, writing-program administrators overwhelmingly express their dislike for the modes as the organizing principle for a reader. Yet, according to several editors with whom I have discussed this informally, modal readers still overwhelmingly command the largest share of the freshman reader market. Miles attributes this to "an endless photocopying cycle" discussed by Perrin (71)—what Lynn Bloom calls the commercial pressure "to clone texts that already have a following rather than to invent works *de novo*" (138). We as reviewers and buyers of these books share culpability for an ironic, unabashedly conservative participation in a publishing process that creates a "pseudo-canon of pseudo-literature" (Otte). This pseudo-canonization extends to the template created not only by the successful reader, but also by the successful rhetoric textbook. The irony further compounds when these books become inadvertent icons of teaching practice, the indirect consumers of the textbook product embedding it ideologically. For some instructors, a particular edition becomes frozen in time, subsequent editions serving only to reinforce through their replication the original framework for teaching, with other editions (that change somewhat) reinforcing the value of the original as a model.

The material conditions that produce textbooks extend still further. In my own experience of gathering texts for an anthology of women's literature, I learned the first lesson of textbook production in that genre: that cost, perhaps even more than canon or literary merit, determines inclusion. Few would doubt the merit of Kate Chopin's *The Awakening;* however, its presence in the public domain, requiring no contribution to another publisher for rights to it, ensures its inclusion in many an anthology or reader. The antithesis? Including the work of some current ethnic writers, whose agents zealously guard copyrights and ask for high permission fees, might prevent inclusion of a lesser-known, equally good writer. Ironically, then, the work of authors who purport to serve democratic ideals might not reach a wide audience of students; however, it is nonetheless publishers who control these permissions' costs and editors and authors who sign the contracts accepting the terms. Rather than democratize writing, e-publishing (even through such highly praised sources as *Slate*) serves as a database clearinghouse to determine quickly which works of literature, for instance, are in the public domain or available as online replications of print media. Certainly e-anthologies and custom-published anthologies that claim to be more democratic than print are bound by the same book publishing structures that still guide royalties and permissions' scales.

As we critique the merely and uncritically replicative qualities of poor pedagogy in new Internet packages, even worse is the reality of truly interactive and "nonlinear" qualities of recent technologies. As Paul Roberts affirms in his essay "Virtual Grub Street: Sorrows of a Multimedia Hack": If the emergence of the so-called new media has clarified anything, it's just how malleable literary standards and professional expectations are, how quickly they can wither or mutate or be ignored altogether in the presence of powerful novelty and cold cash (72). The pleasures of the nonlinear narrative are for the most part untested.

When we consider the ways in which the Internet might help curricula and students evolve "to the natural outcomes unenvisioned even by reader response, what are we advocating?" (Holdstein, "The Politics" 27). Roberts notes: "We can hardly expect musicians or sculptors to allow their work to be pulled apart and reassembled with bits and pieces from other artists. We writers are no less invested in our work and cannot be expected to delight in the prospect of merely contributing to a collective, egoless supertext." To Roberts, perhaps the most destructive irony of the so-called "digital revolution" is "that we so willingly took part in our own extinction" (77). This conclusion is owed less to decision making on the part of those who set standards for good writing, good teaching, and, most of all, to good curricula but more realistically to the forces of economics.

Of necessity, I have condensed an extensive range of scholarship here. As Lester Faigley has written, a choice of textbook is so significant that "teachers answer with the name of a textbook when asked how they teach writing" (133). As this is so, we are remiss to ignore Internet and other web-based ancillaries to textbooks—and web-based products such as Daedalus, Norton Connect, Houghton-Mifflin's Sixth Floor, and so on. Despite a wealth of ways to read against technology, despite twenty years of looking critically at the computer even before the complexities of the Internet, we must be careful to challenge assumptions that Internet ties are somehow magically neutral. Miles articulates well the "cultural reproduction in which textbooks appear to have a one-to-one relationship with the reality of the classroom and programmatic practices" ("Constructing" 30). Certainly the Internet exacerbates this form of reproduction under the guise of ideological neutrality with new questions about authorship, commodification, and, more to the point for some students, access. Further, websites are living documents, not three-year, hard-copy editions. And clearly, much of what now surfaces on the web to accompany composition textbooks illustrates that we have learned little from the early days of "drill and kill," computer-aided instruction on the Apple II+ computer.

In 1985, Marc S. Tucker, then executive director of the Carnegie Forum on Education and the Economy, affirmed the following:

> The outcome of the computer revolution in our schools cannot be characterized as "disappointing" because in fact it never took place.... Very few [publishing] firms were able to turn even a modest profit selling the best software in schools.... The computer is coming into its own... not as a teacher but as an almost universal expressive and intellectual instrument, indispensable in virtually every endeavor of intellectual significance. That is why the first computer revolution...never happened and why the second computer revolution may succeed. (in Holdstein, *On Composition* 13–22)

The revolution may succeed, but perhaps not in the way that Tucker envisions. Indeed, the "success" is the success, as it were, of e-commerce, of the corporation and the corporate marketplace. The Internet has become far less (if it ever was) the free, open, liberating space predicted by writers, such as Esther Dyson, and more a highly structured, cynical reflection of society's ills—a limitless mix of e-commerce, xxx-rated entertainment, and often misguided (and misguiding) sites for information.

Where software developers have for the most part ultimately failed in partnerships with traditional publishers, the alliance of textbook writers and their products with the Internet seems strangely to have succeeded on the apparent presumption that it is "good" to do so. (Although there is little information yet about how effective, even how used, these web-links and web-related sources may prove to be.) And where there are freestanding software products that have become successful, one must question the "corporate involvement" in formerly grassroots, faculty-generated projects (email correspondence with Libby Miles, 5 April 2001).

Take, for instance, a recent mass email sent to faculty by a publisher's representative, with the following letter from a noted textbook author (5 April 2001):

> Some of you have asked for a sneak preview of *The Bedford Handbook, Sixth Edition,* to be published this October. The main thrust of this revision can be summed up in one word: technology. Because most students are now working online, I've extended my book beyond its paper covers by linking it explicitly to its Web site. Throughout the book, "On the Web" boxes take students to locations on my Web site where they will find a variety of supplements to the book: electronic grammar exercises, exercises on avoiding plagiarism and integrating sources, links to libraries, essays called Language Debates, and so on. Because the Web site is an extension of the book, I have written nearly all of its content myself.

The author's good intentions notwithstanding, how ironic that it has taken more than twenty years for what we in the past have lambasted as "drill and kill" and antiprocess when used in stand-alone software to achieve a strange, unearned legitimacy through the otherwise complex locus of the Internet.

In 1987, I wrote:

> What will happen when the text, art, and writing of computer wares go beyond what instructors have now? Clearly, drill-and-practice programs and video textbooks may eventually be seen as the *Fred Ott's Sneeze* [an early film that essentially recorded the process of a man sneezing] of this relatively new technology. (*On Composition* 88)

Apparently not—that is, when grammar exercises that could easily appear in traditional forms of print, indeed, distributed on a ditto master in class, instead acquire the sexiness and desirability of a web link. In 1987, I posited that "[t]he computer could very well lead to less linear methods of writing as it develops further and as teachers begin to make use of its temporal and spatial elements, new dimensions in handling displays and interpreting texts, faster access to more information, and different methods of organizing texts" (88). And how does the single word that drives the development of the Sixth Edition of *The Bedford Handbook* "raise the specter of access and ethics, suggesting both positive and negative issues to consider" (89)? To echo Libby Miles' language about textbooks, it is the technology that is apparently the agent here, not a person's critically analytical adaptation of technology. I also noted in 1987 that "[t]he implications for equal access, an all-encompassing term, are wide-ranging" (89), in 2001, when some students might feel at the margins when directed by their text to a website they have difficulty accessing.

The current alliance between textbook authors and publishers and the Internet in my view illustrates several things. First, and again, that we demonstrate a tremendous discrepancy between what we profess and what we actually do (as with WAC and in assessment, for instance; Holdstein, "The Politics"); and second, that the more things evolve, the more we stay the same. Right now, the web-linked textbook reproduces the conventionally held textbook in its form and goals, with marketability and not sensibility regarding the real promise of the web, the importance of traditional literacies, or alternative forms of teaching as the impetus.

Where is the curricular challenge to the assumption that online access for students is only beneficial? Where do we enact a general concern that Internet access may contribute to an "exteriorization" of knowledge that potentially tempts student writers away from "owning" essential grammatical, logical, critical, and organizational skills with respect to writing? How is this *distancing* from ownership the same whether the grammar exercises appear in a textbook or on the website for that textbook? To what extent are those of us who design and supervise curricula for composition implicated in this distancing and uncritical use of technology to enhance the curriculum?

Do we not merely perpetuate the same, codified endorsement and "cultural reproduction" on the Internet that we've seen in textbook production? In fact, as the examples of electronic grammar exercises illustrate, we even more "run the risk of giving our students messages about writing we do not mean to give— messages we only seem, by our assignment of a particular text, to endorse" (Segal 114). As Miles comments in her *WPA* article, the textbook and the instructor's choice of a particular textbook "is cultural reproduction writ large, in which a tangible commodity can stand in for a series of actions and interactions" ("Constructing" 33). Miles continues, noting that this is potentially more of a problem for instructors who define themselves "through their textbooks," and that "textbooks reproduce what composition teachers do" and "teachers reproduce what the textbooks do. . . . That's how cultural reproduction works" (34). Consider, then, how much more "largely writ" the curricular endorsement of weak curricula and pedagogical practice becomes just because it appears on the Web and is associated with an otherwise established composition textbook— that is, when technology joins corporate interest at the center of a textbook revision rather than a focus on the writing curriculum and effective pedagogy itself.

In 1983, Richard Collier used a case-study approach to look at college students who used word processors. Collier determined that those students revised more and seemed more positive about writing than did their "unplugged" counterparts. However, Collier did not see any particular improvement in his students' writing. More significant than Collier's work—for reasons that soon become clear—is the commentary on Collier's piece by John Pufahl: "In a response, Pufahl notes that Collier neither took part in the computer-writing process nor pointed out to the students where they might need to revise. 'Collier's error in this vision as well as his error in research is that he sees only the technology' " (Holdstein, *On Composition* 53).

Apparently, in both curriculum and classroom, we still see only the technology—in this case the Internet—just as we have seen only the textbook. In her 1991 article, "Texts and High Tech," Linda K. Christian-Smith discusses the actual production of texts: "The set of relations between the people working in publishing and the book production technology endow the textbook with economic and social meanings from the outset. Hence, whenever we read a book we are interacting with the corporate world and its values" (50). The intense focus on profitability by book publishers "is constituting a subtle form of 'censorship' through the narrowing of books published in favor of profitable ones. This emphasis on the mercantile aspects of books clearly links with the computerization of the publishing industry" (51).

Although fabled editor Jason Epstein asserts, on the other hand, that "new technologies" will narrow "the notorious gap between the educated rich and the unlettered poor and distribute the benefits as well as the hazards of our civilization to everyone on earth," he notes that "[g]reater literacy will not reduce the human capacity for mischief any more than Martin Heidegger's philosophical learning kept him from supporting the Nazis" (31). While Christian-Smith in an early discussion of technology and books focuses on production and its implications for labor, Epstein, in his perhaps misguided optimism, begs the question of true access and short-circuits the notion of "literacy," especially if the extended presence of the textbook on the Web glorifies but does not support traditional literacies and good pedagogy. What do we as writing-program administrators contribute to the "greater literacies" of necessary analysis, questioning, and challenging as we design curricula that allegedly complement our theory and pedagogy as we contribute instead to the further, technologically enhanced glorification of corporate textbook production?

In the *New Yorker* (November 2000), John Cassidy cites a former researcher at Bell Laboratories: "We expected computers to bring across-the-board productivity help, work efficiency improvements for small and large alike. This they have not delivered" (116). Cassidy also shares a Y2K epiphany: "Letters produced on a word processor were modified, on average, forty-one times, but with no discernable difference in quality" (116). How surprising that he finds this information surprising. We must, as Libby Miles deftly writes, defuse our own "rhetoric of reproduction" in our practices as program administrators, curriculum designers, "adopters, as formative textbook reviewers, and as consultants" ("Constructing" 31). The extension of print textbooks to web-based ancillaries demands that we destroy the paradigm as textbook-related websites parallel their print sources, endorsing, as Alred and Thelan note, "a theory of writing that is . . . inconsistent and outdated" (472) in an electronic medium that will ironically make it look new.

Works Cited

Alred, Gerald J., and Erik. A. Thelan. "Are Textbooks Contributions to Scholarship? *College Composition and Communication* 44 (1993): 466–77.

Apple, Michael W., and Linda K. Chrisitian-Smith, eds. *The Politics of the Textbook.* New York: Routledge, 1991.

Bloom, Lynn Z. "Making Essay Connections: Editing Readers for First-Year Writers." In Gary Olson and W. Todd Taylor, eds., *Publishing in Rhetoric and Composition,* 133–44. Albany: SUNY P, 1997.

Cassidy, John. "The Productivity Mirage." *The New Yorker* 76.36 (November 2000): 106–12.

Christian-Smith, Linda. "Texts and High Tech: Computers, Gender, and Book Publishing." In Apple and Linda K. Christian-Smith, 41–55.

Eastman, Arthur, et al. *The Norton Reader, Third Edition.* New York: Norton, 1973.

Epstein, Jason. *Book Business: Publishing Past, Present, and Future.* New York: Norton, 2001.

Faigley, Lester. *Fragments of Rationality: Postmodernity and the Subject of Composition.* Pittsburgh: U of Pittsburgh P, 1992.

Gale, Xin Liu, and Fredric G. Gale, eds. *(Re-)Visioning Composition Textbooks: Conflicts of Culture, Ideology, and Pedagogy*. Albany: SUNY P, 1999.

Holdstein, Deborah H. *On Composition and Computers*. New York: MLA, 1987.

————. "The Politics of Composition and Technology: Institutions and the Hazards of Making New." *WPA* 20.4 (1996): 19–31.

Janangelo, Joseph. "Appreciating Narratives of Containment and Contentment: Reading the Writing Handbook as Public Discourse." In Gale and Gale, eds., *(Re-)Visioning Composition Textbooks* 93–112.

McCrimmon, James. *Writing with a Purpose, Fifth Edition*. Boston: Houghton Mifflin, 1972.

Miles, Libby. "Constructing Composition: Reproduction and WPA Agency in Textbook Reproduction." *WPA* 24.1/2 (2000): 29–54.

————. "Disturbing Practices: Toward Institutional Change in Composition Scholarship and Pedagogy." *College English* 62.6 (2000): 756–66.

Otte, George. "Why Read What? The Politics of Composition Anthologies." *Journal of Advanced Composition* 12 (1992): 137–49.

Perrin, Robert. "What Handbooks Tell Us about Teaching Writing with Word-Processing Programs." *Computers and Composition* 6 (1988): 15–26.

Roberts, Paul. "Virtual Grub Street: The Sorrows of a Multimedia Hack." *Harper's Magazine* 292 (1996): 71–77.

Segal, Judy Z. "Textbooks and Subtexts or How to Choose a Handbook." *Journal of Teaching Writing* 14 (1995): 111–27.

Chapter Five

Accountability and the Conditions for Curricular Change

Richard Ohmann

I imagine that almost all academics think of themselves as "responsible" to others, and, if pressed, might allow substitution of "accountable." Responsibility to our employers is contractual, and the professional ethos urges responsibility to students (our clients), to colleagues, and to vague but strong principles of intellectual conduct that obtain in our disciplines. The professional idea calls for responsibility to society as well: We earn our privileges not just by guarding and augmenting our special bodies of knowledge, but by undertaking to put those knowledges to work for the good of all.

"For the good of all" opens up a vast ideological space for disputes that are familiar enough, a space for the antiprofessional cynicism that, as Stanley Fish has argued, festers endemically within professional groups, not just among the envious laity. Still, even cynics tend to think *they* serve the needs of important others; and except in times of deep conflict, such as the years around 1970, professionals with different allegiances live more or less comfortably together, under the capacious roof of that "all."

To speak of professors: most believe that open inquiry advances the interests of a democratic society. For liberals, that may be enough. Conservatives tend to identify the "good of all" with the good of the sovereign individual. People of the left inflect it toward the good of those lacking wealth and power. At this level of abstraction, accountability is not especially controversial, nor exacting. Certainly it was not so for this person of the left. Accountability to my students: plan the course, show up in class, keep it moving, comment thoughtfully on papers, mentor when asked, submit grades, write recommendations—the usual packet of services. To my departmental colleagues: take on my share of core courses and administrative duties. To the administration and trustees: Just don't make scenes, I guess; the thought rarely crossed my mind. To society as a whole: I cheerfully held myself accountable to the wretched of the earth, the workers, the women, the racially cheated and despised, the queers, the reds, all the disempowered. And, aside from the enmity of a very few colleagues and students, this noble commitment was virtually risk-free at Wesleyan University, as were the commitments of faculty conservatives and liberals.

I know that accountability imposes itself more obstinately in the working lives of teachers at less privileged institutions, and teachers without tenure at all institutions. Still, when we faculty members have been able to define our own obligations to society, we have charted a high road—the good of all— that practitioners can travel easily together in spite of different values and allegiances, and without much fuss about the ways our specific work meets those obligations, or doesn't.

This mild regime of self-policing has been under pressure for some time. *Accountability,* a more salient concept than responsibility and obligation in recent decades, is different in major ways. First, as its root suggests, account-ability means keeping score. Not sufficient, in the new regime, to invoke free inquiry, critical thinking, socially beneficial knowledge, and other such ideals, however wide their appeal to the public. Accountability entails being able to show that the efforts of an instructor or department or institution actually did move toward the desired end. That in turn requires framing the goal precisely enough to permit agreement on the state of affairs that would constitute its fulfillment, and on the amount of progress made in its direction at any point. Measurement, in short. And while the measure of success may be crude (e.g., Wesleyan set its sights for a while on reaching at least a certain spot in the *U.S. News and World Report* rankings), it must be quantifiable. Academic resistance to accountability owes in part to that fact: How can the complex things we most highly value be reduced to numbers? we ask.

Quantification of aims and accomplishments may seem less rebarbative to scientists than to humanists. All in the arts and sciences, however, are likely to be put off by the ideas and language of business that have trailed along with accountability in its migration into the university. A 1994 book on *Measuring Institutional Performance in Higher Education* (Meyerson and Massy) works in a semantic medium of "client feedback," "stakeholders," "make or buy options," "output" (of departments), "use synergy," and the like, and carefully recom-mends to educators common business practices such as TQM (total quality management), BPR (business practice reengineering,) and benchmarking (com-paring your performance by quantifiable measures to "best practices" at other in-stitutions). Speakers at an October, 1999 conference on "Market-Driven Higher Education" sponsored by *University Business*[1] used a lexicon of "markets" (e.g., students), "product," "brand" (your university's name and aura), "value added" (including, I guess, to students as labor power), "marginal cost," "deals," and "resource base" (the faculty, chiefly). They taught why to want and how to get "customization," "knowledge management," "just-in-time learning," "strategic partners," "faculty management," good "assessment models" (though some said no good ones exist), "policy convergence" (I took this to mean something like consistency, and the left hand's awareness of what the right hand is doing), and—my favorite—the "Hollywood model" (i.e., the sort of contract put together by actors, producers, etc., in contrast to the antiquated and feckless arrangements most have in higher education for owning and selling knowledge).

Administrators are becoming fluent in this language. It feels alien to many faculty members, and not centrally because of academic distaste for business. Some are hostile to business, some not; but I think all can see that the discourse on accountability is one for managers, not the managed. And while it is no secret that universities have ever-expanding administrations, many faculty cherish the hope that their administrators are managing on behalf of us and the students, taking care of the business side so we can teach and students can learn. But accountability for administrators means managing *us,* not just physical plant and endowment. The literature on the subject may urge them to enlist faculty members in goal-setting and devising measurements, but we are not within earshot of these prescriptions, not part of the intended audience. In short, when politicians or businesspeople or trustees call for accountability in higher education, they are asking administrators to plan, oversee, and assess our labor.

Isn't that what managers do? The accountability movement would be of little interest except that it brings managerial logic into the area of self-management to which all professions aspire, and which the stronger ones were able to stake out in an uneven and conflicted historical process beginning more than a hundred years ago. Accountability, when achieved, turns back that process. Its advocates stigmatize the foot-dragging of professors as whiny and selfish (which it may sometimes be), but more pertinently as *retrograde.* And that it always is—in just the way that Luddite resistance was retrograde in its time and the resistance of doctors is retrograde now. These were and are defenses against new relations of production, imposed from without, to reduce or eliminate the control that groups of workers have exercised over their labor.

That brings me to the last major way in which accountability differs from obligation or responsibility. In the utopian regime of my employment at Wesleyan, or at least in my fantasies about it, I could hold myself responsible to the disempowered, and identify my work with democracy and equality (just as my colleague on the right could identify his with individual freedom). After all, most people here and abroad *are* disempowered. When Lynne Cheney or William Bennett occasionally took hostile notice of my work, that only proved I was doing something right. I and my comrades were on the side of the general public; Cheney and Bennett spoke for an usurping coterie. We wanted to try democracy, for the first time in history; the Right wanted to maintain the rule of the few and call *that* democracy.

But of course there was an obvious problem with this comfortable position: The wretched of the earth do not organize militantly to support academic progressives, or the politics latent in much of our scholarship and pedagogy since the 1960s. Business and the right organize effectively against the academic left. Many of the general public see the world more as Cheney and Bennett do than as we do. That's ideology. That's hegemony. Accountability, in short, is not to the disempowered but to the powerful. There would be no agonizing among professors on this subject, except that boards of regents and trustees, legislative bodies, conservative foundations and interest groups, corporations, and so on want to make teachers and knowledge workers in general more responsive to their purposes, and have power enough to advance that project.

Thirty-five, fifty, or eighty years ago, they not only lacked such power, but had not even hit on the project. Why now? In answer, I will put two skeletal narratives to work. The first can be seen as more or less internal to education. In it, the years 1945 through 1970 brought rapid expansion of the university system. Prosperity and a growing cohort of young people were in part responsible. In addition, the US economy grew fastest in industries, such as communications and petrochemicals, that required highly trained knowledge workers and an enlarged research apparatus. Meanwhile, Cold War leaders mobilized the university to do combat against the Soviet Union and its allies, funding science and technology, weapons research, artificial intelligence, basic computer development, economics, and other fields thought critical to the dominance of capitalism and Western democracy. These new tasks required no dramatic change in the university's structure of relatively autonomous departments, though the change in scale brought talk of, and worry about, the "megaversity." The academic professions flourished, buoyed by proliferation of graduate programs, full employment for new entrants, and public demand for higher education.

Around 1970 the party tired. Public funding became less certain. Graduate programs in many fields were turning out more Ph.D.s than there were jobs: in English and foreign languages the crisis was evident at the 1969 MLA convention, where a caucus of angry job seekers abruptly formed, to the surprise both of the leadership and of dissidents who had come to protest other things. Those other causes also disrupted the postwar complacency of the university and its constituent professions. Civil rights, black power, women's liberation, and antiwar militancy came in from the streets along with open admissions and new student populations. A student power movement germinated within the now-alienating and "irrelevant" megaversity itself. This is a familiar part of the story, abbreviated here in cliché phrases to arrive at the following suggestion: in the late sixties, dissenters within the university both put themselves in opposition to systems of domination outside it and staged a critique of its relations to those systems ("Who Rules Columbia?" and so on). The professions came under assault by many young aspirants and some established members. Secure old knowledges were challenged, new canons proposed. The curriculum, in the broadest sense, changed.

Conservatives, readying to launch their offensive against the liberal welfare state and alarmed at what seemed the rule of liberals in universities, took countermeasures. Some new right-wing foundations zeroed in on education and intellectual life, circulating ideology and attacking the versions of democracy that had grown out of sixties movements. Their work on one front led in time to the culture wars of the 1990s and the attack on "political correctness" and multiculturalism. On another, it produced schemes of privatization. On a third, mainstream conservatives and neoliberals mounted a critique of US education in general (including especially K–12) through commissions and reports that proclaimed our "nation at risk" because of inferior schooling, and called for "excellence." These official reports harmonized with media events like the "literacy crisis" of the mid-1970s and, a bit later, movements such as "back to basics." Schooling became and remains a reliable public media concern. Candidates run for office on school-reform platforms; both Bushes and Clinton have aspired to be "education Presidents." In this context, calls for accountability became ubiquitous. Framed by this narrative, they can be grasped as part of a complex reaction against the social movements of the sixties and seventies and as sallies in culture wars that are often explicitly political.

The other narrative is economic, and embraces far more than the university and the educational system. It too begins with the postwar boom, seen as the cresting both of corporate, Fordist capitalism in the United States and of our dominance in the world economic order. Around 1970, those arrangements began to unravel. The dollar faded against stronger currencies. The US balance of trade turned negative, and has remained so. Unemployment began a steady rise from its 1969 level of less than four percent. Real wages, up substantially since 1945, stalled for a few years after 1970 and then went into a decline from which they have not recovered. The economy stagnated. Both federal and personal debt headed up sharply from the late 1970s on, with corporate debt following a few years later. Productivity growth slowed. The world became far less secure for American capital's project of development in this time of globalization.

Capital responded with strategies, now familiar, that are perhaps creating a new economic order: capital rapidly moving around the globe; proliferating new products and services; elaboration of financial instruments to the point that almost no one can understand them; corporate restructuring and waves of mergers; dismantling the old core labor force and its high wages, security, and benefits; downsizing; temp labor, part-time labor, and subcontracting; and so on. This system, still in formation, has been variously named: globalization, turbo-capitalism, the "regime of flexible accumulation" (Harvey),[2] the knowledge society. That last term predates the others, but may be critical for grasping the place of higher education in the new order. For if knowledge is now not only an accomplice in the making of other goods but itself the most dynamic sector of production, we could expect intense efforts on the part of business to guide its development, control its uses, and profit from its creation and sale. That has implications for universities and faculty members to which I will return.

First, I want to locate accountability in these two narratives. For both of them, the years around 1970 are pivotal; it was precisely then that accountability exploded into the language and politics of education. In June 1970, "accountability" first showed up in the *Education Index* with reference to teaching. The Library of Congress introduced "educational accountability" as a subject heading two years later.[3] To be sure, the word was used much earlier, as its first *Oxford English Dictionary* citation is from 1794. But for nearly 200 years "accountability" has carried a broad meaning: the state of being liable, responsible, held to account for one's actions; it had no special link to education. A keyword search at the University of Massachusetts library turned up 585 book titles, only six of them predating 1970, and none of those six about education. In 1970 appeared professor of education Leon M. Lessinger's *Every Kid a Winner: Accountability in Education,* soon to be characterized as the "bible of accountability." During the next five years, dozens of books were published with titles such as *Accountability and Reading Instruction; Accountability and the Community College; Accountability for Educational Results; Accountability for Teachers and School Administrators; Accountability in a Federal Education Program; Accountability in the Elementary School Curriculum; Accountability, Program Budgeting, and the California Educational Information System;* and *Accountability: Systems Planning in Education*—to mention just some titles beginning with "accountability." Accountability had suddenly become an established idea joined at the hip to education, a recognized field of study, a movement, and a battleground.[4]

By no means did Lessinger's book inaugurate the movement. A 1972 anthology of articles and talks includes a number from 1969 that suggest that accountability—"one of the most rapidly growing and widespread movements in education today"—began "as a flickering spark in the twilight of the 60s . . ." (Sciara and Jantz 1,3). Writers seeking origins tend to mention the Elementary and Secondary Education Act of 1965, later amendments that required program audits, the beginning of the National Assessment Program in 1969, a 1970 speech by President Nixon, and so on. The interesting thing is that abruptly in 1970 it *was* a movement, felt as historically momentous, powerful, and, depending on one's point of view, either tonic or dangerous.

Beyond specific Acts, books, or vague agents, such as "the federal government" or "alarmed administrators," three main forces drove the movement. First was an intense fiscal crisis of the state, caused in part by war-spending, but expressed chiefly as disillusionment with Great Society programs. In a 1970 speech, Terrel H. Bell (then Deputy Commissioner in the Office of Education, later Reagan's Secretary of Education) noted that his department's budget had increased from $500 million to $4 billion a year through the sixties, and that Congress had poured "literally billions of dollars" into the schools, often into "crash programs" for which the schools were "comically unprepared." Money alone would not buy good education (does this sound familiar?). Washington now wanted *"results,"* wanted "to be sure that every dollar invested in an educational program will produce a payoff . . . that can be measured and that can be proved" (Sciara and Jantz 41–47). Nixon's man did not specify which "expensive will-o-the-wisps" Washington rejected, but it is evident from the early literature that accountability was in part a counterthrust against liberatory ideas and experiments in "open education"—that is, against the critique of schooling mounted by sixties visionaries and radicals. That reaction was the second force. The third force—more specific to higher education—was a reaction against "turmoil and disruption on the campuses" and "political action by students and faculty members," which had produced a "mounting distrust of higher education by the public" and an "increasing demand for colleges and universities to justify what they are doing and to disclose the effectiveness and efficiency of their operations" (McConnell 200). In short, it is no coincidence (as Marxists like to say) that accountability emerged and gained strength as a coherent movement exactly when the postwar US economy was tearing at the seams, and when the right began to organize itself against sixties movements.

Origins do not set meanings permanently in place. Acccountability has been and is a contested field of meaning and a terrain of conflict. But I believe the historical conjunction that birthed it continues to inflect and propel it. To put the case bluntly: accountability is most deeply about the right's project of containing sixties movements and about capital's project of recomposing itself internationally, marketizing whatever areas of life had previously eluded that process, and dominating workers of all sorts in ways more pervasive but less confrontational than those that marked Fordism. For this reason, I do not think it will be easy to peel away accountability from "accounting," reclaiming the former as our professional way of taking responsibility for our actions, as Bill Readings hoped we might do.

At this point, several hundred pages might ensue, arguing that the hypothesis organizes a variety of seemingly discrete events and situations into its tidy gestalt. I cannot supply those pages here. In shorthand, here is what I have in mind.

1. The thirty-year job "crisis" for Ph.D.s, campaigns against tenure and for posttenure review, heavy reliance on part-timers and adjuncts, outsourcing and subcontracting many academic and support tasks—these practices respond to local pressures on administrators and trustees, and (one must admit) to self-destructive inertia among the academic leaders. Beyond that, one can see in the casualization of academic labor the same process of dispersal and degradation that capital initiated against the core workforce in almost every industry around 1970. The regime of flexible accumulation brings accountability to us in this guise, whatever the motives of its local agents.

2. These labor practices nest within a far-more-encompassing set of tendencies. The list is long, but let me mention distance-learning, burgeoning adult education, buying and selling courseware, marketing academic

research, corporate–university "partnerships," bottom-line accounting, for-profit universities, the existence today of 1,800 "corporate universities" (GE started the first in 1955). All of these, clearly, support the widespread observation that the university has become more and more like a business—an idea voiced not only by academic critics of the change such as Bill Readings, Lawrence Soley, Cary Nelson, and David Noble, but by advocates, including many speakers at the *University Business* conference and writers for *Business Week* (see, for instance, "The New U"). My second narrative, above, suggests a more encompassing generalization: that capitalism in its new phase extends the logic of the market to encompass areas of production not previously within its scope, and, in particular, seeks to commodify knowledge wherever possible.

3.   From *University Business* of January/February 1999: "In 1955, not a single health care company appeared on the list of the top 50 U.S. Corporations as measured by market capitalization. Today, seven of America's richest companies are in the health care industry. Where the health care market was 40 years ago, the education-and-training market is right now" (Gordon 16). The reorganization and extension of capital's work challenges the professions. Our self-managed intellectual capital (our specific bodies of knowledge), along with our creed of public service, legitimized our partial autonomy for 100 years. The commodification of knowledge and the marketization of professional services are in direct conflict with that autonomy. If medicine, with all its prestige and power, has given up big chunks of its domain, why expect professors to do better in the new regime? In fact, most professions (worldwide) are losing ground (see Krause). Accountability, viewed on the broad canvas painted here, is not just an extra demand on professions. It erodes their historical conditions of possibility.

4.   Primary and secondary education are caught up in the same economic transformation. Channel One, advertising in school corridors, contracts with Coke and Nike are but symptoms: the sale of children's attention to corporations in an effort to ameliorate the fiscal crisis of the state. Marketization works more deeply through the project of companies (like Edison) that seek profit by contracting with school districts to manage learning. Voucher systems, if they gain ground against hot opposition, will be a further step. These are signs of a tectonic shift in the way public schooling sorts children out—that is, reproduces the economic and social system by guaranteeing that the next generation will see much the same distribution of wealth and power as in this, and that inequality will be widely seen as just (i.e., based on merit), or at least inevitable.

5.   Finally, the Culture Wars. The attack on multiculturalism and political correctness this past decade explicitly took on 1960s movements, seen as having all but won the battle for higher education. Furthermore, the germination of this strategy in centers of conservative thought and policy,

from the 1970s on, is well documented. So there is no need to flog the obvious point that it carries forward the *political* project embedded in the accountability movement right at the outset. I want to suggest that between the lines of their crusade for traditional values and great books and free speech, the culture warriors have provided a rationale for "defunding" the public university and putting it in the custody of market forces.[5] This is an all-encompassing hypothesis deserving careful analysis, which I cannot offer. Let it stand as a gesture toward the understanding one might achieve by historicizing accountability in the way proposed here.

Although big narratives can shade into paranoia, courses of action pursued without the (tentative) understanding they provide are likely to be scattered, contradictory, and at worst self-defeating. So I offer these large, pear-shaped thoughts to those enmeshed in a thousand local skirmishes over accountability. Among others, that large group includes people working to revise English, to make it work for or against the corporate university in which some of these skirmishes take place. To such people, the likely readers of this book,[6] I offer a few thoughts about how they might imagine their future and plan their strategies, should they agree with my analysis.

First, it proposes a broad understanding of the whole educational system, under the concept of *privatization*. But battles and futures will differ greatly across the many kinds of institutions that make up that system. Even if, for this book about universities, we limit the scope of the discussion to postsecondary institutions, there are complexities enough. Community colleges, for instance, have always had a relatively direct and simple relationship to the market for education and training. Yes, they have provided a liberal arts core for some students heading toward B.A.s; but for most, the community college is a place to take courses for career-related needs, applying an economic calculus to the purchase of credits, knowledge, and skills. The University of Phoenix, DeVry, and many other for-profit suppliers of immediately useful knowledge will give the community colleges stiff competition, but not oust them from the market, because they are local, handy, effective, and cheap.

At the other end of a familiar spectrum, Princeton, Swarthmore, and the like will continue to experience accountability in only the most genteel and indirect forms. Endowments and loyal alumni will fortify them against harsh competition. But mainly, they will continue to offer an intrinsically scarce good, incapable of mass production: cultural capital—made up of selectivity, name recognition, the right contacts, an education with relatively broad horizons, access to the most prestigious graduate schools, Wall Street firms, and so on. To be sure, the Ivies and the leading public universities are becoming more like corporations, "partnering" with businesses, setting up venture capital offices, subcontracting and outsourcing, selling their curricula by distance-learning, and finding other sources of extra income. But the University of Phoenix will not be elbowing into their primary market any time soon, and they will be able to afford the useless liberal arts, semiautonomous departments, and other paraphernalia of the old professional order.

Between these two locations, life will be strenuous. That is to say, most public and private universities will be scrambling to meet standards of account-ability imposed either by hard-nosed trustees and legislators or by the market itself.[7] Such institutions will look to the bottom line as businesses do, and will decide by that criterion what their English departments are contributing to survival or to profitability. So will community colleges, of course. English de-partments in all these institutions are gradually shrinking (if we count only the tenure tracked), as are most of the other "uncommodified spaces we . . . inhabit" (Downing et al., 5).

The educational and political choices available to people in English studies will differ, depending on how much of their time they spend in uncommodified spaces. For full- as well as part-timers at rapidly marketizing institutions, I see two main ones: obey the market or fight back—or do a little of both. The former entails seeking to give students the kind of practical learning they might otherwise purchase in bits from proprietary schools, or be offered within the corporations where they work. For people in English departments, this strategy will obviously mean an emphasis on writing, not just the basic composition courses, but training in more specialized and saleable skills. Until just recently, I was pessimistic about the second strategy—fight back. The forces arrayed on the other side are powerful, and the sixties' movements that had been our allies in reforming the university are frayed or fragmented. Now, a movement grounded in workplace issues and professional concerns has sprung up from grass roots. I refer to the organizing of graduate students, TAs, and adjuncts of all sorts, which has won stunning victories at campus after campus, and, in modern language fields, built national momentum and successfully commandeered the support of the MLA.

This is a fascinating and explosive moment, I think, since scholarly orga-nizations have in the past stayed as far away as possible from disputes over labor and working conditions. Should the politicizing of such groups move them in this direction, that could point the way toward a reconstitution of the academic profession on more militant lines. Short of such an (unlikely) outcome, unionization among those who otherwise will constitute the cheap labor pool for privatizing education could put up serious resistance to that process. Again, these choices are not exclusive: People teaching English in commodified circumstances can offer courses that respond to job or career needs, and also resist the casualization of academic labor. In fact, as writ-ing programs offer more practical, job-oriented coursework, they had *better* fight against casualization, because the easiest way for the university to sup-ply "demand" in this area is to hire part-timers, either for classroom teaching or for instruction in cyberspace. Ironically, the professionalization and partial autonomy of comp will serve this very, proletarianizing trend, unless people in the field imagine their professionalism in a new way. On the other hand, working alliances of writing instructors, with students as well as with other campus workers, become more plausible in the present situation because all these groups occupy similar, vulnerable positions in the regime of flexible accumulation.

For those who work at least some of the time in uncommodified spaces, and especially for those in colleges and universities able to preserve a liberal arts curriculum and privilege critical thinking, a third main choice (also fully compatible with the fight against casualization) is to continue and advance the ideological critique of oppressive social relations that gained a university beachhead in the sixties and has come to undergird the curriculum in English since—to the disgust of culture warriors on the Right. I have in mind the critique of white and male supremacy, the multicultural critique of canons, history from below, a sour view of American triumphalism, an understanding of culture as a power-laden field of conflict, and so on. By extending this work, particularly into a critique of the university and its role in flexible accumulation, and by mobilizing it in battles over academic and nonacademic labor, practitioners of English may begin—have indeed begun—to disrupt the rules of accountability and open them out to . . . well, the people?

Notes

1. A magazine from the publisher of *Lingua Franca,* sent free to 34,000 college and university administrators—a sign and a facilitator of accountability.

2. David Harvey's analysis has strongly influenced my own.

3. Thanks to Cynthia Spell, reference librarian at the University of Massachusetts, for finding this information.

4. In 1971, for instance, the Educational Testing Service sponsored a "Conference on Educational Accountability," and Ralph Nader organized one on "Corporate Accountability." That phrase sounded in liberal and left circles, but the official discourse about accountability was irreversibly about schooling, not holding the powerful to account.

5. See Lauter for an early and excellent account.

6. Up to this point, most of this chapter was published in *Academe* 86.1 (January–February 2000): 24–29; and in *Radical Teacher* 57 (Fall 1999): 2–7. Thanks to Ellen Schrecker, editor of *Academe,* for encouraging me to write the article, and for permission to reprint it here.

7. For an interesting survey from the corporate point of view, see "The New U."

Works Cited

Downing, David B., C. Mark Hurlbert, and Paula J. Mathieu. "Prospectus for *Beyond English, Inc.*" Unpublished manuscript, 2000.

Gordon, Jack. "Clippings." *University Business* (January/February 1999), 16.

Harvey, David. *The Condition of Postmodernity.* Oxford: Blackwell, 1990.

Krause, Elliott A. *Death of the Guilds: Professions, States, and the Advance of Capitalism, 1930 to the Present.* New Haven: Yale UP, 1996.

Lauter, Paul. " 'Political Correctness' and the Attack on American Colleges." *Radical Teacher* 44 (Winter 1993): 34–40.

Lessinger, Leon M. *Every Kid a Winner: Accountability in Education.* Palo Alto: Science Research Associates, 1970.

McConnell, T. R. "Accountability and Autonomy." In Sciara and Jantz, *Accountability in American Education,* 200.

Meyerson, Joel W., and William F. Massy, eds. *Measuring Institutional Performance in Higher Education.* Princeton, NJ: Peterson's, 1994.

"The New Look of Federal Aid to Education." In Sciara and Jantz, *Accountability in American Education,* 41–47.

"The New U: A Tough Market Is Reshaping Colleges." *Business Week* (22 December 1997): 96–102.

Readings, Bill. *The University in Ruins.* Cambridge: Harvard UP, 1996.

Sciara, Frank J., and Richard K. Jantz, eds. *Accountability in American Education.* Boston: Allyn and Bacon, 1972.

Chapter Six

Excavating the Ruins
of Undergraduate English

Bruce Horner, Kelly Latchaw, Joseph Lenz,
Jody Swilky, and David Wolf

Introduction—Bruce Horner

In 1988, when I came to Drake University—a private, mid-sized Midwestern school with no graduate English program—its English department had about twenty full-time, tenure-line faculty, a regular adjunct, and several part-time instructors. As of Spring 2001, only twelve full-time faculty remain, and several of us are leaving.

This loss of a third of the department's faculty is not the only change the department has experienced. Perhaps most significant, in the first two years following my arrival, the department revised English 001, then required of all beginning undergraduates, from a course emphasizing skills to one emphasizing the interrelationships between reading and writing. Following this, in 1990, the department embarked on a wholesale revision of its curriculum from one requiring majors to take courses in traditional periods and genres to one highlighting theory and the interconnections between reading and writing, significantly broadening the types of texts studied and produced. New courses were developed in literacy studies, popular music, writing, and women's and minority literatures, which contributed to newly developing programs in cultural studies, women's studies, and multicultural studies.

About 1996, first-year seminars began at Drake. These were taught voluntarily by non-English faculty on subjects of their choosing and were restricted to enrollments of twenty; more significant, students could take them as optional substitutes for English 001. A few years later, Drake's general education requirements changed so that English 001 was cross-listed with the first-year seminars (FYSs), and it was the seminar that was required, not English 001 per se.

75

Faculty outside the English department were encouraged and cajoled into proposing versions of FYS to meet their suddenly increased demand. Further, under the new general education program, newly imposed requirements to meet Communications Outcomes–Writing could be met by taking not only English courses but also courses from other departments.

Finally during the past year, Drake University underwent an involuntary program review. In what might seem a textbook case for Bill Readings' critique of the corporatization of the university, faculty, staff, and administrators learned that all academic programs would be assessed for their currency and innovation—whether they were "learner-centered," "values-based," "holistic," "responsive to external demands and needs," responsive and structurally connected to meet the university's internal needs (global/international in perspective); and, above all, achieving "excellence." To achieve "excellence," it was mandated that no less than 20 percent of Drake's existing programs would be eliminated. The faculty's job was not to consider whether such a program review was warranted but to assist in determining which programs would be eliminated, which to maintain at current levels of support, and which to "enhance." Each "unit" was required to provide a description of its programs' histories, external and internal demands, "essentiality," quality of outputs and processes, costs and expenses, and an "opportunity analysis" explaining "what would it take to move the program to the highest level of excellence?"

At the time of this writing, the program review is still in process. The English unit, of which this chapter gives glimpses, has been warned to stop "chart[ing] its own course" and instructed to "consult with other academic units and rethink its programs" and find "ways to be more cost effective." Yet, many of the criteria by which programs are supposed to have been evaluated for their "excellence" are being met in the work English has done—strategies implemented for reaching out to meet external demands; a focus on learner-centered pedagogy; global/international perspectives adopted toward writing; current, even innovative, pedagogies developed.

This chapter thus presents a dilemma that we expect will soon be all too familiar to members of English departments at other institutions: the work faculty do to achieve the seemingly laudable ends espoused by their institutions may have little, no, or even negative bearing on the support they are given. In short, the history of the Drake English department's changes in its curriculum and of Drake's academic program evaluation of English should give pause to those of us following the siren song of calls to be innovative, learner-centered, interdisciplinary, and of course "excellent" at a time of crisis. Institutions may not in fact want what they call for, or may mean very different things by these terms. By "interdisciplinary," for example, those in English may think of scholarly and teaching projects that build on research and research methodologies from a range of disciplines, whereas others may take this to mean essentially interdepartmental endeavors that share resources and cut costs.

In this chapter, each of the four other contributing authors, all faculty who teach or have taught at Drake University, explore their sense of the specific problems and possibilities of developing a curriculum when their academic work was subject to material crisis and change. Like most faculty at small schools, each of them wears a number of different professional hats. Consequently, they bring to bear on Drake's recent history a variety of experiences and perspectives: department chair, practicing poet, director of an interdisciplinary undergraduate program in cultural studies, "freeway flyer" adjunct and literacy center volunteer, magazine business manager, Shakespearean, teacher of writing. Their perspectives are obviously not comprehensive and obviously partial in every sense. Collectively, however, they suggest some of the challenges undergraduate English faculty now face, or will soon face, and the different ways such faculty might engage those challenges. In my concluding remarks following their contributions, I highlight the particular significance of such engagements in light of our ongoing local institutional history.

Repositioning an English Department—Joseph Lenz

I am that Shakespearean alluded to in the introduction. Ironically, it is as the instructor of the much-in-demand Shakespeare courses, the very foundation of what some assume English departments are supposed to teach, that I have currency on this campus—not, certainly, as the chair of an English Department that, in the words of the Program Review report, "charted its own course without careful consultation with other units of the University."

Nearly ten years ago, Robert Weisbuch, then English department chair at the University of Michigan, now president of the Woodrow Wilson Foundation, prayed to "save us, Lord, from the deans, provosts, and presidents who think they know our business better than we do" (53). I was a brand-new department chair at the time, and little did I imagine that ten years later I would be witnessing the erosion of not only the university's largest department but one of its strongest in terms of teaching quality and quality and quantity of professional output. (In fact, even in the current Program Review, English was ranked by the dean as the highest in the college in terms of quality faculty.) Weisbuch was dispensing good advice about the importance of educating administrators about the discipline of English, about not letting the popular press be the only source of information about what English departments are and do, and about thinking carefully and strategically—for the sake of the department and the profession—about who and how we hire. Over the past few years, however, conditions at Drake, and I suspect at other institutions as well, have substantially altered how, when, and who we can hire, opening the process to many besides deans and provosts who "think they know our business better than we do." It is hiring, I believe, that serves as a measure of the health of a department and its status within a university. It is those we hire, and the material conditions under which we hire them, that will set the course for English as we move into the new century.

When I became chair ten years ago, the English department was vibrant. We had twenty tenure-line faculty who were inaugurating our newly revised major, which embraced theory and abandoned, more or less, constituting English study by period or genre or author. We were responsible for teaching the only course required universitywide: "Freshman Seminar on Reading and Writing," a course that would serve as the model for the first-year seminar described in the Introduction. Many department members were active as teachers or administrators in various interdisciplinary programs—Cultural Studies, Women's Studies, Latin American Studies, the Humanities Center, the Honors Program, and so on. Others were experimenting, even then, with computer-assisted education and hypertext. We had 165 majors and a small (thirty students) M.A. program. Securing permission to hire was relatively easy. If the department lost, say, an Americanist, we could point to the vacancy and replace her; if enrollment of first-year students was burgeoning, we could point to the freshman writing requirement and add a position. In fact, in my first year as chair we did just that, advertising for and hiring one person in American studies and one in composition studies. At that time we dealt almost strictly with the dean. The positions were "ours" because they were replacements for faculty who retired. We pointed to enrollment figures to secure permission to hire, and that was done six months in advance of the September deadline for the MLA Job Information List. We were in charge of our program; we knew best what our students needed and how to constitute English studies at Drake.

All of that has changed. Hiring, and by extension control over the department's own discipline, has become subject to corporate decisions by those who may know little or nothing about that discipline. Now, to get approval to hire, every department chair in the College of Arts and Sciences must submit position requests by September 1. All requests, no exceptions, are subject to group discussion and priority ranking by the department and program chairs, the college's Planning and Review Committee, and the deans of the other colleges. Typically there may be fifteen requests for new or replacement positions in the college, with as few as six or seven being approved. In short, I must convince the chairs of Chemistry, Political Science, and Music that the English Department's need for someone to teach American Studies is more pressing than their need for someone in biochemistry or international relations or piano pedagogy (all growing programs). Moreover, a position in one department may be reassigned to another program or department or eliminated altogether. This is precisely what happened in 1999. We proposed two tenure-track searches to fill vacancies created by a resignation and a retirement. One position was defined as a "fiction writer with teaching interests in American literature, preferably before 1900," the other as "professional writing." Both positions were tied to a new Writing major and minor we were developing. We were not certain that we would get both positions, but we were surprised when our colleagues across the college ranked the professional writing position as the least needed in the college (seeing it as merely "service" to the schools of business and pharmacy).

In the end, the fiction writing search was approved, but only on a visiting, one-year status, not tenure-track, and the professional writing position was rejected, the line itself reassigned to the program in Environmental Science and Policy, which was attracting many students.

Even when a position is approved, the participation of those outside the department does not end. As a general rule, new faculty should be able to cross-list some courses in other departments like Environmental Policy or Women's Studies. Thus, the search committee is required to involve faculty from other programs. A few years ago when we hired a linguist, a colleague from Education participated in our search because students seeking language arts teaching certification must take a linguistics course. The end result is that we have increasingly less control over how we define a position, whether we secure the position, and who we eventually hire to fill that position, as more and more people "who think they know better" become involved. This isn't necessarily a "bad" thing, but it does demand that we reconceive the relationship between the department and the university that contains it.

Of course, the very fact that the hiring process has been transformed over the past ten years is evidence that the relationship between the department and the university has already changed. Some of these changes, like the competition for positions, are budget-driven. Like the rest of corporate and academic America, downsizing and cost-effectiveness are the current themes. A vacant position in one area is an opportunity to reclaim or reassign that budget line. This is precisely how we have lost one-third of our faculty. No one has been fired, no one terminated. But as faculty retire or resign, the positions are reclaimed by the central administration, or reassigned.

More important, however, the department has redefined itself and its position in the university without, perhaps, adequately explaining that redefinition. To some extent, we have become victims of our own success. For years we argued that writing was not the sole responsibility of the English Department, that students can and should write in all of their courses, and that professors in other disciplines are better equipped to instruct students about the conventions of writing in those disciplines than are English professors. Simultaneously, *on principle,* we refused to hire part-time instructors or grad assistants to staff courses not integral to our curriculum. We "won" the argument, but now at Drake there is no freshman comp course but rather the interdisciplinary "first-year seminar." Similarly, the written communication portion of the General Education requirements can be satisfied by a host of courses, English and non-English alike. Further, in order to concentrate our resources on undergraduate education, we dropped our M.A. program in 1995. As a result, as already noted, seven tenure lines have been lost since 1992. A department that taught more than 700 students in a first-year writing course now teaches about 220 in first-year seminars. Where once we had 165 majors with 30 grad students, we now have 90 and no grad program. Not only do we have less political clout—no one questioned our need for faculty when there was a first-year writing requirement—we have undermined our credibility as the arbiters of all things related to writing. If other faculty can teach writing in their courses, what do we need an English department for? This is not a rhetorical question.

This question is even more pointed when others look at how the department has defined itself and do not recognize "English" as they may have experienced it in their undergraduate years. To paraphrase Stanley Fish, "How do you recognize an English program when you see one?" We have reshaped English study at Drake to stress theory—the critical awareness of the processes of producing, reading, circulating, and interpreting texts—rather than coverage of traditional periods, genres, authors. The position just defined—"a fiction writer with teaching interests in American literature, preferably pre-1900"—is a case in point. Ten years ago we would have seen these as two separate areas and thus two separate positions, keeping "writing" and "literature" distinct. In the past ten years, however, we have tried to erase that distinction, making "writing" and "reading" an integral part of all of our courses. Our own promotional copy—the public face presented to current and prospective students—proclaims:

> [W]e have shifted our focus from a study of texts as containers of meaning (nuts to crack or puzzles to solve) to a study of the critical thinking process by which writers and readers activate meaning through language. In our courses you are likely to become adept at developing and employing a set of critical practices in reading and writing. Thus, what you learn about engaging with texts in Writing About Songs does connect in important ways to what you will do in Postcolonial Literature.

So defined, we become vulnerable to those who question our "need" for someone in American Literature or a fiction writer or a Shakespearean when "anyone" will do, including perhaps someone not in English at all. No longer conforming to our colleagues' idea of what English is supposed to be and do, we have, in their view, lost our direction and our purpose. While we have redefined ourselves, we have done a poor job of explaining and—forgive me—marketing ourselves to our institution.

Our future is now strongly in doubt. During the current program review process, the Provost, with backing from a faculty committee, concluded that English must find ways to become more "cost-effective" (while simultaneously providing needed low-enrollment, and hence, writing courses for general education that are not cost-effective). The catch-22: *"No replacement tenure-track positions will be approved until these issues are addressed"* (Program Review Report [italics mine]). Three new resignations by tenured faculty bring to five the total number of vacancies the department now has. I and my (ever-diminishing number of) colleagues have been struggling over the past few months trying to preserve our sense of what English studies should be while at the same time trying to address the never-specified concerns of "those who think they know better." However elegiac this may sound, I am not writing an epitaph. After all, I am the department's Shakespearean, and if the last act sometimes loads the stage with bodies, it can also be the scene of restoration and resurrection. On the positive side, if we are granted permission to replace, we will have an opportunity—with the infusion of fresh ideas—to begin a process of reconstruction similar to what we experienced in 1989, when five new members joined the department.

The decline in department status may be sharper here at Drake than elsewhere, but still it reflects the evolution of the profession and the reconceptualization of the academy. The "English department" as an academic administrative unit is little more than a hundred years old. And many would argue that, while it served its discipline and its function well during the twentieth century, its time, if not passed, is passing. (This of course is true for most discipline-defined departments.) A variety of forces—economic, political, disciplinary—are at work to reshape English Departments and to integrate them into the colleges that contain them. As a quick glance at the MLA Job Information List will testify, new faculty are increasingly asked not only to fill a variety of different department needs but to support other college or university programs as well.

How does the changing curriculum affect why we hire? How does the trend toward interdisciplinarity influence who we hire? How do new technologies (e-mail, videoconferencing, electronic portfolios, etc.), on the one hand, and decreasing budgets, on the other, alter how we hire? The English Department of the twenty-first century may not exist at all, giving way to a more fluid structure that encourages, perhaps even requires, faculty to realign themselves continually in relation to their colleagues, not only in English but across the college, the university, and perhaps the community. Again, this prospect is not imaginary but very real. As I write, the Program Review Committee has issued its latest proposal, one that will reduce Drake's six colleges to four. Instead of discipline-based administrative structures (Arts & Sciences, Business, Education, Journalism, Pharmacy, and Law), we may have, instead, amalgamations that recall Gerald Graff's description of the "aggregate" English Department. One college would consist of History, Accounting, Marketing, Sociology, Education, Economics, Management, and Anthropology, among others. (Go figure.) English, so the proposal goes, would be located with Music, Theater, Art, Philosophy, Journalism, Religion, and Graphic Design. This is just one of several possibilities. The challenge we face now, in other words, is not simply to restructure English but to re*educate* our institution about the shift in English studies, and, at the same time, to re*imagine* ourselves as something other, or more, than *English* professors working in, or for, the needs of English as a discipline, a major, and a department.

Guerrilla Teaching—Kelly Latchaw

I have taught at Drake University, on a part- or full-time basis, for three years. The current forecast for next year, always relevant to the temporarily employed, is to staff the department with five tenured, two untenured, two partially retired, and five temporary full-time faculty. I closely observed the program review process, in part in order to assess the potential for tenure-track employment here.

While the review has failed to eliminate the English department, it has put a freeze on tenure-track hires pending the department's demonstration of its relevance to the rest of the university. This means that, at least for now, temporary faculty will play a significant role in curriculum development and in repositioning the department in the eyes of the rest of the university, even without participating in the official committees set up for these purposes. The courses we design, the extracurricular work we do on campus, and the students we teach will comprise nearly half of the department's most visible interactions with the rest of the university.

Nontenure-track faculty, including graduate instructors, may be uniquely positioned to contribute to the development of a curriculum that is flexible enough to respond to the increasingly broad range of social and material realities our students bring with them to college. We are the subset of the faculty most likely to encounter transitional, at-risk, and nontraditional students because we manage the bulk of the entry-level and remedial courses at many institutions. While tenure-track faculty at some institutions may also teach these courses and work with these students, they are likely to devote their time, energy, and other resources to their upper-level, field-specific classes. The adjunct or TA generally does not have this option.

My adjunct position places limits on the time, energy, bureaucratic authority, and economic resources I can put into my classes, and I have always been open with students about how these factors affect my teaching. It has always been a part of my teaching to discuss with students how we, as collaborators in the learning project, can develop strategies to work with instead of against constraints. As an adjunct, I am aware that by employing nontraditional assignments and assessments, I am taking a risk with my livelihood that a tenured colleague need not fear. There is a culture of fear that shapes the teaching of the adjunct—whether it is fear of being further alienated from one's colleagues by taking risks or revealing nontraditional practices, or fear of losing one's position and paycheck as a result of such revelations—that can produce either conservative classroom practices or self-silencing in pedagogical discussions. This fear may be more or less tangible, depending on one's circumstances and one's chutzpah, and it may be ameliorated by an awareness of the place of the adjunct in the cost-cutting schemes of most institutions. I am lucky in that Drake has provided me with a great deal of social and institutional support for my teaching. This has made it easier to develop relationships with my students necessary to engage their material social realities as well as my own. I have learned to deal with the culture of fear in large part by regarding myself as a "guerrilla" teacher, one who comes in to stir up the students' expectations and concepts of education rather than as a part-time laborer or temporary replacement. But my lifestyle and work history give me the flexibility to take risks that many adjunct colleagues do not have.

Of course, as an adjunct, practicing such flexibility can be both challenging and risky. The challenge often lies in determining the institutional goals of the course and how it fits into the overall curriculum, since often these are "unwritten rules," which are more readily picked up by faculty engaged with the institution as a whole. The risk comes from flouting conventions and traditions, which can lead to questioning an educator's practices. For tenured and, often, even tenure-track faculty, this questioning can take the form of dialogue with one's colleagues. For the adjunct, it is more likely to simply result in one's name being moved to the bottom of the reserve list.

As an adjunct, I often do not know whether, or what courses, I will teach in any given semester until as little as a week before classes start. I have taught as many as six different courses at a time, so I often use this as a way of discussing with students the value of time management, practice, and adaptability in writing. I tell them about when I composed introductory materials on legal pads in airports, on grocery receipts in doctors' waiting rooms, and on borrowed computers before I could afford one of my own. I also tell them about how my understanding of the function of these materials, and hence my composition process for them, has changed over the years that I have been teaching. When I started, I felt the need to envision every class session in its entirety and include great detail in course goals and policy statements. I have since learned that it is both impossible and counterproductive to control a class too closely.

Adjunct faculty have no turf to defend. We generally receive teaching assignments based on departmental need rather than on individual training or interests, and we rarely have the opportunity to design or establish new courses or extracurricular activities that might be threatened by proposed changes. We are normally excluded from the formal channels of institutional politics that engender and preserve inter- and intradepartmental rivalries. As individuals excluded from the administrative system of the department and the usual avenues of curricular and professional development generally, we have neither a definite history (except insofar as many institutions place limits on the number of semesters we may work for full-time salary and benefits) nor a tangible future in institutional terms, as evidenced by our contracts, our promotion status, and the systems by which our performances are reviewed.

At Drake, various quarters of the university voiced objections to the revised English curriculum. Specifically, many students and advisors from other departments wanted to reinstitute canonical literature courses. Individual administrators did not perceive in the department's curriculum a grounding in Western culture. Even faculty in the new first-year seminar were at a loss as to where to send students they believed needed support for basic writing skills. In the face of these objections, adjuncts assisted the department by refocusing their teaching so that permanent faculty would not have to back away from its more progressive curriculum.

While the program review process may have put the adjunct faculty in this department in an unusually strong position to covertly influence the future of English studies here at Drake, the dependence of many institutions on such faculty to fulfill their various obligations makes us a widely available, if much overlooked, resource. Although the material conditions of English studies generally require the adjunct, we are rarely acknowledged for our contributions and almost never included in official departmental and universitywide decision-making bodies. As individuals, we may not be permanent at any given institution, but as positions we most certainly are.

Welcome to the Club?—David Wolf

So begins Adrienne Rich's essay, "How Does a Poet Put Bread on the Table?"— a very old question indeed:

> But how does a poet put bread on the table? Rarely, if ever, by poetry alone. . . . Of other poets I know, most teach, often part time, without security but year-round; two are on disability; one does clerical work; one cleans houses; one is a paid organizer; one has a paid editing job.

I have "put bread on the table" by teaching at the college level for the past ten years, holding a variety of temporary positions since earning an M.F.A. in 1991. All of my teaching positions have at least been full-time, benefited stints. So I am fortunate in that I have not had to endure the underpaid, piecemeal semesters of part-time college teaching so common today. Perhaps I also feel fortunate in that as a writer who once made his living in the corporate world of magazine publishing, I find such a situation far from deplorable, at least far less deplorable than my nonwriter, tenure-track, and tenured academic colleagues find my situation. From their perspective I am an exploited professional, desirous of the security of tenure, a reluctant member of the growing new world order of faculty temps. Those who see me as such are more often than not lifelong academics who progressed traditionally from undergraduate to graduate work and on into the profession as professors of English language and literature. This was not my path.

After receiving my B.A. in 1982, and after a year of minimum-wage underemployment, I moved to New York to seek a career in publishing. I landed a job in an ad sales department of a major group magazine publisher and remained in the business end of the magazine world for five years. I did, however, work for four different companies in those five years. Such was the dynamic world of media mergers and acquisitions during the 1980s.

I left because I decided to pursue an M.F.A. I had been out of college for seven years when I entered the creative writing program at Michigan where I first taught creative writing. However, I knew what the future teaching prospects were for an M.F.A graduate with no book and only a handful of small magazine publications. I was in the process of lining up some part-time composition teaching work when I was hired as a visiting assistant professor at Drake.

The position was full time, with benefits, and consisted (for the year) of four sections of introductory creative writing, one section of freshman English, and the advanced undergraduate poetry workshop. To say the least, I felt very fortunate and continued to feel that way as Drake hired me for the next three years and provided me with the opportunity to develop and teach a variety of courses alongside the service and composition courses that made up the bulk of my duties. Yet during this time I was becoming aware—and being *made* aware from my colleagues—of the politics, hiring "rules," and complexities (or inconsistencies) of employment in my new field. At one level, I could not help but compare this world to the corporate context, where the notion of tenure still seems baffling, if not horrific. As a poet, I knew that I needed *at least* a book (better yet, two or three)—from a highly respected publisher—to even entertain applying for a tenure-track position in creative writing.

Yet my full-time tenured colleagues, both at Drake and those teaching in the area, seemed concerned, even apologetic for my situation. I became aware of the limit placed on renewable contracts and all of the reasons for the limit from everybody's perspective—the tenured faculty, the administration, the A.A.U.P., and so on. Each year, when asked by those on the outside whether I was still at Drake, I would reply, yes. The follow-up question grew predictable: "Any chance for a tenure-track job?" My usual answer: "Currently no." As the years passed, and I moved into my nonconsecutive fifth and sixth (and final) years at Drake as a visiting professor, I would still get the inquiries, yet my clipped responses were met by academics with increasing dismay, as most shook their heads in pity and some even whispered that I should sue. That seemed extreme, though I know why career academics feel that way. The proliferation of such visiting, part-time, nontenure-track positions can be seen as threatening to the long-term viability of tenure. If colleges and universities can exploit the labor glut of highly qualified new M.F.A.s and Ph.D.s, hiring and dismissing according to supply and demand (like any other red-blooded capitalist organization), who needs tenure?

Perhaps I have accepted the situation more because I *entered* the profession as an aspiring writer, fleeing the stultifying and anti-intellectual confines of corporate existence, looking for a way to put bread on the table. Due to a variety of factors—from mergers and takeovers to internal management shifts and the general demands of profitability—one's job is never secure in the corporate world, indeed in the nonacademic world in general. Everyone is on a yearly contract of sorts in the form of the annual review. I certainly do not celebrate such a world; indeed my teaching and writing and very presence in the world continue to stand in critical opposition to the destructive range of values that produce and are produced by a world so enamored of commerce. Still, my experience with the corporate world leaves me less shocked than my career academic colleagues with the labor practices of the contemporary academy.

I have been a prime example of the flexible worker these past ten years, though again, much more materially fortunate than my part-time colleagues.

I have been reappointed as early as the fall prior to the next academic year, and as late as a week before the start of fall term. I have worked as a freelance writer, editor, copyeditor, proofreader, and fact-checker when not employed as a college instructor. Currently, I hold a renewable contract at Simpson College, where my duties include the teaching of composition and other writing courses and some literature. I am hopeful that things will work out at Simpson in the long run, although it's unclear what "the long run" means anymore, as evidenced by the changes at Drake in its pursuit of excellence (or "flexillence," as I prefer to call it).

I finished my last visiting year at Drake before the completion of its program review. My colleagues' revelations in this article about the process and the results of that review are certainly illuminating to me. I hope the department can achieve the "restoration and resurrection" Joe speaks of, renewing itself either in a more self-directed way or in meaningful (i.e., not market-driven) interdisciplinary concert with other areas of the university. But it is ironic, to say the least, that the bottom-line world of corporate human relations I fled more than a decade ago seems increasingly to be ruling my current profession. I endured and helped execute a few too many corporate downsizings during my publishing career to say to my academic colleagues something so crass and insensitive as "Welcome to the club." I'll leave that to the deans, provosts and presidents, and the faculty committees—or, as they are called in the corporate world, upper management.

Perceiving English: The (In)Visibility of Curricular Reform—Jody Swilky

> *English:* The perception is that the program has charted its own course without careful consultation with the other units in the university. The number of majors has declined significantly. The department must consult with other units and rethink its program.
>
> —*Academic Program Review: Report of the Provost*

The recent program review at Drake evaluated the performance of academic departments during the period from 1997 to 2000. While the "perception" stated in the provost's report is of an English department operating without concern for its institutional interdependence, since the mid-1990s my colleagues and I have engaged in discussions with other departments and most of the university's professional schools concerning the growing need for curricular reform in response to recent changes in general education requirements and a decline in the university's student population. By fall 1998, English faculty were teaching new and revised writing courses aimed at strengthening connections between the needs of students in the professional schools (i.e., journalism, education, and business) and the needs of English majors and other students enrolled in the College of Arts and Sciences. A year later my colleagues and I were receiving favorable feedback from students, faculty advisors, and administrators within and outside our college. These contrasting perceptions of the English department during the late 1990s pose the question of how the department's work on curricular reform, as I am representing it, could be real yet virtually invisible.

The English department had become less visible because of institutional limits placed on its functions, reductions in its faculty, and declining enrollments at Drake. The university's revision of the ways students could fulfill general education writing requirements meant English faculty no longer were the only teachers of these courses, which had proven to be a way in which students became interested in English as a major or minor. In addition, cuts in departmental tenure-track lines began prior to any significant drop in majors, and such reductions made it difficult to offer the full range of courses that might attract students to the English major. Finally, although the number of English majors decreased, many other humanities' and social sciences' departments experienced comparable declines in majors, and there were decreases in students in most of the professional schools.

It was these material changes that prompted the English department during the mid-1990s to consider how it might apply its faculty's expertise in writing to meet changing institutional conditions and student needs. Conversation and debate focused on how to develop new courses that would strengthen and expand existing areas that faculty were committed to, such as literacy studies and creative writing, creating curricula that would better meet the needs of majors and students in multiple colleges. For example, in the fall of 1998, I developed and began teaching an upper-level seminar ("Writing, Literacy, and Schooling") concerned with the practicalities and politics of writing, and devoting considerable attention to the concerns and needs of prospective secondary school teachers. This course was designed to serve the different needs of education students, traditional English majors, and Cultural Studies concentrators, as well as connect with and build on two existing English courses concerned with literacy studies. Another new course focusing on writing in electronic media was designed to meet the interests and requirement needs of English majors as well as those of students pursuing degrees in the schools of journalism and fine arts. We also began designing a writing concentration that allows students to fulfill requirements by taking writing courses offered by English, other departments in the College of Arts and Sciences, and the professional schools.

The purposes of this reform would seem to be in sync with the goals outlined in the university's mission statement. According to the provost's report, the value of an academic experience is determined in part by how well it responds to "student needs and interests," contributes "to the programmatic needs of other parts of the university," and prepares students "for the needs of the workplace." The seminar I designed was influenced by requests of practicing and prospective teachers for more courses at Drake that afforded teachers opportunities to develop pedagogical strategies working with high school students.

In addition, there was considerable interest in understanding more about the politics of schooling, particularly how local and national policies and trends affect classroom practice. Other than a course that trained tutors for the department's writing center, the university was not offering courses in the teaching of writing, and there was no course that provided in-depth attention to the teaching of English.

According to the provost's report, an educational experience should be informed by a "structure and philosophy that encourages and enables connections to other fields" and, where appropriate, "integrates these connections programmatically," as in "multi/interdisciplinary programs." The upper-level seminar I have been discussing underscored the interdependence of knowledge by having students read and write frequently about how multiple fields (i.e., educational psychology, sociology, literary theory, journalism and literacy studies) offer competing perspectives on writing, literacy, and schooling. In addition, the seminar was designed so that students might fulfill multiple requirements through a single course, such as those of a professional college (teacher education), a major they are pursuing (English), and an interdisciplinary concentration (Cultural Studies).

During the period of 1997 to 2000, feedback about this course acknowledged its relevance to the university's mission, particularly the concerns of meeting "external demands and needs" and making "internal connections." In written course evaluations, students regularly recommended the course and almost unanimously stated that their collaborative work with high school students, study of competing perspectives on literacy and schooling, and their research projects built on work they were doing in other courses would help prepare them for graduate school or the workplace. Advisors in the school of education recommended the course to students and sent expressions of approval to my chairperson. After consultation with the School of Education, the English department began developing a new course that affords multiple student audiences—tutors working in the university writing workshop, English majors interested in studying composition in graduate school, and education majors preparing for student teaching—more opportunities to study the teaching of writing. Last year I was asked by the provost, who had spoken favorably about my collaboration with high school teachers, to work with a group of high school seniors scheduled to take courses at Drake, including an introductory reading and writing class which I would be assigned to teach.

This recognition of my work, or of other English faculty's contributions to curricular reform, has been noticeably absent from the university's public forums on program review. Worse, when the department chairpersons, program directors, and the dean of the college met to discuss the reports prepared by the college's academic units, the English department came under attack for its alleged failure to fulfill those traditional service functions that frequently distinguish it from other disciplines. Instead of assessing the pertinence of recent reform in English to the university's mission, or recommending innovative possibilities for meeting the needs of other academic units, this discussion focused on the department's "inadequate" attention to teaching canonical literature and the "limited" value of its writing courses. One person claimed that English was no different than the other humanities departments because it no longer had an "object" of study—that is, literature. Our chairperson challenged this misconception by explaining how we still teach literary works but they were no longer packaged in the familiar course containers of traditional periods, genres, and authors. Our chair also explained that a significant reduction in faculty lines since the mid-1990s affected the number of courses, and hence the amount of literature, the English department could offer over an academic year. His explanations were met with silence.

From a different angle of attack, one person criticized the size of the department's writing classes, claiming she regularly taught history classes twice as large while performing the same work English faculty do in writing courses—"correcting grammar, spelling and punctuation in blue books." Someone who had participated in a summer writing workshop led by English department members who could speak more knowledgeably about how English faculty structure writing assignments, read and comment on multiple drafts, and conference with students, challenged this misrepresentation of the English faculty's labor. However, there was no response to her comments.

This narrow view of English devalued the department's efforts to build on the innovative curricula offered by interdisciplinary programs during the first half of the 1990s. The English department had a long-standing commitment to women's studies, cultural studies, and multicultural studies—programs with many of the defining features of the university's mission statement: "learner-centered," "holistic" classroom experiences; teaching informed "by current knowledge and strategies of the field(s)," which takes place in "new and more effective learning environments"; and educational experiences that make "connections to other fields" and afford students opportunities "to apply their learning to real-work tasks." Despite their pertinence to the university's mission statement, these programs, like English, has experienced reductions in faculty and student concentrators since the mid-1990s.

The program review at Drake University has augmented an atmosphere of competition for resources and protection of territory, which certainly influenced the assessment of the English department's performance. The fact that the term "perception" was not used in evaluations of other academic units leads me to believe that issues, such as class size and ideological differences about what and how the department should teach, have influenced what the provost's report recognizes. That is, what is officially invisible in this process may have as much influence on assessment as what the department's report made visible through evidence, such as the high quality of the faculty's scholarship and teaching, which was supported by student testimony and data. This was confirmed when the Review and Priorities Advisory Committee presented with such evidence in the English department's response to its evaluation, answered that while it found the department's response "thoughtful and helpful" and "appreciated [the department's] current efforts to address [noted] issues," all of that was irrelevant. For in its final assessment, the committee "affirmed the original recommendation *as worded*" (President's Report [emphasis added]).

In the end, the department's experience with the academic program review suggests we must work differently if we are to have a chance to illuminate the value of curricular reform in English. We need to consider the nature and direction of curricular reform in light of what we have lost or given up—that is, our function as the primary designers and teachers of university writing requirements. How do we respond to the perceptions of the department's expertise brought about by the outsourcing of writing? We also need to consider the limitations of developing individual courses that are not perceived as part of a program vital to multiple needs and demands of colleges or the university. And as my chair has painfully learned, we need to be careful how we name what we do and how that might mislead others about our work. Attention to these concerns may help us better negotiate the tensions of departmental purposes and institutional pressures, and thereby have more control over the ways in which our work is perceived.

Epilogue—Bruce Horner

In the popular imaginary, the "university" typically brings to mind Research I schools—the "big tens," perhaps, or the illustrious Ivies. And it is on such schools, and particularly their graduate components, that much attention has always fastened. Concomitantly, small universities like Drake and the hundreds of even smaller liberal arts colleges are sometimes denigrated as intellectual backwaters and are also often seen as academic havens sheltered from the successive perils of publish or perish, political correctness, and corporatization now visited on their more high-profile competitors—places where traditional academic life can still be found preserved, if sometimes in somewhat ossified form.

As this essay should make abundantly clear, such a vision is deeply flawed. Indeed, precisely because they are less "visible," schools like Drake are nowadays more, not less, vulnerable to the forces for corporatization of the academy on which this book focuses. Because they are in a sense under the radar of media attention, they are often financially vulnerable, desperate to improve their standing vis-à-vis their many competitors, and willing to make dramatic structural and/or curricular changes that would provoke serious and unwelcome public scrutiny if undertaken at a more visible (e.g., state-supported) institution. For that very reason, the recent history of English at Drake merits attention for what it may tell us of how corporatization may and can work when its actions are "excavated."

I would like to highlight three implications of the recent history of Drake's English department. First, there is a significant gap between how traditional academics and corporatizing university administrators understand not just "excellence" but such concepts as "interdisciplinarity," "flexibility," "innovation," and "holistic learning." The English faculty's excellence, as measured by traditional criteria of scholarship and teaching, counted not at all in the university's assessment of its value. Nor did the innovations and commitment to interdisciplinary ventures expressed in its curricular revisions. Indeed, some innovations can work against a department, as suggested by the complaints about the small enrollments in English writing classes required by its innovative pedagogy, and the "loss" of turf resulting from the English department's innovative attempts to get others to share responsibility for writing instruction.

Second, work that carries little or no status in traditional terms, at least within English departments, may carry high status outside English. Drake's English department lost both students and status within the institution when it lost what had seemed to at least some in the department its burdensome chore of teaching English 1 to all Drake undergraduates. English 1, it turns out, though low in official status within the department, served unofficially, and even unwittingly, as a means of recruiting English majors and securing the goodwill of other departments and schools in the university.

Third, occupying and imagining one's work "profession" in traditional academic terms of the tenured professor can blind one to the pressures of corporatization. From their position as adjuncts "outside" the institutions they teach "in," Kelly Latchaw and David Wolf respond to the changes at Drake far more dispassionately than their tenured colleagues Joseph Lenz and Jody Swilky (and, for that matter, myself). Contrary to the latter's expectations (in hindsight, naive) that their efforts at designing innovative curricula and courses would be recognized and amply rewarded by the institution, and their sense of betrayal when no such recognition was forthcoming, both Latchaw and Wolf have very low (and in hindsight, enlightened, reasonable) expectations about how their work will be valued by the institution and hence, are less shocked by the program review. More, they maintain an important distinction between the value they place on the work they do as teachers and the ways in which the institutions where that work takes place may, or may not, value their work. Latchaw describes herself as a "guerrilla" teacher who returns the flexibility—a.k.a. impermanence—of her position with flexibility in the approach she takes to her work. And Wolf, from the perspective of his experiences in the corporate world, responds wryly to the situation of his tenured colleagues that they may, in the new "long run," have to get used to it. Flexibility may, in other words, become necessary not just in how one works but in how one perceives one's work "in" English.

More generally, all these writers demonstrate a recurring disjunction between, on the one hand, how faculty may perceive and value their work and themselves as workers, and, on the other, how they and their work are perceived and valued by others, a disjunction with which they must come to grips—for both their own sake and for the sake of what they do value. Much of the work that consumes the energies of faculty and students remains invisible, "covert" in all senses, especially insofar as it is work for and with undergraduates—non-preprofessional, with no immediate direct results to be ascertained from it. So long as it is not "packaged" into an institutionally recognized commodity form, such work will not be recognized; and so long as recognition is withheld, so too will be the material support for continuing it. In other words, whatever use-value work may have for those faculty and students participating in it, the exchange value (or lack thereof) it possesses within the institution will depend on those with the institutional social capital to recognize—and thereby confer—such value. Faculty can and do often attempt to understand and pursue their work in ways that seems to "fit" with institutionally sanctioned goals. Sometimes, other, unofficially sanctioned goals of the institution take precedence. But more troubling, the institution's definition of the goals it proclaims officially may differ radically from how faculty define them. Thus, when institutions call for collaboration, outreach, and the like, faculty should be wary. They may not say what they mean, and they may not mean what they say. In official pursuit of "excellence," and in the name of encouraging faculty to develop interdisciplinary pedagogies of outreach centered on learners, programs can be cut, tenured faculty fired, releases eliminated, departments dissolved, positions removed, staff outsourced, faculty self-governance weakened, and administrators' power enhanced—all outcomes feared as likely to result from our own institution's review.

Finally, it seems crucial for those faculty who remain committed to pursuing the value they see in their work to learn how to make the work of such pedagogies visible as material—to demand that the benefit of their work comes at a cost for which institutions are held responsible. In some instances, this might mean repackaging that work as commodities to sell back to institutions for enhanced support (i.e., to insist on the exchange value of that work). In other instances, it will mean taking more seriously *as* labor the labor teachers and students perform through coursework. While I do not support the elimination of tenure, as some on the left have recommended as a way of further reinforcing faculty's sense of the "flexible" commitment their institutions have toward them, the adjunct/tenured distinction blinds us to that shared status and from facing clearly the problem of what "academic work"—to many at best an oxymoron—does, can, and will mean. Excavating that meaning will itself mean extricating ourselves from our illusions about ourselves, our work, the academy, and its ruins.

Works Cited

Graff, Gerald. *Professing Literature: An Institutional History*. Chicago: U of Chicago P, 1987.

Weisbuch, Robert. "Recruiting in Ignorance." *Profession* 91 (1991): 53–55.

Chapter Seven

"No Chains Around My Feet, But I'm Not Free"
Race and the Western Classics in a Liberal Arts College
Pancho Savery

Reed College is a small, private, liberal arts college in Portland, Oregon. It has a long tradition of combining an innovative core curriculum with contemporary humanistic educational reforms. Reed doesn't have fraternities, sororities, eating clubs, or big-time organized sports. What Reed has is Hum 110, which is required of all first-year students. The course has been in existence since 1943 (the college was founded in 1908 and started offering classes in 1911); and, according to the college catalog, it places primary emphasis "not upon information, important as that may be, but upon the development of disciplined thinking and writing through the interpretation of works of art, literature, or other means by which people have expressed themselves and ordered their lives, individually and socially" (Reed 63). The first semester looks at Greek civilization from Homer to Aristotle, and the second semester looks at Rome from Augustus to Augustine.

The course has served as a model for similar programs across the country, and has been retained long after others have been abandoned. Faculty from several departments teach the course, which emphasizes an interdisciplinary approach to the classical world. There are lectures three times a week at 9 A.M. attended by the entire first-year class and all the faculty in the course. For an additional three hours a week, each faculty member leads a small conference of sixteen students. Students write four papers in the fall and three in the spring, and there is a midterm and final each semester. Faculty are required to have a half-hour paper conference with each student for each paper. There are frequent

93

faculty meetings to discuss how to approach texts; these are particularly useful for faculty members new to the course. At the end of each semester, there is a staff meeting to plot next semester's syllabus.

After the first year in the course, new faculty are required to lecture. No one owns a particular lecture spot; and while faculty generally lecture within their disciplines, this is also often not the case. So art historians lecture on history, literature professors lecture on art history, and philosophers lecture on literature. Students and faculty see how different disciplines approach their work. There is a chair for the course who is elected for a two-year term, but this person does not have any real say in what the context of the lecture is. She or he coordinates the course, choosing lecturers, cajoling people to fill empty lecture spots, running the subcommittee that makes up paper and exam topics, and acting as a mentor for faculty new to the course.

One of the results of this cross-disciplinary organization is that there is not the kind of departmental isolation that exists at a lot of colleges and universities. Faculty interaction is furthered by the fact that the main organizational unit at Reed is not the department, but the division. The English department is part of the Division of Literature and Languages, which consists of English, classics, French, German, Spanish, Russian, and Chinese. Additionally, offices are not grouped by departments. My nearest neighbors are in history, religion, philosophy, and Russian. Thus, the interdisciplinary nature of Hum 110 (which counts for 60 percent of my teaching load) is repeated in the rest of one's academic life at the college.

Because Hum 110 is such a significant part of one's academic life at Reed (the normal teaching load is Hum 110 and one English course), and because most faculty come to Reed with little to no knowledge of the topic, a significant portion of an MLA interview focuses on it. Many faculty, as I did, have a dual response to the course. On the one hand, there is a sense of getting to read texts one always wanted to read and knew one should read; and on the other, there is the real fear of taking on an entirely new field which includes quite long and difficult texts. In moments like these, I can always respond by recounting my own experience.

I came to Reed having read exactly two texts on the fall syllabus, *Oedipus Rex* and *Antigone*. I was overwhelmed by the syllabus and struggled in my first year to keep up with the reading assignments. It actually took five years of teaching the course before I felt completely comfortable with Plato, Aristotle, Herodotus, Thucydides, Homer, Hesiod, Heraclitus, and all the dramatists. The staff meetings helped enormously, because you realize you aren't alone. It is also pedagogically good to be in exactly the same place as your students. Struggling together, over texts which sometimes your students have read before but you haven't, creates an equality in the intellectual enterprise. Two other things help enormously. The first is the existence of the lectures, because you can always go into the classroom and begin by asking what people thought of the lecture. The second is Reed's tradition of conference education. When I first got to Reed,

I thought the word "conference" was just a fancy elitist word for "seminar." But in fact, it isn't. A seminar can just mean a small class where the teacher is still in charge and does all, or most, of the talking. But at Reed, more is expected of the students. As Peter Steinberger notes:

> At Reed we follow an unconventional tack, and we do so self-consciously. To be sure, there are as many kinds of Reed conferences as there are Reed professors. But they all tend to share this belief: that undergraduate education is most effective when students develop, articulate, criticize, and defend their own arguments. A conference is, in effect, an academic version of the blind leading the blind. Students—all of whom have a comparatively limited acquaintance with the subject matter—are responsible, through discussion, for formulating and evaluating theories and interpretations.
>
> Understood in this way, education at Reed is an eminently practical activity because it gives students an ongoing experience in the actual practice of making and evaluating arguments. What better way to understand a set of analytic tools, concepts, and theories than actually to engage in the analysis itself? (18)

At Reed, we consider this the real definition of the Socratic method. This term, however, has been corrupted by law schools and popularized in the film, and later television series, *The Paper Chase*. The professor, the source of knowledge, remains in control, and nothing approaches equality. Martha Nussbaum puts it nicely when she says, "We have not produced truly free citizens in the Socratic sense unless we have produced people who can reason for themselves and argue well, who understand the difference between a logically valid and a logically invalid argument" (35–36). This involves students taking active roles, not the all-too-common passivity of the classroom. As Stanley Aronowitz argues:

> "Mastery" cannot be achieved by ways of learning that are largely passive, such as being fed information through lectures or, what amounts to the same thing through textbooks. There is no substitute for the encounter with complex arguments made through the use of rhetorical strategies that can themselves be studied. (190)

Students come to Reed knowing that the expectations are high and where it is not only expected, but required, that they talk in class. Students who are unprepared for this or are too shy to talk consistently don't choose, for the most part, to come to Reed. Teaching in such a system is incredibly exciting, ideal really; and this makes teaching a course entirely outside your field not as daunting as it otherwise might seem. All students who apply to Reed know about Hum 110, and many choose Reed because of this course. This is clearly different from colleges and universities that have a freshman English requirement. At such places (and I taught at one for fifteen years), freshman English usually means Freshman Composition, which is taught mostly by faculty who are not full-time, get paid by the course, have limited benefits, often teach at several places simultaneously; and who therefore don't feel or have time to feel any departmental loyalty or commitment, don't come to departmental meetings or functions, and exist as second-class citizens. The thinking was that virtually anyone can teach composition, but only those with Ph.D.s and tenure-track lines can teach literature. This kind of class bias, in which literature "professors" were managers and composition "teachers" were workers, mirrored class biases in the larger world and helped contribute to the kinds of intradepartmental splits that led to talk of the "university in ruins."[1]

Another split that often develops in English departments is that between literature and creative writing people. Everyone in Reed's English department participates in the humanities program. We have no composition. We have no part-time faculty. Creative writing faculty are fully integrated into the department. We have no war between theorists and nontheorists.

This sense of equality is a feature of the College in general. The faculty truly govern. All major decisions are made by two elected faculty committees. One makes all personnel decisions and the other makes all decisions regarding academic planning and policy. Individual departments don't make tenure recommendations, nor do department chairs. In fact, department chairs have no real power; and, for the most part, serve bureaucratic functions. Faculty members constitute one-third of the budget committee, which makes decisions on tuition and all major expenditures. Reed also has an egalitarian salary structure. There is a graduated series of ranks that every faculty member goes through, and there are no salary discrepancies. Everyone is on the same scale, even holders of endowed chairs, and the college has a policy of not matching offers from other institutions. The upside of this is that as a faculty member you feel that you have some real say in how the college is governed. While there are other institutions with a similar salary structure, they are mostly public institutions. Furthermore, there are few institutions at which faculty have as much power as we have at Reed. It is one of the things about Reed that keeps faculty members from leaving for other institutions with significantly higher salaries.

For all of its academic rigor, egalitarian structure, and wonderful students, there is, however, a gaping hole in the quality of the education offered. Reed's faculty of 126 includes three African Americans (2.4 percent). In the combined five first-year classes between 1996 and 2000, there were 10 African Americans out of 2,029 students (0.5 percent). How is it that in the twenty-first century these numbers are possible? The reasons are, I think, obvious.

One is the all-white nature of Hum 110, and this can serve as a fitting symbol for the entire institution, where the lack of an African-American presence is painfully obvious. There are no African-American administrators; there are few courses that touch on African-American life; there aren't even any African

Americans who cut the grass. Why would any African-American student look-ing for a supportive environment want to come to a place that is less diverse than their high school? Whatever efforts the admissions office makes to attract diverse students to Reed is almost bound to fail.

The only viable solution is the, by now, somewhat cliched phrase from *Field of Dreams:* "If you build it, they will come." By this I mean that rather than focusing on a diverse student body, the focus needs to be put on recruiting faculty. Students have choice about where they will go to college. Newly minted Ph.D.s tend to have less choice and are more likely to take on the challenge of coming to a rigorous institution such as Reed. They may be willing to take on the task of creating a more diverse environment. It is here that the governance structure gets in the way. At a more traditional institution, the dean or president could put pressure on departments to define faculty lines in such a way that there would be a greater chance of hiring minority scholars. At Reed, that probably wouldn't be tolerated. The faculty would feel that their autonomy was being usurped. The problem is that when the faculty have the opportunity, they usually let it pass. Two recent examples are illustrative.

When the Art department had an opening in the modern period, it adver-tised for someone knowledgeable in twentieth-century European art. It could have advertised for someone who could teach African or African-American art. Why didn't it? The department has only four faculty members (14 of Reed's 24 departments have no more than 4, while 20 of 24 have no more than 6) and each of those members has to function as a generalist as well as a specialist. One person covers ancient and medieval, the second does the Renaissance through the eighteenth century, and the third covers everything from the nineteenth cen-tury forward. (The fourth person covers Asian art in conjunction with Reed's relatively new program in Chinese humanities.) The department isn't in a posi-tion to ask for an additional position in African or African-American art because it doesn't have enough students to justify a new line. So, short of an outside donor or a sudden rise in students taking art history courses, or the college's endowment doubling, this won't happen. African and African-American art are luxuries it might be nice to have. But why does it have to be thought of this way?

I teach August Wilson, but is it so surprising that I also teach Ibsen and Chekhov? Is it so strange to think that one capable of teaching Bearden could also teach Matisse? Clearly, that is the case. The Art department's thinking was that a specialist in African or African-American art would not be able to do anything else. This would be a racist assumption, given the fact that these art historians would be trained at the same institutions as their white counterparts, and thus would be knowledgeable about European as well as non-European art.

When the college created several new faculty lines in order to decrease the student–faculty ratio to 10:1, the committee in charge of allocating the new positions announced that diversity would be one of several criteria used to award the lines. In response, the Sociology department submitted a proposal and wrote a job ad which read in part:

> We are seeking applicants deeply committed both to teaching academically oriented undergraduates and to conduct basic research in the sociology of work, organizations, and markets. The successful candidate should have a substantial interest in race and ethnicity in an American context, with emphasis on economic sociology as a vehicle for understanding the situation of African Americans.

The proposal was accepted and the department was awarded one of the coveted new positions. A month later, the department informed the committee that it was changing the job ad. The new language read as follows:

> We are seeking applicants deeply committed both to teaching academically oriented undergraduates and to conducting basic research. Preference will be given to applicants prepared to teach courses in social stratification and some combination of the following areas: race, gender, ethnicity; occupations, organizations, markets; political economy.

Clearly, there is little connection between these two descriptions. The first is seeking a candidate who specializes in African-American material while the second is not. Because of the change in the description, members of the department were asked to come to the committee's next meeting with an explanation. The straight-faced explanation given was that the discipline of sociology did not organize itself in racial ways, and that no self-respecting sociologist would describe his or her work as race-based. To think this way was to go against the founding fathers of the field, Emile Durkheim and Max Weber.

In Amiri Baraka's poem "Class Struggle in Music (2)," a man walks into a bar and can only truly convey the way he feels by reciting a litany of Thelonious Monk titles: " 'Rootie Tootie, motherfuckers,' he/began, 'And Straight, No Chaser,' he went on. 'Nutty,' he called looking at/the colorless negro piano player from No Heaven" (The Music 102). I thought of this poem at that moment and of DuBois, E. Franklin Frazier, William Julius Wilson, Charles S. Johnson, Paul Gilroy, Stuart Hall, Orlando Patterson, and Elijah Anderson— eminent sociologists whose works deal with race. There was also the question of why the department wrote the original job ad if the discipline doesn't deal with race. I made clear that I would not support this change, but the other members of the committee were reluctant to tell a department how to define itself, and the change went through. Of course, no specialists in African-American material applied for the job.

Reed has been mostly white for nearly all of its existence. (There was a time in the late sixties when there were African-American students and even a Black Studies program. But the program disappeared during hard financial times; and gradually, so did the students.) Even so, there is also a feeling that Reed is a unique educational institution—because of the Humanities program, the requirement that all students write a senior thesis, and the fact that students are never given their grades[2]—and that not everyone has what it takes to make it at Reed. Thus, it would be un-Reed-like for the institution to target any group and actively say, "We want you." The result is that the college can simultaneously remain mostly white in the students, faculty, and curriculum while also claiming, in the abstract, to be in favor of diversity. Thus, there is no real argument to be made about affirmative action; the college does not practice discrimination or engage in unfair employment practices.

Whenever the topic of Hum comes up at a job interview or campus visit, the topic of diversity invariably follows, and it is always the candidates who bring it up. When I give them the facts, they are amazed that in a world in which, according to the Association of American Colleges and Universities, "62 percent of the 543 institutions they surveyed have or are developing a diversity requirement" (Greene A16); and the National Association of Scholars complains that English majors "are more likely to encounter the writings of Toni Morrison and Zora Neale Hurston than those of Mark Twain, Henry Fielding, and Jonathan Swift" (Leatherman A19), Reed seems, at least on the surface, to be far behind the times.

Even a Reagan-appointed federal judge, Patrick Duggan, has ruled in the case of the University of Michigan that a "racially and ethnically diverse student body produces significant benefits such that diversity, in the context of higher education, constitutes a compelling governmental interest" (Wilgoren, "Affirmative" A32). He also "cited research that students 'who experienced the most racial and ethnic diversity' exhibited sharper critical thinking skills, because heterogeneity eliminated 'group think'" (Steinberg, "Defending" 29). Reed certainly has an investment in thinking of itself as a school on the cutting edge. After all, the 1998 *Princeton Review* named Reed the best academic institution in the United States, regardless of size, and developing sharp critical-thinking skills is what Reed considers its educational experience and mission to be about.

More recently, an article in the *Boston Globe* highlighted a book by Donald Asher, *Cool Colleges for the Hyper-Intelligent, Self-Directed, Late-Blooming, and Just Plain Different,* which names Reed as the top college in America. What is impressive to Asher is that "Reed is not afraid to stand up and say it is interested only in the student's mind. The school exists for the life of the mind. Reed is the epitome of an ivory tower" (Weinstein C7). If Stanley Aronowitz is correct, we live in a world where, according to a vice-president of the University of Chicago, "I don't know how many students we can attract if we go after those who only seek the life of the mind" (135), because there is "not much evidence of real learning taking place at most postsecondary institutions" (143). In a world of grade inflation, Reed does not give students their grades. In a world of vocational training and long-distance learning, there is nothing of the sort at Reed. In a world in which colleges and universities stake their reputations on

U.S. News & World Report's ranking, Reed refuses to participate. In a world of nontenure-track, part-time instructors, Reed doesn't have any. In a world in which how many books you have published determines whether you get tenure, Reed is a place where you can get tenure without writing books.

Reed has figured out, again to quote Aronowitz, that "real thinking entails marching to your own drummer, ignoring rules the thinker regards as arbitrary. In the service of reflection, the thinker may even choose to be less 'excellent'" (159). What Reed hasn't figured out is that, in the words of Judith McLaughlin regarding Brown's hiring Ruth Simmons as president, "access and excellence can coexist" (Steinberg, "Brawn" A14). Although Humanities 110 isn't the cause of the problem, it is in many ways the biggest symbol of it.

Humanities 110 is called on to do a number of tasks. It is the one intellectual experience that all students share, and this is the first place where we promote and foster the idea and ideal of an intellectual community. It is the students' introduction to Reed's conference method of teaching. It is the place where the primary writing instruction takes place. The course is not only an in-depth introduction to Greek (fall) and Roman (spring) civilizations, but also an interdisciplinary introduction to the humanities and the different disciplines that comprise it. This is an enormous burden for one course to assume; and generally, it fulfills its functions well. But again, the key problem is diversity.

In the second semester, an attempt at diversity is made. The focus of the semester is Rome, but Rome not just from the perspective of Romans. The first third of the semester does consist of classic Roman texts: Virgil, Livy, Tacitus, Augustus, Ovid, Lucretius, and Seneca. The second and third parts of the semester look at Rome from the perspective of those on the periphery: first, Jews and Christians (The Hebrew Bible, The New Testament, The Tractate Avot, and Josephus's *The Jewish War*); and then the perspective from North Africa (Apuleius, Perpetua, Anthony, and Augustine's *Confessions*). While it is true that this is not as diverse a list as it could be, it nevertheless conveys an essential truth—the Roman Empire was not an isolated monolith. There were people and perspectives at the center of that experience, and there were those who were, for a variety of reasons including being victimized by it, on the periphery. I must say, however, that I don't think the multicultural focus of this semester is the result of enlightened opinion. Rather, I think there is a general consensus that the Roman material is not as interesting as the Greek. Proof of this is that the fall syllabus has changed little, while the spring syllabus has changed several times. Most recently, for example, the semester ended with Dante rather than Augustine.

The real key to the course is the fall semester, which only covers Greece from the perspective of the Greeks, beginning with Homer's *Iliad* and ending with Plato's *Republic* and Aristotle's *Nichomachean Ethics*. In this semester, other than the Persian enemies in Thucydides and the exotic Egyptians in Herodotus, one is led to believe that Greece existed by itself as the lone outpost of civilization amidst various groups of barbarians. While it is true that the initial lecture of the course promises that the material will be problematized, that, in fact, doesn't happen enough. While it is true that there is one lecture on the invention of the polis that makes it clear that the notion of Greek democracy is a myth and that women were marginalized; that another points out that Greek civilization was created in an environment in which as much as a third of the population were slaves whose labor created leisure for others to think, build, and write; and my lecture on Herodotus and Martin Bernal's *Black Athena* challenges the entire idea that Greek civilization is the bedrock of all we are, these are a minuscule percentage of the lectures given.

One argument is that there is a value in spending an entire semester on one culture, looking at it in depth from a number of standpoints: literary, historical, musical, philosophical, architectural, art historical, military, and so on. I completely agree that there is value in doing this. One can also argue that this particular period produced an exceptionally rich body of material that has not been matched elsewhere. I also agree with this. I additionally feel that you can't critique the canon of Western thought if you aren't thoroughly familiar with it. But does it follow that that culture has to be looked at in such a way that all the other cultures it dealt with, was influenced by, was surrounded by, and was a product of, are completely ignored? I don't think so.[3]

Greek culture did not have the strict disciplinary divisions we have, nor did it have the same notion of aesthetics. It was a culture that thought about itself. For these reasons (and more), it provides an opportunity to learn not only about it, but also about ourselves and how and why we are different. Or as Aronowitz says, the knowledge of the canon "provides the basis for any critique and transvaluation of that canon" (169). In a recent class I taught on African American aesthetics, a student wrote an essay analyzing King's "Letter From Birmingham City Jail." She focused on the passage where King makes clear that the tradition of civil disobedience is an old one, citing Shadrach, Meshach, and Abednego's refusal to obey Nebuchadnezzar, the Christians' submitting themselves to the lions, and Socrates' defiance of Athens. She was able to write a good paper because she was familiar with these allusions. They are all texts in Hum 110. This example is one of many any Reed faculty member could cite. It is wonderful to be in the classroom and have students recognize the allusions to classical texts.

I don't think, however, that these are the only or even the main reasons why Greece is studied. I do believe that there are certain commonplace beliefs underlying the course and that, for the most part, they are as alive now as they were when the course was started. One of these is that our civilization was founded on the bedrock of Greece and, to a lesser extent, Rome. The job of the course should therefore be to acquaint students with this tradition. If students don't feel this tradition alive in themselves, the course will make that happen. A second related principle is that because these works are so crucial to our identity, it is the mark of an educated person to be familiar with them. We cannot be the best thinkers without knowledge of these texts. Finally, our literary tradition is based on these texts, and writers constantly allude to them. To fully understand the texts, we must also understand those texts to which they allude.

I have no problem with the idea that these are important texts that everyone should read. However, I wouldn't go so far as to say that one could not be considered "educated" without having read them. That's elitist. The idea that all "we" are came from Greece or that the Greeks "invented" rationalism is not only the worst form of elitism, but also smacks of racism.[4] It isn't, again, *that* these texts are being taught, but *how* they are being taught and contextualized.

When faculty candidates come for campus interviews and we get a chance to talk alone, I am often asked how I really feel about Reed or why I continue to stay, given the lack of diversity. The first answer is that I didn't come to Reed naive. I came intending to check it out to see if I liked it, knowing that if I stayed, I would have to engage in a long-term effort to help make the college more diverse. I have been here long enough to think the struggle is worthwhile. It is because of the tremendous students the institution attracts and because of the intellectual atmosphere maintained by the college. This too is the result of Hum 110.

This brings us to Lenin's question, "What is to be done?" Reed needs to understand its mission not just in educational terms but in social and moral terms. In *A University for the 21st Century*, James Duderstadt, whose idea of a university is very different from mine, nevertheless articulates a point on which we do agree:

> American colleges and universities are founded on the principle that they exist to serve their society through advancing knowledge and educating students who will, in turn, apply their knowledge for their own advancement but also to serve others. Hence, higher education, indeed all educational institutions, are responsible for modeling and transmitting essential civic and democratic values and helping to develop the experience and skills necessary to put them into practice. In this sense, then, higher education's commitment to reflect the increasing diversity of society in terms of both our academic activities and the inclusiveness of our campus communities is based in part on the American university's fundamental social, institutional, and scholarly commitment to freedom, democracy, and social justice. (194)

For whatever reason, Reed's actions do not reflect this vision. Somehow, Reed seems to think that it can educate its students to cope with a diverse world by giving them "four years with a 'white, homogeneous, and upper-middle class' educational home" (Nussbaum 270).

In a special issue of *Daedalus* on residential liberal arts colleges, Peter Gomes asserts: "If elite residential colleges have a consensus on anything in addition to the rationale for their own survival, it has been on the values and virtues of diversity as an institutional goal" (110). How ironic is it that not only does this not appear to be the case at Reed, but that this issue of *Daedalus* is edited by Reed's president? By diversifying our campuses, we put students in a situation in which they can best learn. The world they will graduate into is and will be an increasingly diverse one. As Nancy Cantor argues, "Our country entrusts our institutions of higher education to stretch and challenge the minds of undergrads, not to present mirror images of ourselves" (Evelyn 18). In addition, Annette Kolodny notes, "By diversifying the faculty, we provided role models who helped open up the pipeline into higher education for previously underrepresented groups" (187).

Smith College president, Ruth Simmons, began "a 'personal crusade' to bring disadvantaged students to her campus and similar institutions nationwide" (Wilgoren A10). Smith and other colleges have also set up relationships with private high schools and community colleges as institutions from which to draw students. At Reed, the president initiated an historic campaign to reduce the student/faculty ratio to 10:1. Reed's president could also make diversity an issue worthy of an historic effort. In place of such an effort, my picture has appeared for the past several years in almost every major Reed publication including the course catalog, the graduate catalog, and the annual Reed calendar.[5] These pictures convey an image of Reed that does not exist. I was once told by a first-year student that my picture in the catalog was one of the reasons he decided to come to Reed. Situations like this can lead to what Gramsci has termed "pessimism of the intelligence." Fortunately, Gramsci's dialectic also includes "optimism of the will" (175).[6] Reed is one of a handful of schools that has the opportunity to have "learning" as its agenda as opposed to "education" (Aronowitz 1). While I am willing to struggle for this, I am not willing to be used. When Kenneth Nunn resigned as associate dean at the University of Florida's law school because he was the only African American teaching in a faculty of fifty, he said, "I did not want to serve as window dressing to make it seem there was a concern for diversity that I did not think was present" (Glaberson A12).

At the beginning of the twentieth century, in the second chapter of *The Souls of Black Folk,* W. E. B. DuBois announced: "The problem of the twentieth century is the problem of the color-line" (54). As the twentieth century drew to a close, many people suggested that in the new century, class would be the dominant issue because many of the racial problems that existed at the beginning of the century had been conquered. After all, the chains of slavery had long been removed, laws had been passed, and there was a healthy black middle class. The reality of the world, however, is that this is not close to being true. Wage deferential, life expectancy, wealth, infant mortality rates, and the absence of African Americans in the new reindustrialization make it clear that "the problem of the twentieth century" has not disappeared with the dawn of the new millennium. In addition, my own experience at Reed leads me to the conclusion that it's much too early to retire DuBois' words. The color line is still very much in existence.

In "Concrete Jungle," Bob Marley put it best, "No chains around my feet, but I'm not free." We must be very careful in assessing the world. Too often, it's easy to be blinded by surface changes and think because things have changed for some, they have changed for all. Many colleges and universities have made much more progress than Reed has; but that doesn't mean that, except for Reed, the problem is solved. Reed has a problem, but Reed isn't the problem. Reed is a sign that the problem continues, and that no one is free until everyone is free.

Notes

1. According to Bill Readings, spurred by economic changes, the contemporary university is a "university in ruins": departments are given prominence and rewards in terms of how much they bring in; there is a preponderance of nontenure-track faculty; students are primarily concerned with their vocation; the minimum publication for tenure approaches two books; significant grade inflation is designed to keep students, who are really consumers, happy; scholarships are given out on the basis of merit, not need; there is a move to online education; and schools are obsessed with their ranking. Readings writes:

> My argument is that the University is developing toward the status of a transnational corporation . . . [T]eaching cannot be understood either as structurally independent of a generalized system of exchange or as exhaustively contained within any one closed system of exchange. This, it seems to me, is the situation in which we find ourselves now, one of both limitation and openness. We are more free than we used to be in our teaching, but we can no longer see what it is that our freedom is freedom from. (164)

For responses to Readings, see Delany, Green, LaCapra ("University"), Miller, and Royle.

2. To keep the focus on learning and critical thinking, as opposed to credentializing, there is no dean's list, honor roll, or graduating with honors. In 1999–2000, the average GPA was 2.9, a figure that has remained constant for seventeen years. In that same time period, only five students have graduated from Reed with perfect GPAs of 4.0.

3. I recently came across a course syllabus from 1943. The first week of the course was devoted to Egypt and Babylonia and included reading the *Code of Hammurabi*. The second week included a discussion of the "Aegean and Oriental Background of Greece." Apparently, faculty knew something in 1943 that has since been lost.

4. For another take on this topic, try Hanson and Heath's *Who Killed Homer?*

5. For a discussion of the "multicultural wars," see Carby and Jacobson.

6. The slogan "Pessimism of the intelligence, optimism of the will" is associated with Gramsci, but the phrase actually belongs to Romain Rolland and was appropriated by Gramsci.

Works Cited

Aronowitz, Stanley. *The Knowledge Factory: Dismantling the Corporate University and Creating True Higher Learning.* Boston: Beacon, 2000.

Baraka, Amiri. "Class Struggle in Music (2)." *The Music: Reflections on Jazz and Blues.* Amiri Baraka and Amina Baraka. New York: Morrow, 1987. 100–103.

Carby, Hazel V. "The Multicultural Wars." *Black Popular Culture: A Project by Michele Wallace*. Ed. Gina Dent. Seattle: Bay P, 1992. 187–99.

Delany, Paul. "The University in Pieces: Bill Readings and the Fate of the Humanities." *Profession*. Ed. Phyllis Franklin. New York: MLA, 2000. 89–96.

DuBois, W. E. B. *The Souls of Black Folk* (1903). New York: Signet, 1969.

Duderstadt, James J. *A University for the 21st Century*. Ann Arbor: U of Michigan P, 2000.

Evelyn, Jamilah. "In Defense of Diversity." *Black Issues in Higher Education* (16 April 1998): 18.

Glaberson, William. "Accusations of Bias Roil Florida Law School." *New York Times* (30 October 2000): A12.

Gomes, Peter J. "Affirmation and Adaption: Values and the Elite Residential College." *Distinctively American: The Residential Liberal Arts Collges* (special issue). Ed. Steven Koblik. *Daedalus* 12801 (1999): 101–19.

Gramsci, Antonio. *Selections From the Prison Notebooks* (ed. and trans. Quintin Hoare and Geoffrey Nowell Smith). New York: International Publishers, 1971.

Green, Daniel. "Opinion: Abandoning the Ruins." *College English*, 63 (2001): 273–87.

Greene, Elizabeth. "Most Colleges Require Diversity Education." *The Chronicle of Higher Education* (3 November 2000): A16.

Hanson, Victor Davis, and John Heath. *Who Killed Homer?: The Demise of Classical Education and the Recovery of Greek Wisdom*. New York: The Free P, 1998.

Jacobson, Jennifer. "In Brochures, What You See Isn't Necessarily What You Get." *The Chronicle of Higher Education* (16 March 2001): A41–42.

Kolodny, Annette. *Failing the Future: A Dean Looks at Higher Education in the Twenty-First Century*. Durham, NC: Duke UP, 1998.

LaCapra, Dominick. "The University in Ruins?" *Critical Inquiry*, 25 (1998): 32–55.

———. "Yes, Yes, Yes, Yes . . . Well, Maybe: Response to Nicholas Royle." *Critical Inquiry*, 26 (1999): 154–58.

Leatherman, Courtney. "English Curriculum Favors Morrison Over Swift, Report Says." *The Chronicle of Higher Education* (2 June 2000): A19.

Marley, Bob, and the Wailers. "Concrete Jungle." *Catch a Fire*. Island Records, ILPS 9241, 1973.

Miller, Richard E. "'Let's Do the Numbers': Comp Droids and the Prophets of Doom." In Phyllis Franklin, ed., *Profession*. 96–105. New York: MLA, 1999.

Nussbaum, Martha C. *Cultivating Humanity: A Classical Defense of Reform in Liberal Education*. Cambridge: Harvard UP, 1997.

Readings, Bill. *The University in Ruins*. Cambridge: Harvard UP, 1996.

Reed College Catalog, 2000–2001. Portland Reed College, 2000.

Royle, Nicholas. "Yes, Yes, the University in Ruins." *Critical Inquiry*, 26 (1999): 147–53.

Steinberg, Jacques. "Brown U Breaks Ground in Picking Black as Chief." *New York Times* (9 November 2000): A14.

———. "Defending Affirmative Action With Social Science." *New York Times* (17 December 2000): 29.

Steinberger, Peter. "Small is Beautiful: Reed Aims for a Ten-to-One Student/Faculty Ratio." *Reed Magazine* (August 1999): 16–18.

Weinstein, Bob. "College Beyond the Ivy League." *Boston Globe* (4 March 2001): C5+.

Wilgoren, Jodi. "Elite College's President Takes to the Road to Attract the Disadvantaged." *New York Times* (12 October 1999): A10.

———. "Affirmative Action Plan is Upheld at Michigan." *New York Times* (14 December 2000): A32.

Chapter Eight

A Symposium on "What Will We Be Teaching?: International *Re*-Visions in University Level English Curricula"

David Stacey, Claire Woods, and Rob Pope

International hybridization moves quickly in the ever-more-corporate academy. In this symposium, we look for some of the light in the shadows of this brave new world. The good news is, English has moved beyond itself. In the United States, cross-cultural aspects of contemporary composition studies occupies our attention; around the world, departments and universities connect to one another on the Internet. We can do more nowadays than inquire about literacy in other national traditions. We can begin to share the experiences of international others, as a more complicated "we" begins to collaborate to study and teach language, literature, and writing.

We offer observations on what might be an emerging Anglo–American–Australian synthesis of composition, or writing, or possibly even *re*-writing studies. Initially, we describe a new B.A. in Professional Writing and Communication within the School of Communication and Information Studies at the University of South Australia. We then explain how Rob Pope's work at Oxford Brookes University, in England, synthesizes the theories and practices of *re-writing*. Finally, we reflect on what we can do in the United States, where the "university in ruins" has given way to *English, Inc.,* to renew the teaching of writing.

A Teaching Team Creates a New B.A.

Claire Woods, David Homer, Mia Stephens, Ruth Trigg, and Paul Skrebels call themselves a teaching team. Over the past seven years they have developed a program in Professional Writing and Communication at South Australia. In 2000, they won two major Australian University teaching awards, the Discipline Award in Humanities and the Arts, and then the Prime Minister's award as "University Teachers of the Year." Claire, speaking for the team, assumes the narrative "we" for the first segment of our symposium.[1]

Australia does not have a tradition of writing programs/communication studies, so drawing on the individual team members' experiences in the United States, Australia, and the United Kingdom, we began to design a new B.A. degree with multiple majors and an emphasis on writing. But we began in tabula rasa, in a sense, because our university does not have a department or area named "English." The teaching team thus developed an undergraduate award that has not been burdened by some of the discipline-based conflicts besetting English departments around the Western world. The team has not had to deal with the issues of composition versus literary studies as has been the continuing scenario in the United States, nor has it had to join the battle between English and cultural studies, which has been part of the academic scene in the United Kingdom, United States, and Australia. Free of these pressures, we have tried to stress the interdisciplinary nature of all knowledge about texts, and to give students a particular "geography" in writing/reading/discourse studies: a geography that draws inter alia on ethnography of communication, anthropology, communication and cultural studies, literary studies, and a revised notion of rhetoric.

These name the five foundational foci or perspectives on which the award is built. In one sense, it could be argued this is an English degree in another guise. In another, it is something different, for we are concerned with the "arts of discourse *and context*," the "enlarged conception of rhetoric" offered by Richard Andrews, which incorporates writing, reading studies, *and* language studies (18). A resultant "larger" rhetoric may be the foremost among five equal foci; nonetheless we strive to integrate first, an ethnographic perspective drawn from the ethnography of communication; second, a focus on the construction of knowledge and the discourse of the disciplines; third, a deliberate orientation to language studies—language structures and language in use; fourth, an obvious focus on text and discourse studies (writing and reading practices); and fifth, a specific encounter with and investigation of texts, literacies, writing, and reading practices in context. We engage our students in literary practice—in the reception and production of texts.

The disciplinary footprints for our degree come less from the vocationally oriented world of public relations or management communications, and more from the bases of our teaching foci. For us, *text production* means not only making literature but also making texts for professional, community, business, political, scholarly, personal, or recreational purposes. *Text reception* means not just reading literature but, more widely, reading texts of all kinds in cultural contexts. We want to foster critical and creative perspectives on discourse in use and literacy practices in context. We ask students, for example, to read and write a short story or poem, contribute a piece of creative nonfiction to the student electronic magazine, investigate an aspect of language use, design and write a public document, undertake research on an aspect of literacy in the community, or conduct a communication project. This might involve producing a newsletter for a charity organization, editing a family history, or writing an instruction manual in "plain English." When they render the world on paper or online, they must critically consider their audiences and the social and cultural context for the discourse.

We are interested in enabling students to be the ethnographers of their own situations—whether these contexts are disciplinary areas and their discourses or the community and professional contexts in which they find themselves. Each of the courses that students take in some way demands that they adopt something of the perspective offered by "doing" ethnography and the rhetorical endeavor—(writing) ethnography. Such a perspective engages students directly as writers representing either their thinking about an issue, or their interaction with the information they gather from other writers, researchers, or the information they gather as part of their own investigations of specific situations, contexts, or topics. As students carry out a project or conduct research in a context, they confront the issues involved in gathering data, handling information and constructing a written report, and considering the reader and the persuasiveness of the text.

If *tekhne* is the art and craft of writing, one important way it can be engaged in is through the exploration of the interactivity of the text. We connect the rhetorical sense to the role of ethnographer: What decisions are made in the writing? What is omitted? What included? What is fore-grounded? What is peripheral? How is the case made, the position argued, and so on? These considerations bring the reader–writer to the interface between language and literature/text, and demand, in our view, a conscious blurring of the critical and creative faculties.

Writing as Re-*Writing*, or *Textual Intervention*

Re-*Writing Texts, Re-Presenting Courses*

A project at Rob Pope's institution, Oxford Brookes University, an ex-Polytechnic in the United Kingdom, explores the interrelations between pedagogic and curricular issues surrounding the concept of re-*writing.*

The initial prompt for this project was the recognition that many beginning students needed additional support when encountering a substantially new textual activity. The core course for first-year English undergraduates called "Texts, Problems, and Approaches" was designed to introduce students to ways of reading and writing about literature. The activities were the critical–creative rewriting of literary texts, including imitation, parody, adaptation, *re*-genreing and "intervention" (the deliberate dis- and re-location, de- and re-centering of a text). The aim was to provide examples of previous student work in an effective, enjoyable, and hopefully inspiring manner, while avoiding any sense that faculty were supplying preferred "models" to be slavishly imitated. This material was developed in conjunction with an advanced course reserved for Independent Study in which students gather, edit, and eventually publish work from the earlier Texts, Problems, and Approaches course.

Viewed as a whole, this project performs a variety of functions. For the students who contribute materials, it is an opportunity to revisit and reflect on what they have done and to show and share their work; they also acquire a portable and presentable record (as well as souvenir) of part of their degree work. For those who put the materials together, it offers some practice in action research and reflective practice while developing skills in editing and publishing; it also serves as an assessed part of their coursework. But the most obvious beneficiaries are students new to the course the following year. They get access to actual examples of *re*-writing along with "course-wise" advice from their predecessors. Meanwhile, Lecturers, who seem to serve best as hands-off consultants rather than hands-on supervisors in such matters, get substantial teaching and learning resources as well as make invaluable contributions to course development.

Projects in which students gather, edit, and internally publish their own and other students' coursework are still curiously rare in English studies in United Kingdom higher education. Partial parallels can also be found in the practice of editing and publishing texts generated in creative writing courses. Nonetheless, in English studies at large, the massive resources of students' own work and their considerable potential reserves in energy, commitment, and enthusiasm often remain untapped. Such resources and reserves are especially valuable—and often all the more necessary—when students are encouraged to work with texts in relatively new and potentially intimidating ways. They are appropriate when the course being *re*-presented (and in effect *re*-written) is itself centrally concerned with the *re*-writing of texts.

Re-Writing Texts

At its most basic, re-writing takes the form of such familiar activities as note-taking, book review, and the redrafting of essays and reports.[2] All these involve processes of textual transformation, whether of someone else's words or one's own. Working from this basis, the emphasis can be gradually shifted to more critically searching and creatively demanding strategies. In general terms, these involve such things as: reading and researching between the lines—for what is not said, or merely implied, or utterly excluded; playing devil's advocate—deliberately taking up a contrary, alternative, or unorthodox position; recasting in a different genre or medium, for another purpose and different people—for instance, a technical report transformed into the script of a Television program; exploring play-spaces, posters, and transparencies—thereby realizing complex or contentious issues in collective dramatic and visual forms in which everyone has a hand and a say.[3]

Each instance of re-writing must be accompanied by a commentary. The functions of the commentary are various, and can be as analytically and theoretically demanding as the nature of the course requires. But whatever the level, the basic aims are similar: (1) to make the principles informing the re-write explicit; (2) to discuss the problems and possibilities encountered during the process of composition, including *de-* and *re*-composition; and (3) to explore the relations between the text as read and the text as re-written, in its initial moment(s) of production and its subsequent moment(s) of *re*-production.

This procedure has been used to underpin various English courses and projects at Oxford Brookes, ranging from first-year compulsory introductions through advanced, second- and third-year elective courses built round re-writing strategies, and even into an M.A. course dedicated specifically to the practices, methods, and theories of "Changing Literature." The only differences are in the kinds of contextual knowledge and degrees of theoretical sophistication called on. For, whatever the level and whatever the precise terms in play, the commentary is the place where students will almost inevitably engage central issues such as the death of the author/artist, the rebirth of the reader/viewer, the nature of cultural re-production and intertextuality, the play of difference and the exercise of preference, de- and re-centering, textual change as a function of social exchange, the nature of value, and genre and gender. What's more, students will tend to engage with such issues more convincingly and with more commitment through re-writing than in the standard abstract essay or critical reading. For, in their own re-writes, they have, themselves, already been grappling with them in the practical graft and craft of composition.

In all these ways, then, the combination of "re-write plus commentary" offers a synthesis that is practical and theoretical, creative and critical. What's more, systematic re-writing can really sharpen a sense of language as discourse. The questions that follow may be put to the re-write of any stretch of text, long or short. And again, depending on the course, the responses in the commentary may be more or less technical and more or less theoretical. The questions include:

- Why this word (or argument, or evidence) and not some other?
- How would such alternatives make a difference?
- What if the aim or purpose of this text were different—if it were to present a different point of view or promote different attitudes?
- How would you change the text to open up different perspectives and offer alternative valuations? And how would this interfere with the present logic and structure?
- What other pieces of knowledge would you need to carry through these changes? And where can you find them? How would you deploy them?
- Who else might need to write or read such a text?
- What else might be done with it?

Re-Writing Courses Across and Between Institutions

Two students (Elaine Hunter and Helen Datson) asked a tutor (me) to help them gather re-writes from the course they were just finishing. This course—Texts, Problems, and Approaches—has the theory of intertextuality and the practice of re-writing as its two informing principles. To this end, most of the texts are studied in pairs: *Hamlet* with *Rosencrantz and Guildenstern*, *Jane Eyre* with *Wide Sargasso Sea,* Chaucer's *The Clerk's Tale* with Churchill's *Top Girls.* Students are also required to generate corresponding "re-writes plus commentaries" of their own. Elaine and Helen wanted to review the first-year course. Their initial reason was that they themselves found the whole matter of re-writing both frightening and fascinating. From this beginning sprang a full-blown independent study project drawing on the written work of some ten students.[4] The project was published in paper form, and subsequently electronically on the university intranet, and was enthusiastically received by students in the Texts, Problems, and Approaches course the following year (1999–2000).

At Oxford Brookes, there are currently a number of widespread changes planned in English for 2001 to 2003 and re-writing will be central to these. There therefore will be an opportunity and need for a *re*-run (and *re*-design) of the project with different texts and new students. In addition, there are plans to combine this project with another, larger one dedicated to the building and provision of re-writing materials on the Web. This is in its early stages but is planned to involve collaboration with a range of UK institutions and networks—the English Subject Centre of the Learning and Teaching Network, the National Association of Writers in Education, among others.

Meanwhile, we are looking to build links with colleagues doing similar things beyond the United Kingdom and Europe. In the first instance, this means firming up links among programs and courses at institutions in the United States and Australia as well as the United Kingdom. In particular, we aim, first, to pool "re-writing" strategies and materials with a view to students studying the same texts in different countries sharing their work electronically, and secondly, to pilot a cross-institutional project "re-presenting" related courses for subsequent years of students, initially electronically and perhaps subsequently in paper format.

The *University in Ruins; English, Inc.;* and Curricular Models From Far and Wide

David Stacey writes for the group.

> Markets and modems, in the era of the New World Disorder, push and pull people and countries in different directions, and the choices individuals and groups make when faced with novel challenges matter. (Wasserstrom 4)

At David's institution, several new computers lay idle in their boxes for months. "Behind the Redwood Curtain" in northern California, technology is consciously avoided. "I'm from Humboldt County," declares the archetypal (and sometimes real) student, "I don't have to do this computer crap." At David's former Midwest institution, the dean and the English department vie with each other to break out the shiniest new interdisciplinary, digital media program in the state, seeking to outflank an equally technology-focused neighboring state university.

The regional, state-funded, comprehensive university moves ever farther into corporate culture, becoming, as Bill Readings argues, ever more a business unto itself, and no longer merely the ideological arm of industrialized national culture. In the North American university we inhabit, a new structure of feeling: a congeries of nostalgia, excitement, ambivalence, confusion, resistance, and surrender. This new structure of feeling is, as Raymond Williams explained, social, hypothetical, emergent, and powerful; furthermore, it is to be associated wholly with the intersections of capital and technology.

Functioning in what Readings famously termed the *ruined* university, teachers, scholars, and students of writing need to acknowledge this new mood, mode, and medium of operation of social life in the university, along with the fact that it is indeed technology that introduces this ubiquitous *newness* into all our systems. In the face of full-blown momentous change, Readings himself advocates what he calls "institutional pragmatism"—a kind of postironic acceptance of cultural work based on accountability rather than accounting (17). Readings was trying to work through certain postmodern vagaries of definition to a place where culture matters again. The perplexities that confronted him in this task are felt on the pulse of our everyday work lives, most specifically and interestingly in the way that technology structures feeling.

On Netscape, David's graduate students peek in on and join the threaded online discussions of secondary education undergraduates in a course taking place at his former institution, both levels of students playing out their ambivalence in the face of sometimes radical shifts in what they expected "English" to be. At contemporary state universities, such scenes are a snapshot of academic life "in the ruins," where a range of confusing feelings and behaviors now define the day. Some students, to take another example, resent the teacher who insists on their participation on the class listserv, Web postings, and synchronous e-discussions, while others, blessed with a seemingly innate techno-savvy, scorn the stodginess and always-one-step-behind feel of many serious educational intentions on the Internet. Some professors disdain or eschew computers altogether for serious educational applications, while some adolescent students develop personal identity by demonstrating an "attitude" toward computers and the way they complicate traditional student–teacher relationships.

Given these changes, how do we accept the attendant complexities of felt experience, how do we thrive in a markedly discomfiting structure of feeling, and how do we make our work with culture (or "writing") matter? In this chapter, we have two examples from elsewhere of "what is to be done." The first presents team teaching that successfully *re*-conceives English studies as *Professional Writing,* and the second presents curricular reforms that set into place sequenced courses that deconstruct and reconstruct themselves. In the first instance, we in the United States may not have the material conditions in place to so thoroughly do the job. The University of South Australia teaching team does not work atop the history and tradition of internal academic politicking and public scrutiny that we have in the United States, thus they are free to recombine things in ways that may not be available to American academics who want to *re*-do writing in the English department. In the second case, Rob's unreconstituted love of literature and the unapologetic situating of his whole enterprise in "English Studies" might strike compositionist sensibilities as an improper place to locate the beginnings of our methodology and methods.

These are some of the constraints. The opportunities lie in the occasions we now have to use the resources of the computer and the Internet to achieve an international hybridization of courses in curricula. If we cannot adopt programs and curricula in their entirety, we can re-write texts and courses across and between institutions, even and especially when to do so means constructing linkages between vastly different locales.

In 1994, on the LINGUIST email discussion list, I "met" Sharon Goodman, a graduate student in linguistics studying with Roger Fowler at the University of East Anglia. I asked her if she would be interested in tutoring one of my students in an Advanced Composition course. In the ensuing conversations among students, tutor, and teacher in Missouri and England, all parties discovered something interesting. Our latent cross-cultural differences, revealed in our use of language to communicate on email, were of more importance and interest than the ostensible content of the language study lessons on which we were working. In other words, we learned more from reflecting on how we were trying to talk to one another in this strange fashion through this unfamiliar new medium, than we did studying our stuff in usual ways, with or without the help of email (Stacey, Goodman, and Stubbs).

Other, frankly wonderful, surprises have befallen me and my students as we communicate via the Web. In 1997, using a Web-posting system developed by a colleague and our students at Missouri Western State College, a class of writing students conducted a conversation among themselves about Mary Louise Pratt's concept of the "contact zone," and about Joseph Harris' published critique of the use of Pratt's concept as a metaphor for a basic writing class—*with* Joe Harris, who, invited, swooped out of that distant and mystifying region inhabited by "authors who write the books we read," to talk with students at the website where they had been discussing his work. It was brilliant, as they say in the United Kingdom, to see the responses among first-year composition students (many of them nontraditional students) when they discovered that their ideas and writings were important enough to engage the author of their subject.

Several years ago we constructed a website intended to draw together Rob's theorizing with the Australian team's eclectic breadth of practice with American entrepreneurial know-how. We gave it (to attract some local funding) the rather ostentatious title of "The Online Center for the Study of Textual Intervention." An extant rough copy of the site still exists at *http://www.mwsc.edu/~center/*.

We wanted this site to be a place for that inter-institutional, transnational, and potentially cross-cultural ground of interaction Rob sees as the next step for the Oxford Brooks project. We had also envisioned classes devised and taught by Claire and David Homer in Australia made available to students in England and Missouri, and then potentially elsewhere. Our grander visions have not come to fruition—yet—but we did manage to demonstrate the possibility of serious intercontinental curricular hybridization. We put into place the opportunity for engaging those re-writing strategies and materials developed in Australia and England. The "Center" (ironically named for something so radically de-centering) can still be used to start students who are studying the same texts for different courses in different countries, and sharing their work electronically.

Recently, I was expounding on these "alternative modes" to one of my colleagues. After listening, he insisted these add up to little more than the transfer of skills and methods already used in writing workshops and literature classrooms. He may be right, for both Rob and Claire blur the rather clear and fast distinctions between critical and creative writing that we maintain in our North American curricula. However, it seems to me that my colleague may be thinking about new things using old categories. In setting up the online Center, I discovered that textual intervention, as described by Rob, does indeed "push the envelope" of our understanding of "what goes with what," as Kenneth Burke would say, in the curriculum of an American English department. Further, if writing (or re-writing) were ever to replace literature or culture as our primary god-term (Burke again), to the extent that it has done so in Claire's program in South Australia, we would achieve a critical mass of change and would be standing on qualitative new ground in a rather "brave new world."

Notes

1. For further information about the B.A. (Professional Writing and Communication), see Claire Woods.

2. Extended definitions and expositions of critical–creative re-writing can be found in Pope, *Textual Intervention,* summarized in his *The English Studies Book* (242–50, 265–69). Also see Corcoran, Hayhoe, and Pradl; Evans; and Nash and Stacey (182–225).

3. Such broad strategies can generate specific re-writing activities—working with alternative summaries and paraphrases to draw attention to different aspects of the text; changing titles and openings or writing alternative endings; writing preludes, interludes, and postludes to extend the text beyond the events it represents; changing some "turning point" in the narrative to explore alternative premises or consequences; changing the

direction of a scripted drama or transcribed conversation by intervening in a single "move" or "exchange"; converting narrative into drama or drama into narrative; imitating a text using another as model to re-cast it in a new manner; using parody by exaggerating certain features of a text, or introducing incongruous frames of reference; use of collage; use of hybrids by re-casting two or more related texts to produce a compound; converting word to image, music, movement, or other media such as film, video, photography, painting, and sculpture; music, dance, and performance; even clothes, architecture, smells, touches, and tastes—that offer alternative ways of interpreting texts.

4. For extracts from student re-writes (plus commentaries) from this course and others, see Avery, et al., and Pope, "Re-write Chaucer!"

Works Cited

Andrews, Richard, ed. *Rebirth of Rhetoric: Essays in Language, Culture and Education.* London: Routledge, 1992.

"Artisans Who Create and Challenge," with David Homer *TEXT* (*www.gu.edu.au/art/ text/april98/woods/htm*), 1998.

Avery, Simon, Cordelia Bryan, and Gina Wisker, eds. *Innovations in Teaching English and Textual Studies.* London: Staff and Educational Development Association, Paper 108 (1999) 171–79.

Corcoran, Bill, Mike Hayhoe, and Gordon Pradl, eds. *Knowledge in the Making: Challenging the Text in the Classroom.* Portsmouth, NH: Boynton/Cook, 1994.

Evans, Colin, ed. *Developing University English Teaching.* Lampeter: Edwin Mellen P, 1995.

Nash, Walter, and David Stacey. *Creating Texts: An Introduction to the Study of Composition.* New York: Addison Wesley Longman, 1997.

Pope, Rob. *Creativity: A Critical History.* London: Routledge (forthcoming), 2002.

———. *The English Studies Book.* London: Routledge, 1998.

———. "Re-Write Chaucer! Creativity and Criticism, Interpretation and Performance in the Teaching and Learning of Medieval Literature." *World and Stage.* Eds. Greg Waite and Jocelyn Harris. Otago: University of Otago P, 1999. 65–92.

———. *Textual Intervention: Critical and Creative Strategies for Literary Studies.* London: Routledge, 1995.

Readings, Bill. *The University in Ruins.* Cambridge: Harvard UP, 1996.

Stacey David, Sharon Goodman, and Teresa D. Stubbs. "The New Distance Learning: Students, Teachers, and Texts in Cross-Cultural Electronic Communication." *Computers and Composition* 13.3 (December 1996): 293–302.

Wasserstrom, Jeffrey N. "China: Beyond the Matrix." *The Nation* (7 May 2001): 32–43.

Woods, Claire. "Bridging the Creative and the Critical." In *L1- Educational Studies in Language and Literature.* 2001: 55–72.

———. *Communication and Writing: Footprints on a Territory.* Hawke Institute Working Paper Series No 2. Magill, South Australia: Hawke Institute, University of South Australia, 2000. Also available online at *www.hawkecentre.unisa.edu.au/institute.*

————. "Review, Reflection, and Redirection in a Writing Program," *TEXT* (1999)—*www.gu.edu.au/-art/text/april99/woods.htm.*

————. "Students and an Undergraduate Program in Professional Writing and Communication: Altered Geographies." *TEXT* 1:2 (1997)—*www.gu.edu.au/-art/text/oct97/woods.htm.*

————. "The Art and Craft of the Honours Thesis: A Rhetorical Enterprise," *TEXT* (2000)—*www.gu.edu.au/-art/text/oct00/woods.htm.*

Chapter Nine

Curriculum for Seven Generations
Derek Owens

An Emerging Conversation

Within this decade, the term "sustainability" will offer a potential concurrence among composition studies, literary theory, cultural studies, postcolonial studies, gender studies, and service learning. A concept that has already significantly influenced scholarship in architecture, ecological economics, environmental education, and planning, sustainability has the potential to create contexts for new research and pedagogical explorations in English studies. It would interpose a different kind of crisis into our conversations, larger than any other crisis so far associated with our discipline.

One already sees this term, or at least concerns associated with sustainability, surfacing in recent composition and rhetoric titles (Brown, Dobrin and Keller, Dobrin and Weisser, Herndl and Brown, Killingsworth and Palmer, McAndrew, Roorda). My objective here is not just to urge faculty and students to consider the implications of sustainability for their research and their teaching, but to argue that an unrealized, latent sustainable curricula already runs throughout American English departments. Ours is a discipline better suited than many to model sustainable curricular reform, and as such is positioned to play a key role in the promotion of a sustainable ethos throughout higher education.

The purpose of exploring connections between English studies and sustainability would not be to save English from its own crises for its own sake, but to teach and research notions of sustainability because they are vital and cannot be ignored. Focusing on local and global crises that transcend disciplinary boundaries and reach into the lives of our students and their communities might further strengthen our students' and the public's perception of our discipline's raison d'etre.

Sustainability, Briefly

Sustainability, defined in broad strokes, is about achieving intergenerational and intragenerational equity: living in ways that do not jeopardize future generations and addressing the relationship between poverty and ecosystem decline. Sustainability means resisting a consumer culture for simpler ways of living that have minimal negative impact on existing resources and ecosystems. Living sustainably means working toward social justice—ensuring that poorer people have the necessary skills and resources to live safe, productive lives. It means understanding one's impact on local environments and seeking to lessen the negative effects of that impact. It also means replenishing limited resources in the course of our daily activities. While there are competing definitions of weak and strong sustainability that I will not explore here,[1] I will let the concept of sustainability imply the need to critically examine the short- and long-term impacts of our contemporary consumer habits and lifestyles on current and future generations.

My own tendency to make sense of sustainability is to begin developing a more intimate knowledge of one's local environment: one's neighborhoods, communities, watersheds, cultures, and economy. Sustainability also requires one to distinguish between elements of social and material culture that ought to be preserved and cultivated, and those that work against sustainability—to construct a sense of values related to sustainable goals. Seen through a sustainable lens, for example, preserving a family's oral histories promotes sustainable values (Art Spiegelman's *Maus,* for instance, or a freshman's interview with her grandmother). Knowledge of sustainability implies an awareness of how educational institutions ignore the need to think sustainably, as well as a familiarity with arguments for sustainable pedagogy (Bowers, Merchant, Orr, Ryan, Smith, Trainer). Sustainable thinking also leads one to examine future employment options with an eye toward their role in furthering or hindering a sustainable future: Sustainability-minded students would be ones not simply interested in getting "good jobs," but seeking careers wherein one could further sustainable objectives (Hawken, Lovins, and Lovins; Shrivastava). Sustainability also requires one to think like a futurist, imagining near-future conditions based on available information (Bossel, Linden, Schwartz).

The concept of sustainability is sometimes characterized in a native American context. The Iroquois have often been characterized as a culture that, before making any major tribal decisions, first considered the potential impact of those decisions on the next seven generations. Since the most widely circulated definition of *sustainability* is meeting "the needs of the present without compromising the ability of future generations to meet their own needs" (World Commission 43), one can see how this Iroquois Gen 7 vision gets associated with the goal of imagining a sustainable future. Although this two-dimensional rendering of what Shepard Krech calls the "Ecological Indian" is arguably romantic, if not unintentionally racialized—more than a few Native American tribes radically changed their landscapes, cultures, and futures by altering and depleting local flora and fauna—this seventh-generation perspective remains a useful metaphor for imagining and designing curricula that might cultivate a sustainable ethos.

Sustainable thinking, a cognitive balancing act where local and global (or, more precisely, microlocal and macrolocal) realities are constantly considered in conjunction with one another, lends itself to Bill Readings' call for "a certain rhythm of disciplinary attachment and detachment" (176). Educators, particularly those in higher education, need to redefine themselves as both specialists *and* generalists: to pursue specific disciplinary preoccupations while at the same time designing curricula that seek to counter the ruination of our communities. No department or discipline can afford not to explore ways in which sustainability—which is at once an aspiration, a responsibility, a myth, and a design principle—might manifest within its curricula.

A Discipline Suited to Sustainable Thinking

English studies is a logical site for fostering conversations about sustainability. Appendix A demonstrates the degree to which many fields, methodologies, and specialties already established in English studies have emerging counterparts directly and indirectly related to sustainability. In the left column in this appendix are listed "Existing Zones in English Studies," and it includes fields and thematic foci typically represented in English studies curricula. The right column lists sustainable complements, many of which have surfaced in the last decade, and others which, in my opinion, are on the verge of surfacing more predominantly within the work of English studies. In essence this appendix depicts a second "sustainable" map, existing just beneath the surface of the more obvious landscape of English studies.

Appendix B looks more closely at actual undergraduate and graduate courses currently taught in American English departments between the years 1999 and 2001. According to the *Peterson's Guide to Four-Year Colleges, 2001,* there are 1,233 American colleges offering English majors, with an extra thirteen institutions offering majors in English Composition (I exclude colleges listed in *Peterson's* located in Canada, Mexico, Puerto Rico, and Europe). The *Peterson's Graduate Programs in the Humanities, Arts, and Social Sciences, 2000,* lists 427 programs in the United States offering graduate degrees in English. Of these programs, both graduate and undergraduate, I have visited approximately 200 English departments with course offerings listed on the World Wide Web[2] and gathered from 150 of those colleges approximately 200 courses with titles that could lend themselves to sustainability-oriented conversations, readings, and projects. Appendix B lists the titles of courses exactly as they appear on the World Wide Web; the categories under which I have grouped them for the sake of clarity are my own (admittedly arbitrary) headings. Some of the courses listed are clearly oriented to sustainability: "Current Issues in

Eco-Criticism," for instance, and "Environmental Writing." But most are not obviously "about" sustainability in any explicit sense. Although it's unlikely that sustainability is being addressed in these courses, their titles, regardless of the intentions of faculty who designed them, imply logical sites for discussions and readings pertaining to sustainable concerns.

The listings in Appendix B are not comprehensive. In most cases departmental websites listed only recent or current course offerings; consequently complete departmental course archives were usually unavailable on the Internet. However, given that I have only viewed the course listings at approximately 200 colleges—just one-sixth of the departments currently offering majors or graduate degrees in English—the number of potential sustainability-oriented courses cited in Appendix B might lead one to project that more than 500 courses now on the books in English studies could feasibly serve as sites where sustainable concerns could enter into the course. When we include more generically titled courses in introductory and advanced composition, literary theory, creative writing, critical thinking, teaching and pedagogy, and also those featuring service learning initiatives—courses the likes of which I have not compiled within this appendix—the number of classrooms where students and faculty could feasibly explore sustainability in English studies is even greater. One might even conclude that nearly half of the courses currently offered in English departments nationwide lend themselves, at least in part, to discussions and writing projects for furthering the understanding of sustainability.

A significant vein runs through contemporary English studies curricula, one that can only get richer as more faculty replicate and add to this already diverse collection of courses. What's more, it is difficult to imagine other departments offering this degree of variety. This is why I anticipate English studies playing an increasingly prominent role in shaping the curricula of higher education, particularly core curricula, as faculty, students, and the public become more aware of the need to think and act sustainably.

Sustainable Pedagogical Objectives

I imagine four predominate objectives in a sustainable curriculum: awareness, preservation, preparation, and implementation. The first entails understanding the concept of sustainability and its daily relevance for our private, public, and professional lives. After awareness the issue of preservation surfaces, forcing us to consider cultural and environmental resources within our at-risk local environments. Preparation points to the need to anticipate the short- and long-term futures of our communities, private lives, and chosen professions. Implementation refers to the need to act on observations about sustainability arrived at as a result of contemplating the status of our local needs and environments.

An initial step in promoting sustainability is to create classroom environments in which faculty and students become familiar with the concept of sustainability. The most obvious English courses are those structured around immediately recognizable "green" themes and vocabularies: ecocomposition, ecofeminism, ecorhetoric, ecotheory, landscape, nature writing, and regionalism. One would also expect literary theory courses including ecocriticism within their overview to provide introductions to the concept of sustainability. Less obviously, however, a variety of courses pertaining to composition, rhetoric, culture, and communities are potential sites for pedagogies aimed at making students more aware of the complex interrelationships among mind, body, and place.

Once students and faculty understand some of the fundamental principles of sustainability, the issue of preservation becomes more acute. Since sustainability is about preserving the needs of future and present generations, questions of value are implicit within discussions of sustainability, along with the issue of distinguishing between needs and desires. Logical opportunities exist for introducing the concept of sustainability in virtually any course where the current and future lives of our students, their families, or their neighborhoods becomes a topic of conversation and writing. Any course where students are encouraged to explore and justify their own evolving value systems provides opportunities where faculty might work sustainability into classroom discussions. More than simply fostering an appreciation of "place-based writers" and "nature writing," place-centered courses can provide incentive for students to investigate their towns, neighborhoods, and blocks in what might ultimately become acts of self-construction and redefinition. Also, any course concerned with the investigation of culture or the preservation of identity and language provides opportunities for students to preserve and archive cultures, especially through the act of making oral histories. In some ways a preservational ethic implicitly counteracts the fetishization of the individual by resituating individuals within a network of cultural, ecological, economic, and geographic exigencies.

Courses encouraging students to critique their field's relationship to work and its role in the development of a sustainable economy are crucial. They create a forum for understanding the history of one's chosen discipline, as well as assessing the social and economic implications of their chosen profession in light of future trends. Departments, through their course offerings, have a responsibility to help prepare undergraduate majors and graduate students for a range of current and future career possibilities in rapidly changing economic and technological arenas. Thus, investigations of ecological economics, future studies, information technology, media studies, sustainable business opportunities, teaching, and other potential career paths suited for students with expertise in the production and interpretation of text are necessary not just for the pragmatic purposes of helping our students get jobs, but also so that English faculty might continually have a context for reassessing their role in preparing students for a changing economy.

With the rise in service learning throughout undergraduate curricula, and especially in composition, there are growing opportunities for students to work toward constructing sustainable environments. Any course in English studies that promotes service-learning or internship activities offers students opportunities to play active roles in adult and community literacy, involvement with electronic community networks, neighborhood revitalization projects, building green campuses, engagement with regional planning initiatives, maintenance of community archives and oral histories, and so on.

Two Examples of Sustainable English Courses

In *Composition and Sustainability: Teaching for a Threatened Generation,* I discuss how research in sustainability, as well as the insights of my students, led me to design introductory writing courses around the theme of sustainability. Here I wish to highlight two cultural studies courses I taught within my English department during the fall 2000 and spring 2001 semesters, respectively: "Constructing Suburbia" and "Writing the Future." I offer these courses not as models, obviously, of what faculty interested in sustainability "ought" to be doing: In the spirit of sustainability, these courses have been informed by my own local interests and needs as well as those of the students I teach at an urban university in Queens, New York City. One would not necessarily expect such courses, or the course materials I use, to surface in classes taught elsewhere. My objective here is simply in the spirit of sharing, in hopes that future contexts might arise where other English faculty might offer their own sustainability-informed courses.

Constructing Suburbia

Since an increasing number of my students come from suburban environments, as do I, I was eager to create a course with suburbia as a focal point. I designed a course in which, as a class, we would explore manifestations of suburbia in film, literature, and television, and students could spend the entire semester researching their own neighborhoods. It was not a requirement, obviously, for students enrolled in the course to live in the suburbs; as would be expected for the urban university where I teach, half of the students lived in New York City. Obviously this only served to enhance the course because students from the suburbs could compare their neighborhood portfolios (which consisted of written accounts, oral histories, photographs, and videos) with those of their urban classmates. Ultimately the primary objective of the course was for students to begin thinking more critically about their own neighborhoods and communities: their histories, their current status, and their likely futures.

I framed the course with the following brief introduction, included in the syllabus:

> *Suburbia.* Lawns, nuclear families, driveways. Backyard barbecues, cocktail parties, two car garages. A controlled landscape of cultural homogenization and class conflict. A laboratory for the marketing and

assimilation of post–World War II consumer desires. A state of mind. A genre filled with cliches. Romanticized and demonized, parodied and condemned, embraced and revised—suburbia is an evolving idea, a mirror at once reflecting what people fear and what they long for. We all know the genre of the Western, even if none of us have ever encountered that fantasy landscape of cowboys, buttes, and coyotes. But while more Americans now reside in suburbs than in cities, the concept of "the suburban"—as a genre unto itself—has yet to find its way into the vernacular (as in, we watched a suburban on TV last night). This class will explore "the suburban" in a variety of media: novels, film, television, sociological research, and planning. Whether lurking in the background or self-consciously presented as a central character, the more one looks the more one finds suburbia manifesting in all manner of media. We'll look at a handful of such texts, critiquing them in the context of our own personal understandings of suburban, urban, or rural living.

The course was divided into themes, most of which featured scenes from films and television shows. I began with past and recent depictions suburbia: a 1967 special issue of *LOOK* magazine, followed up by a 2000 special issue of the *New York Times Magazine*. After this we read Fitzgerald's *Great Gatsby* for insights into an earlier, presuburban vision of Long Island, along with a 1946 issue of *LIFE* magazine depicting Long Island's North Shore. To highlight class and cultural conflict in suburbia, scenes from the films *Avalon, A Raisin in the Sun,* and *Goodbye, Columbus* were shown; and we read Sandra Tsing Loh's novel *If You Lived Here You'd Be Home by Now.* Following this we looked at the design of suburbia, reading *Suburban Nation: The Rise of Sprawl and the Decline of the American Dream* (Duany et al.), Wetherwell's "The Man Who Loved Levittown," watched the monorail episode from *The Simpsons,* and looked at excerpts of a *SimCity* software manual from the early 1990s.

We spent several weeks examining ways in which mothers, fathers, neighbors, and children are portrayed in suburban films, during which we watched scenes from *The Graduate, The Stepford Wives, American Beauty, Serial Mom;* clips from *Home Improvement* and *Rugrats* episodes; and *The Ice Storm* in its entirety. One week we explored the nature of absence in suburbia, using Donna Gaines' *Teenage Wasteland: Suburbia's Dead End Kids,* and scenes from the film *SubUrbia.* A section on suburban monsters included excerpts from the films *Poltergeist, Edward Scissorhands, Blue Velvet, Parents,* and an *X-Files* episode in which Scully and Mulder go undercover in a gated community.

At the course's conclusion we watched an episode from the Home and Garden Television Network on "The New Suburbia," a CNN episode on rising sprawl in Atlanta, and discussed several websites celebrating suburban culture. Throughout we read chapters from The *Geography of Nowhere: The Rise and*

Decline of America's Man-Made Landscape (Kunstler), *Crabgrass Frontier* (Jackson), *Picture Windows* (Baxandall and Ewen) and *Borderland* (Stilgoe). Students submitted five response journals (minimum length five pages) in which they recorded their thoughts and observations in response to the course materials.

The variety of sources (and especially the frequent filmclips) helped to keep students enthusiastic throughout the course. But what made the class so successful was not so much the usage of these materials, but the students' evolving portfolios, which they shared with one another at intervals throughout the semester. Students were required to not only write about their neighborhoods, but investigate the histories behind them; interview friends, relatives, and neighbors; and photograph or videotape their communities. The results were invigorating: because St. John's University is located in Jamaica, Queens—dead center in the most multicultural population not only in the United States but, by some estimations, the Western Hemisphere. Throughout the course, and especially during the final two weeks when students presented their finished portfolios (and brought in food to share from their neighborhoods), we saw a range of communities through the eyes of students, their families, and neighbors.

- A videotape of elderly Greek men in their local barbershop telling stories about the old neighborhood

- A photo-essay about a neighborhood not far from campus where Asian women worked in garages converted into sweatshops

- Stories and photos of the architecture in "old" Howard Beach, and the mafia presence circulating throughout that community

- A video tour of a poor and working-class Bronx neighborhood through the eyes of a student who had, by the course's end, realized how much she loved her community, which had such a stronger sense of community than any of the suburbs explored in the course materials

- A video tour of a Long Island suburb, in which the student visited the places where, as a teenager, she had sought to find a place of her own (the second story of a neighbor's garage, a crawlspace beneath a viaduct, a street corner)

- Town "newsletters" and "newspapers" of Floral Park and Howard Beach, slickly designed and completely fabricated by students, which revealed insights into community neighborhoods, events, and controversies

- Gripping accounts of violent drug communities run by Italian American working-class teenagers in Throgs Neck

- Investigations into the racism found in a Nassau County town of Elmont, which characterized its poorer, more ethnic neighborhoods as "Hellmont"

- One transfer student's look at gang communities, suburban track housing, and working-class suburbs around West Hollywood

- One person's account of former high school classmate who had recently been convicted of a homicide committed in suburban Bergenfield, New Jersey
- One student's video tour of her crime-ridden neighborhood in South Ozone Park, including interviews with her younger nieces and nephews who had been mugged and/or assaulted within several blocks of their houses
- Another student's inquiry into the mixture of boredom, drug culture, and consumer addiction in an affluent Texas suburb

Student evaluations of the course went through the roof—half of the students expressed that this was the best course they'd taken in three or four years of college. I call attention to this without reservation or awkwardness, for it was clear to me that the reason for their excitement was a response to the opportunity to discover so much about where their peers lived and what they thought about those places. Ideally, in the future such a course would involve an optional service-learning component, in which students might begin to investigate opportunities to engage in community revitalization and cultural preservation. (The course did feature this option—but since most of my students work at least twenty hours a week in addition to taking a full course load, there was simply no time to successfully pursue such service-learning projects.) But the course turned out to be an example of how a course focusing on the analysis of literary and visual sources could be a catalyst for students becoming more aware of the strengths and weaknesses of their own communities.

Writing the Future

The following semester I taught a course that examines a new literary genre, what I call the "near-future narrative." This isn't the same as classical science fiction—the course was not about colonies on Mars, time machines, or the Star Warsy brand of science fiction. Instead we examined writers interested in the relatively near future: cyberpunk authors like William Gibson (*Neuromancer*) and Misha (*Red Spider, White Web*); authors of speculative fiction like Octavia Butler and Nalo Hopkinson, who paint postapocalyptic portraits of life several decades hence; and short stories by the visionary writer J. G. Ballard; as well as those by African American writers of speculative fiction housed in the anthology *Dark Matter* (Thomas).

What made this course different from many science fiction courses was that we discussed these texts in conjunction with nonfiction works on the near future, including excerpts from the latest *State of the World* (Brown et al.); Hartmut Bossel's *Earth at a Crossroads: Paths to a Sustainable Future,* Bill Gates' *The Road Ahead;* Eugene Linden's *The Future in Plain Sight;* Bill McKibben's *The End of Nature;* excerpts from *The Cyborg Handbook* (Gray); and a number of newspaper and magazine articles on biotechnology, energy, future studies, globalization, information sciences, and nanotechnology. Whether fictional accounts drawing on present-day conditions or nonfiction predictions culminating in future fictions, all of these works constitute a hybrid genre of near-future narrative. The purpose was to expose students to this body of literature, and, more important, to provide them with tools and examples by which they might begin constructing their own future scenarios of life several decades from now.

As I write this, the course is still in progress—it began in January 2001, certainly an apropos time to investigate perceptions of the future. In addition to writing five journal responses to the readings, students have been writing ongoing future scenarios in which they situate themselves twenty-five or thirty years in the future and explore what they imagine to be their worlds at that point in time. The purpose of these writings is not for students to describe what they hope or fear will come to pass, but rather to come up with a "best-guess" narrative based on their reading of the course materials. Students are also engaging in a second project in which they imagine ways of pursuing future careers—even careers not yet currently invented—and follow their needs and desires, but simultaneously do not escalate ongoing socioeconomic and environmental crises. Although these projects have yet to be submitted, I can comment on their future scenarios, which are eye-opening for a variety of reasons.

The most startling feature of the narratives is that the majority of the students anticipate bleak futures: futures grimmer, more environmentally compromised and technologically oppressive than the present. It is also fascinating to read accounts by writers between the ages of eighteen and twenty-two where, usually for the first time in their lives, they reflect on the fact that they will some day be approaching middle age, living in landscapes radically different from the ones they now inhabit. Some students have become increasingly depressed at the future conditions described in the *State of the World* report, coupled with the horrific landscapes imagined by Octavia Butler or the editorials and articles archived at *www.dieoff.com*. Plus, there have been a series of conversations in class and during one-on-one conferences at which I've attempted to help students reconstitute this unease into a sense of fascination as well as urgency regarding their complex and shifting present environments.

The risk of such a course, and particularly the materials I'm using, is that students respond to the material with what one student aptly characterized as a "fuck it, I mean, what can I do" attitude. However, part of the value in a course like this is to bombard students with well-informed near-future forecasts, like those found in *State of the World,* and at the same time introduce them to works by writers who imaginatively fashion these contemporary fears and exhilarations into constructive scenarios and fictions. In other words, pedagogical environments need to be designed where students, encountering for the first time disturbing predictions of short-term futures, must have room to articulate the cynicism that understandably manifests itself in encounters with such materials. They will then, hopefully, move beyond that cynicism by constructing imaginative future scenarios informed by their own desires and needs.

It is too early for me to determine how I've succeeded at these goals; the evaluations for this course won't be submitted for some time, and I can't tell to what degree my students are envisioning their futures through constructive eyes. I am convinced, however, that pedagogical spaces like this—where forward-looking texts are presented in a manner in which students can begin imagining their own futures—are necessary in a sustainable curriculum.

Curriculum for Seven Generations

If English studies is in a state of crisis, then this crisis is dwarfed by a tapestry of local and global ecological, economic, material, and psychological crises created or exacerbated by unsustainable global forces. We will likely witness more upheavals in the next several decades than at any time in human history.[3] Ultimately, we cannot treat our professional and disciplinary crises as if they were separate from those resulting from living in an unsustainable world. Both concerns need to be explored concurrently. Meeting our personal needs as researchers and educators, while also addressing the needs of future generations, is, I think, the primary challenge now confronting English professionals. My own contribution in this chapter barely addresses the seriousness of our current situation: What is at stake here will involve more than simply creating new courses in which sustainability makes an entrance into our classroom conversations. The first step might be to situate our immediate objectives within the long-term goal of building a sustainable culture. How might a cultivated exploration of sustainability provide us with new opportunities for research and publication? What are the numerous, and, as of yet, unarticulated ways that the project of English studies is already implicitly about qualities associated with sustainability: preservation, cooperation, diversity, collaboration, intuition, cultural critique, scenario-building, social justice, critical education, and service? How might an embrace of sustainability help our discipline, and the academy, be seen as more relevant—and especially more locally relevant—in the eyes of the public?

In one of the more important titles on sustainability, *Earth at a Crossroads: Paths to a Sustainable Future,* Hartmut Bossel explores two future scenarios. If we continue on our current course of unsustainable development—a "Path A" characterized by increasing competition—the results will be devastating to current and especially future generations. An alternative "Path B," one where competition has been replaced with partnership and cooperation, points in a radically different direction toward a sustainable future. To appreciate, let alone move toward, this new path will require, among other things, adopting a whole-systems approach to interpreting present conditions and imagining sustainable future scenarios. It is unlikely the answers to the questions that confront us will come from students and scholars specializing in just one facet of a discipline; to paraphrase Buckminster Fuller, more expert generalists, not specialists, are required. What we need is to think in terms of systems, and to constantly relate our private desires as researchers and educators to the requirements of our immediate environments. While the tasks ahead are nothing if not overwhelming, the exigencies of the contemporary moment present all of us in English studies with new challenges that must be seen as opportunities for further reconstructing the mission of English in response to looming environmental catastrophes. Given the enormous range of courses and research conducted in English departments, ours is a logical and fecund site for such necessary work.

Notes

1. See Chapter 2, "Sustainability," in *Composition and Sustainability: Teaching for a Threatened Generation* (Owens).

2. Nicolette Porochnia and Brian Quinn assisted in this research.

3. Readers who find this claim exaggerated are directed to *GEO-1: 1997 Global State of the Environment* by the United Nations Environmental Programme *(www1.unep./unep/eia/geo1/index.htm)*; the Union of Concerned Scientists' document, "World Scientists' Warning to Humanity," from November 18, 1992 *(www.earthportals.com/Earthportals/ucs.html)*; the Worldwatch Institute's annual *State of the World* and *Vital Signs* series, as well as their new releases at *www.worldwatch.org*; archives housed at *www.dieoff.com*; and daily news sources found at *www.envirolink.com*; and the Environmental News Network *(www.enn.com)*. For a compendium of news stories that have influenced my own sense of urgency, see Appendix A in *Composition and Sustainability* (Owens).

Appendix A

Existing Zones in English Studies		*Emerging Sustainability-Oriented Zones in English Studies*
composition	→	ecocomposition
creative writing	→	ecopoetics
electronic writing, publishing	→	community networks
feminist theory, gender studies, queer theory	→	ecofeminism, ecological feminism
folklore, anthropology, postcolonial studies	→	indigenous sustainable cultures in less-developed countries
literary history, (new) historicism	→	environmental history; oral histories
literacy	→	community and environmental literacy
literary theory	→	ecotheory, architectural theory, planning theory

Marxism; capitalist critique	→	ecological economics
memoir, nonfiction	→	place-based writing
professional, technical, workplace writing	→	critiques of work; green and sustainable business; third-sector careers
race, class, culture	→	social and environmental justice
regionalism	→	ecocriticism; green cultural studies
rhetoric	→	ecorhetoric
science and literature	→	ecology; environmental studies, cybernetics
service learning	→	community revitalization, sustainable neighborhoods, economic renewal
utopian studies, apocalypse literature	→	future studies, scenario building
writing across the curriculum	→	sustainability across the curriculum
writing pedagogy	→	sustainable pedagogy

Appendix B
"Sustainable" Courses Currently Offered in 150 American English Departments

Cities and Suburbs

American Cities

Cities and Cultures

The City and the Country

City of Text

City/Story/Spectacle: Studies in American Lit and Culture, 1865–1910

Coming of Age in the City

Constructing Suburbia

Everyday Life and the City: The Urban in Literature and Architecture

Fictional Geographies

Global Cities: Paris and Cairo

Imagining the City

Small Town, Big City: The Sense of Place in Twentieth-Century American Literature

Medieval Writers and the City

Modern and Postmodern Cities

Suburban Culture

Sub/urban Literature and Culture

The Urban Experience

Walk on the Wild Side: Modern Literature of the City and the Body

Communities, Neighborhoods, and Regions

Collectives of the Poor in Latin America: Performing Community

Hillbilly Highway: Appalachia and America

Literature and Family

Literature of the Hudson River Valley: An Environmental Approach

Literature of Vermont

On the Road: Journey Literature and Music

Postcolonial Memory: The Poetics of Home

Studies in Ethnic and Regional Literature

The Writer in the Community

Culture and Environment

American Everyday

The Art of Modern Crisis

Between Aztlan and Queens: Latina Culture and the Making of Space

Cross-Cultural Literacies

Culture at the Turning Point

Ethnic Communities: The Melting-Pot Revisited

Ideologies of Nature and Culture in Early Modern

Literature of the Encounter

Them and Us: Revisiting the American Dream

Ecocriticism and Ecorhetoric

The Construction of Nature in Word and Image

Current Issues in Eco-Criticism

Ecocriticism

The Environmental Imagination: Green Writing and Ecocriticism

Ethics, Rhetoric, and Writing

Politics, Criticism, Literature

Reading the News, Understanding the Media

Rhetoric and Geography: Discursive Constructions of Real and Imagined Places

Rhetoric and Public Life

The Rhetoric of Making a Difference

Rhetoric of Politics

Writing and the Public Interest

Ecofeminism

Ecofeminism: Reading and Writing Nature

The Nature of Gender/The Engendering of Nature

Rhetorics of American Feminisms

Women's Narrative of Survival

Apocalypse When? Gender at the End of the World

Economic Critiques of Globalism and Commodity Culture

American Literature and Corporate Culture

American Modernism and the Market

Commerce and Culture

Commerce, Luxury, and Consumption in the Early Modern Era

The Consumption of Culture

Cultural Pluralism: From Modernity to Globalization

Culture and Capitalism

The Culture of Capitalism

Currencies of Culture

Desire in America

Economics and the Literary Imagination

Emotions/Economics in American Literature

The Function of Literature in an Age of Global Capitalism

Global Culture

Global Markets and Alternative Literatures

Globalization, Literature, and Culture

Globalization, Place, and the Poetics of Cultural Identity

Images of Empire

Literature of Empire

Narrating the Empire

Novels of Development

Pedagogies of Empire

A Poetics of the Language of Desire

Portable Property

Power/Desire/Culture

Problems in the History of Consumption

Resistance Literature of the United States

The Simple Life

Theories of Globalization and Postcoloniality

Visions of the Global

Working Class Literature

Education and Literacy

Community Service

Composition in the Public Sphere

Literacy Politics in the United States

Literacy and Technology

The Meaning of Literacy

Teaching Literature in Community

Books of the Environmental Movement

Culture and Imperialism

Enlightenment and Disaster

Romanticism and Environmentalism in Britain

Utopian Practices: Reformers and Utopians in Twentieth-Century American Literature and Culture

Health and Spirituality

Buddhism and American Culture

Caring About Health

Contemplative Practice

Expository Writing: Caring about Health

Literature, Medicine, and Ethics: Narratives of Injury and Repair

Indigenous Cultures

Ancient and Contemporary Voices

Folk Material Culture

Native Images

Studies in Native American Literature

Institutional and Professional Critique

Critical Theory Workshop: The Institution and Disciplines of the University

Developments in English Studies

History and the Future of the Profession

Professing English

The Rhetoric of Change in the Academy and the "Real" World: Bonds, Embattlements, and Bridges

Rhetoric of Work and Labor

We're Doing What?

Writing for the World of Work

Land and Landscape

American Landscape: Changing Conceptions of Natural Beauty, 1820–1920

Body, Land(scape), Identity

Finding, Founding, and Figuring America

The Land in American Experience

Landscape and Literature

Landscape Art in Cultural Perspective

Landscape as Character

Landscapes of Identity in Early Twentieth-Century American Fiction

Law of the Land: The Literary and Legal Invention of America

Nineteenth-Century Landscape: The Limits of Standardization

Postcolonial Geographies

Reading the Built Landscape

Reconceiving the US Frontiers and Frontier Theory

Romantic Landscape

Local and Regional Writing

Bay Area Literary Scene

Life and Literature of the Southwest

Literary Locals

Mountain Area Writing Project

Reading New England Landscape

Representing Pittsburgh: Text and Image

Topics in Appalachian Studies

Writing About the "Real Florida," or This Ain't No Disneyland

"Nature," Literature, and Writing

American Nature Writers

American Nature Writing

Ecological Literature

Environmental Literature

Green Romanticism

Into the Wild

Literature and the Environment

Literature, Environment, Place

Literature, Wilderness, and the American Imagination

Native American Literature: Alternative Visions of Nature and Culture

Nature and the Modern Poet

Nature in Literature

Nature/Poetry

Nature Writing & Environmental Concern

Nature Writing and the Nature of Writing

Nature Writing in America

Reading Nature

Visions of Nature

Writing Nature

Writing/Reading the Environment

Writing Yourself, Writing the World

Place Studies and Geography

Environmental Writing: Writing on Place

Ethics of Place

Introduction to the New Cultural Geography: Theories of Space and Spatiality

Farm Literature

Literature, Environment, Place

The Natural Environment and the North American Literary Imagination

Place and American Culture

Poetics of Space, Prose of Things

Our Place in Nature

The Sense of Time and Place

Topics in Expierential Education: Writing About Place

Writing about Places

Science and Technology

Cyborg Culture

Darwin Among the Poets: Monkeys, Cats, and Black Holes

Evolution, Ecological Imagining, and Biopoetics

Feminist Theory in Science

From Brains to Clones: Science in the Media

Literature and Science

Narrative in the Human Sciences: Models of Knowledge and Resistance

Science Writing: The Environment

Scientific Technical Writing

Social Implications of the Internet

Technoculture

Twentieth-Century Reconceptions of Knowledge and Science

Social Justice

Culture, Democracy, and the Public Sphere

Literature and Human Rights

Realism and Cultural Violence

Violence and Community

Writing and Preparing for the Future

Career Development for English Majors

Contemporary Media Theories

Creative Writing and the Profession

Cybermedia

Desktop Publishing and New Media

Extremities of Drama: Revolution, Terror, Apocalypse

Futures of American Studies

Introduction to Professions in Writing

Media Theory and Knowledge

Mediated Composition

Millennial Fevers

Viewing Tomorrow: Reviewing Technology

Writing Cyberspace

Writing Beyond the Academy

Writing and Emerging Technologies

Writing for Your Life

Writing the Future

Works Cited

Ballard, J. G. *War Fever.* New York: Farrar, Straus, Giroux, 1990.

Baxandall, Rosalyn, and Elizabeth Ewen. *Picture Windows: How the Suburbs Happened.* New York: Basic Books, 2000.

Bossel, Hartmut. *Earth at a Crossroads: Paths to a Sustainable Future.* New York: Cambridge UP, 1998.

Bowers, C.A. *Educating for an Ecologically Sustainable Culture: Rethinking Moral Education, Creativity, Intelligence, and Other Modern Orthodoxies* Albany: SUNY P, 1995.

Brown, Lester R., Christopher Flavin, Hilary French, et al. *State of the World 2001.* New York: Norton/The Worldwatch Institute, 2001.

Brown, Stephen Gilbert. "Composing the Eco Wars: Toward a Literacy of Resistance." *JAC: A Journal of Composition Theory* 19 (1999): 215–39.

Butler, Octavia E. *Parable of the Sower.* New York: Warner Books, 1993.

Dobrin, Sidney I., and Christopher J. Keller. *The Nature of Writing.* Albany: SUNY P. (forthcoming), 2002.

Dobrin, Sidney I., and Christian Weisser, eds. *Ecocompostion: Theoretical and Pedagogical Approaches.* Albany: SUNY P. (forthcoming), 2001.

———. *Natural Discourse: Toward Ecocomposition.* Albany: SUNY P. (forthcoming), 2001.

Duany, Andres, Elizabeth Plater-Zyberk, and Jeff Speck. *Suburban Nation: The Rise of Sprawl and the Decline of the American Dream.* New York: North Point P, 2000.

Gaines, Donna. *Teenage Wasteland: Suburbia's Dead End Kids.* New York: HarperPerennial, 1991.

Gates, Bill. *The Road Ahead.* New York: Penguin, 1996.

Gibson, William. *Neuromancer.* New York: Ace Books, 1984.

Gray, Chris Hables, ed. *The Cyborg Handbook.* New York: Routledge, 1995.

Hawken, Pual, Amory Lovins, and L. Hunter Lovins. *Natural Capitalism: Creating the Next Industrial Revolution.* New York: Little, Brown, 1999.

Herndl, Carl G., and Stuart C. Brown. *Green Culture: Environmental Rhetoric in Contemporary America.* Madison: U of Wisconsin P, 1996.

Hopkinson, Nalo. *Brown Girl in the Ring.* New York: Warner Books, 1998.

Jackson, Kenneth T. *Crabgrass Frontier: The Suburbanization of the United States.* Cambridge: Oxford U P, 1987.

Killingsworth, M. Jimmie, and Jacqueline S. Palmer. *Ecospeak: Rhetoric and Environmental Politics in America.* Carbondale, IL: Southern Illinois UP, 1992.

Krech, Shepard. *The Ecological Indian: Myth and History.* New York: Norton, 1999.

Kunstler, James Howard. *The Geography of Nowhere: The Rise and Decline of America's Man-Made Landscape.* New York: Touchstone, 1993.

Linden, Eugene. *The Future in Plain Sight: Nine Clues to the Coming Instability*. New York: Simon and Schuster, 1998.

Loh, Sandra Tsing. *If You Lived Here You'd Be Home by Now*. New York: Penguin, 1998.

McAndrew, Donald A. "Ecofeminism and the Teaching of Literacy." *College Composition and Communication* 47 (1996): 367–82.

McKibben, Bill. *The End of Nature*. New York: Anchor, 1999.

Merchant, Carolyn. *Radical Ecology: The Search for a Livable World*. New York: Routledge, 1992.

Misha, *Red Spider, White Web*. Portland, Oregon: Wordcraft of Oregon, 1999.

Orr, David W. *Earth in Mind: On Education, Environment, and the Human Prospect*. Washington, DC: Island P, 1994.

Owens, Derek. *Composition and Sustainability: Teaching for a Threatened Generation*. Urbana, IL: NCTE, 2001.

Readings, Bill. *The University in Ruins*. Cambridge: Harvard UP, 1996.

Roorda, Randall. *Dramas of Solitude: Narratives of Retreat in American Nature Writing*. Albany: SUNY P, 1998.

———. "Sites and Senses of Writing in Nature." *College English* 59 (1997): 385–407.

Ryan, Paul. *Video Mind, Earth Mind: Art, Communications and Ecology*. New York: Peter Lang, 1993.

Schwartz, Peter. *The Art of the Long View*. New York: Currency, 1991.

Shrivastava, Paul. *Greening Business: Profiting the Corporation and the Environment*. Cincinnati: Thomson Executive P, 1996.

Smith, Gregory A. *Education and the Environment: Learning to Live with Limits*. Albany: SUNY P, 1992.

Stilgoe, John R. *Borderland: Origins of the American Suburb, 1820–1939*. New Haven: Yale UP, 1988.

Thomas, Sheree R., ed. *Dark Matter: A Century of Speculative Fiction from the African Diaspora*. New York: Warner Books, 2000.

Trainer, Ted. *The Conserver Society: Alternatives for Sustainability*. London: Zed Books, 1995.

Wetherell, W. D. *The Man Who Loved Levittown*. Pittsburgh: U of Pittsburgh P, 1985.

World Commission on Environment and Development. *Our Common Future*. Oxford: Oxford UP, 1987.

Chapter Ten

Concentrating English
Disciplinarity, Institutional Histories, and Collective Identity
Amy Goodburn and Deborah Minter[1]

Universities are increasingly pressured to model themselves after corporations. This chapter represents one effort to identify pressures that were formative in the work of a group of faculty working to develop a concentration in "Writing and Rhetoric" as part of a larger departmental initiative to revise the undergraduate major at the University of Nebraska–Lincoln (UN-L). By examining some of the conversations associated with the process of creating the concentration, this microethnography suggests that while the formation of curriculum can be read in terms of corporate influences, faculty can and do intervene in administrative structures that press toward increasing corporatization. While it is true that corporate pressures represent the effects of one very powerful discourse of value and collective identity in contemporary American culture, postsecondary curricular reform can be usefully understood as a site of multiple discourses of value and identity that faculty negotiate in the process of making curricula. The point of this essay is not to provide a model curriculum, but to show how reflecting on group processes can build a collective consciousness about the multiple pressures on curriculum in one's own institution and make visible opportunities for intervening, rhetorically, in the press toward corporate management of teaching and learning.

Pressures on Curricular Work

In their study of university administration, Currie and Vidovich define features of *corporate managerialism,* a term they use to describe a particular orientation toward decision making in higher education. They argue that corporate managerialism takes its name from the institutions on which it is modeled, emphasizing "efficiency (minimizing costs) and effectiveness (maximizing outcomes)" (114). A recent UN-L planning document that outlines criteria for evaluating and prioritizing academic programs offers an example of such emphases. Among the nine criteria presented as "the framework within which each campus will reach holistic judgment about programs and set priorities that will guide resource allocation and program development" is "Need and Demand." In responding to this criterion, faculty are asked to assess their programs in terms of "distinctive market niche," "special strength in the market," and "number of competing programs in the state, region, and nation" (Commission for Development of Criteria for Evaluation and Prioritization of Academic Programs).

This internal UN-L planning document reflects the codification of corporate managerialism as a means of academic planning. Public discourse surrounding our institution reflects the kinds of critiques of higher education that press for market-driven, corporate models of efficiency. One of the state's most widely circulating newspapers recently ran a four-part exposé on the status of UN-L in comparison with other research institutions. While some have suggested that the criticism was politically motivated, headlines, such as "State's Flagship Mired in the Middle," "Low Research Rating Self-Inflicted," and "Campus Culture Keeps Best from Shining," nonetheless provide an example of a common rhetorical trope: Identifying an institution's research ranking as the only "product" worth maximizing and citing inefficiency to explain rankings that disappoint (Cordes and O'Connor).

This larger institutional discourse of market-driven efficiency as well as public and institutional anxiety about the university's research profile emerges at a time when our department wrestles with some of the same kinds of shifts that North and colleagues have recently documented for English studies as a field. As North's account of English departments would suggest, our department has recently experienced considerable turnover of faculty (several left for "greener pastures of higher salary," in the words of one local newspaper, as well as many faculty retirements). Recent hires with research specializations reflective of current trends in English studies (hires, for example, in postcolonial literature, theory, and composition) as well as shifting research interests (into areas such as gay and lesbian studies or disability studies) of long-time faculty resulted in course offerings that reflected disciplinary shifts by the accretion of new courses, rather than by comprehensive review of the curriculum. The department had, for some time, grappled with slight declines in enrollments (a frequent measure of "demand" for a particular program).

A 1997 external review of the department provided the institutional exigency for curricular reform. The review, supportive of the department overall, was critical of its course offerings. The reviewers asserted that the curriculum represented "a list or bank of 177 separate courses rather than a sequence formed in response to an educational vision," invoking the imperative of an educational vision while also signaling (perhaps unintentionally) a kind of curricular inefficiency (Morris et al., 5). The reviewers also took up the department's commitment to smaller class sizes, which, to their understanding, results in a teaching load that "makes it difficult for faculty to maintain sustained research, hinders the department's ability to compete with other Research I departments for excellent new hires, and puts the department's teaching load out of synch with university norms" (5). The reform process, described by many as "closely managed," began almost immediately on the heels of this review.

By Spring1999, a structure for a revised major had been approved by department vote. In addition to retaining what department documents term "a historical literature core," the major would now include two majors-only courses (an introduction to English studies and a senior capstone course) to address concerns for coherence and community-building that surfaced both in the external review and in the department's annual survey of graduating English majors. Second, majors would now be required to take one course in each of three designated areas: Linguistics, Writing, and Rhetoric; Literary/Rhetorical Theory; and Culture, Ethnicity, and Gender. Finally, the major would now require a twelve-credit hour concentration in one of the following areas of English studies: Gender and Textuality, Writing and Rhetoric, Creative Writing, North American Literatures, British/Commonwealth since 1789, Film Studies, Early Literatures in English, Theory/Criticism, Preprofessional, and/or Ethnicity and Race.

Processes of Developing the Writing and Rhetoric Concentration

Within this reform process, the six rhetoric and composition faculty (ourselves among them) began negotiations to develop an undergraduate concentration focusing on composition and rhetoric. Four were untenured assistant professors and two had tenure. We chose to develop this concentration by meeting together (about once a month). Between meetings, we corresponded via email and talked informally. What struck us initially were the ways in which the six of us struggled to work together as a group—a discovery that was all the more surprising given the general commitment to collaboration that we shared, and our groupwide interest in making our research and teaching commitments visible to students and colleagues. One member described the process as "bizarre and contentious." Another wrote that it was "disheartening and painful." And a third said,"I was always a little on edge when we would come together. I sort of looked forward to it and dreaded it at the same time. . . . At times there would be overt flare-ups, or just some tension beneath the surface."

This discomfort surfaced almost immediately when we shared our dream plans for the concentration. Some argued for various versions of a "rhetorics and poetics" model to speak across the disciplinary distinctions of literature, rhetoric, and creative writing. Another hoped to build in more opportunities for students to study the uses of literacy in their lives. A third hoped to maintain the workshop model that informed the existing composition courses. The challenge was not the irrelevance of any proposals. In fact, each one invoked a whole set of respected scholarly conversations surrounding the key terms. Rather, we debated how these various visions might play out in the local contexts of our classrooms. Perhaps the best example of these discussions surrounded the required first-year writing courses and their relationship to the intellectual work we could imagine for the concentration. The first-year courses became a visible illustration of what was possible (and problematic) about the workshop method. They also served as touchstones to the complex economies of writing instruction. A concentration in our area would likely draw more of us out of the first-year courses, moving at least one member of the group to argue for a serious reconsideration of the first-year writing requirement while others pressed its defense. Writing later about these conversations, one group member explained:

> There were . . . outspoken critics of some of the most visible aspects of the writing curriculum. . . . On the one hand, their critiques were compelling. On the other, they were dispiriting—partly because I felt . . . really involved in the very courses and orientations they found wanting.

In retrospect, the dynamics of our conversations mirrored those that John Ramage described in his recent account of establishing a writing certificate program at Arizona State University. Ramage argues that insofar as major theorists (in the field of composition especially) have already constructed particular curricular features (such as the abolition of first-year writing) as logical extensions of the move to program-status, faculty undertaking the collective establishment of a concentration in writing should be prepared for the likelihood of such debates (137). While Ramage's observations help us to identify one source of the tensions that surfaced, our interviews with faculty suggest that the administrative directives for the concentration contributed to these tensions.

While developing this concentration, administrative pressures on the process seemed to shift. Initially, faculty were directed to develop concentrations using only those courses that were currently in the course catalogue. The directive to work with existing courses had specific effects on our conversations. The writing and rhetoric courses already "on the books" were created before four of the group members had begun working in the department and did not necessarily represent all of our conceptions about how a sequence of writing courses should be organized. For others, the courses that they could most imagine teaching were not present in the curriculum at all. As one group member described the process: "We had been asked to list our investments, our dream plans, but I couldn't see myself in the courses already on the books."

"Being faced with this task seemed kind of strange," another member responded when interviewed. "We aren't going to re-envision courses as we redo this major, we're just going to shift the courses around . . . I kept on thinking, 'OK. So why am I here?' "

Beyond grappling with administrative mandates, our group processes were also profoundly shaped by the different institutional and disciplinary memberships that defined each of us individually. These differences in perspectives affected the process when we collectively determined which courses might count for the concentration. The group had several discussions about the role of creative writing courses. Initially, most members relied on their teaching experience to identify courses for the concentration—courses that were, for the most part, specifically named as composition or rhetoric courses in the existing curriculum. The effect of this "first pass" at identifying courses was an emerging concentration focused primarily in terms of nonfiction expository writing, preserving some of the preexisting norms (within the department and across the field of English studies, more generally) that separate creative writing from composition.

In one discussion, a newer faculty member asked about the absence of creative writing in the concentration.

> It's still not clear to me where, if anywhere, do creative writing courses (or courses that may include creative writing) fit in?...I would want students taking a writing concentration to learn about how poetics figure in all of these activities—culturally, institutionally, disciplinarily, academically, professionally, personally....The language used in our last meeting for the kind of writing we'd have students do was "nonfiction."...Now, if that's what we want, OK....But I do want to be clear on what we're after here—a writing studies or discourse studies approach...or a more narrowly defined persuasion and exposition deal? (2 February 1999)

Another group member responded via email:

> I think the connection between rhetoric and poetics is extremely important, especially for undergraduates....Additionally...I'd like to add (like you couldn't see this coming) just a whisper of my favorite word—history....I am, like [the speaker quoted above], willing to live with the more narrowly defined persuasive/expository focus...for a while...and always with the explicit knowledge that it's something I'd like to see changed. (2 February 1999)

Both group members in this exchange delineated subtle but discipline-significant distinctions ("exposition" as opposed to "writing studies" in the first case; a call for more attention to the history of rhetoric in the second) as a means both of locating themselves in relation to the emerging concentration and articulating its limits. The willingness to name such distinctions allowed us, as a group, to discuss what was at stake in these subtle departures from a concentration that might otherwise reflect only the list of existing composition and rhetoric courses that most of us were regularly assigned to teach.

One of the stakes involved was resources: Department administrators had framed the concentrations as an important means for determining course rotation and arguing for additional hires. Theoretically, then, thinking intradisciplinarily (or including courses from "outside" the discipline of rhetoric and composition, narrowly conceived) meant risking some access to these kinds of resources. Ultimately, we agreed that including some creative writing courses in the Writing and Rhetoric concentration offered a way to figure the term "writing" more broadly, shifting away from discrete boundaries between genres and focusing instead on the rhetorical purposes that prompt writing.

Like the task of choosing courses relevant to the emerging concentration, the process of naming the concentration involved similar negotiations of professional commitments. In many ways, the process tapped our desires to name ourselves in terms of our disciplinary interests and the type of connections we hoped to eventually create across the department. For instance, one faculty member suggested the title "Writing, Rhetoric, and Literacy," understanding that the inclusion of the word "literacy" in the concentration title might announce (to students and faculty) possible connections across writing and literature courses and create opportunities for additional literacy-oriented courses. For this faculty member, the term "literacy" carried out important cultural work—connecting reading and writing in the academy to school (K–12) and community literacies. Another member forwarded "Writing, Rhetoric, and Culture" for many of the same reasons that "literacy" was championed. Our shared commitment to the pedagogical force of this work led us toward terms that would best name *for undergraduates* the work they could expect to do in this concentration and a desire to know more about how students might name their own interests. As one group member wrote in an email to the group: "Do we have a sense of how many students are currently interested in the Writing and Rhetoric concentration? . . . I think it would be productive to discuss with interested students what their hopes/goals for such a concentration are and to develop our curriculum with this feedback in mind" (11 November 1999).

Though our polling of interested undergraduates was limited to informal surveys of our own classes, we sensed some mismatch between how we might name our disciplinary interests and how undergraduates might see themselves in those names. While the department frequently referred to us as the Rhetoric and Composition group, we believed that the term "composition" might not have much meaning for undergraduates beyond their first-year writing courses. In the end, we settled on the title "Writing and Rhetoric" because these two terms seemed the most recognizable to undergraduates at our institution, and we believed that they signaled both the content and practice at the center of this concentration. In this way, pressures to create a more marketable major or concentration that could have driven us to different kinds of conversations about titling the concentration were overshadowed by our collective sense that the work of developing this concentration—identifying and imagining the courses that would comprise it, naming it, and so on—was important professional and pedagogical work. At the same time, our different understandings of the professional and pedagogical significance of this work led to strained and sometimes frustrating conversations.

Clearly, managerialist tendencies were at work in the administrative directives to do this work quickly. Each of us, however, came to this work with various discipline-specific commitments and a desire to establish composition and rhetoric as a vital area of study for undergraduates in ways that would also speak to our colleagues in the department. This collective desire required us to contend with the range of discourses about writing and writing instruction available to our students, our colleagues across the department, and to those who specialize in composition and rhetoric. To some extent, then, the corporatizing pressures were negotiated through our range of professional commitments and the multiple discourses through which we carried out that work. Our point is not that disciplinary discourses and pedagogical commitments are somehow outside of or immune to such pressures. Rather, each discourse ascribes value differently, and the task of developing a concentration in Writing and Rhetoric as part of a larger departmentwide initiative required us to confront those differences and make choices about how to represent writing and rhetoric as an area of undergraduate study.

Researching Curriculum: An Opportunity for Reflection and Intervention

If disciplinarity was one of the discourses in play, offering alternatives to the values of efficiency, our research into this curricular work revealed that disciplinarity, alone, could not account for the struggles we faced in our group. This moment of curricular revision foregrounded, sometimes in painful but ultimately important ways, the importance of attending to group identity as faculty engaged in representing our shared intellectual commitments. To understand why our group operated as it did, we interviewed other members about how the process of developing the concentration shaped their notions of group identity. It was surprising to see the variations in experience and perspective that emerged during these conversations:

> I don't believe there is (or ever was) a "six of us" . . . But I do believe that forging a workable "six of us" would force us to confront some serious intrafield differences. Which would be fine, except . . . I wonder why, with the current constraints on our work, we'd want to put ourselves through that. . . . We certainly share enough commitments—to teacher education, to the composition classroom . . . to do some good work together.

Another member agreed that there was frustration among the faculty working together to develop the concentration:

> [P]art of the difficulty in coming together . . . is that I assumed a group identity but others didn't. Because we never articulated these differences in our thinking about our roles, they didn't come to the fore in a way that might have been productive for helping us think through what, exactly, a writing/rhetoric concentration might mean.

This member searched for a way to articulate the ways that this process of curricular reform felt different from earlier curricular work in the department:

> I . . . felt that I was being socialized and welcomed into a group— and it was a socialization that I valued, even [as] . . . an outsider and sometimes critic of the work . . . I don't think we need to necessarily hold the same values or even have the same research interests as long as we are willing to come together and work to negotiate, articulate, represent the work of composition and rhetoric as a discipline/field that is worthy of study and research.

Another member located her reading of the group dynamics in terms of disciplinary memberships and the role that the arrival of three new faculty played:

> The process of constructing the concentration . . . came at a very interesting time in terms of the composition and rhetoric faculty . . . I think it was crucial having an infusion of new faculty at that moment, and it has taken us almost two years to get around to really talking more—or understanding more about people's ideas of what it [the concentration] should be. . . . It starkly pointed out . . . the ways that my own education had been shaped in different ways.

As this member notes, generational differences within the group shaped disciplinary memberships in difficult but also generative ways. A year later, another group member said: "Even as late as the end of last year, I really wouldn't have said we were a group. I think I feel more like some of us are a group and some of the others are invested with the idea that we are a group. That's what makes it so hard." In retrospect, though, this faculty member came to consider the six to be a group distinct from the rest of the department:

> Who we are as a group does represent a very different view of English studies than the department is necessarily comfortable with. . . . We are all in that flexible, extended position. . . . Interested in theory and the text and writing and I think that's very different from the department's identity, although that seems to be shifting as well.

As this faculty member notes, the ongoing flux in the department's faculty research interests and approaches makes it difficult to pin down a monolithic "department identity." The transitional state of our faculty, with many retirements by colleagues who specialized in a literary period (eighteenth-century British, for example), coupled with the hiring of faculty who name their research interests in terms of methodological approaches (e.g., postcolonial theory or rhetorics and poetics) has created generational differences in how faculty name and view their work. This flux further complicates the task of constructing concentrations designed to "pin down" areas for undergraduate study.

Researching this curricular moment has offered us important insight into the variety of disciplinary understandings and institutional experiences that we represent as a group of faculty in the field of rhetoric and composition. In our interviews, we came to see how specific institutional and historical contexts (different for each group member) inflected individual understandings of composition and rhetoric as a discipline in relation to other areas of study in English. The emergence of composition and rhetoric as a respected area of scholarly work, its institutionalization in our particular department and in the variety of graduate programs through which we were educated, means that all of us have lived through very different trajectories of the field. This increased awareness, while it does not necessarily reduce our differences, helps us value and take account of them.

Perhaps any work in curricular (re)formation involves an accounting for the varieties of ways in which the work *could be* carried out, and for the significance of the choices that are actually made. Our experience with writing an undergraduate concentration in writing and rhetoric, and our research into that group effort, has led us to believe that one reason so few extended discussions of actual curricular development exist is because of the rhetorical challenges posed by writing about difference and group negotiations among departmental colleagues with whom one is continuing to work. In fact, in writing about our group's processes, we believe it is important to note that our version of this curricular reform is necessarily situated from our own perspectives. While we have tried to honestly represent the process through which our group worked, we acknowledge that others involved in this process might not have experienced it in the same way. Ethical issues of representation, a central concern in any ethnographic inquiry, remain equally vexing when one is writing about one's own community. However, we also view this chapter as an important rhetorical intervention in a professional life that hinges on our separate accomplishments and individual work profiles.

Although our process in constructing the Writing and Rhetoric concentration was painful and sometimes contentious, we are ultimately hopeful about how reflecting on and understanding this experience can impact our future work together. In their recent *CCC* essay, "Institutional Critique: A Rhetorical Methodology for Change," Porter and his colleagues describe institutional critique as a rhetorical practice that can mediate "macro-level structures and micro-level actions rooted in a particular space and time" (612). They describe such critique as both a method and a practice that "insists that institutions, as unchangeable as they may seem (and, indeed, often are), do contain spaces for reflection, resistance, revision, and productive action" and thus can be rewritten through rhetorical action (613). Taking up these authors' charge, we have begun to consider how reflecting on the process of constructing the concentration has been such a form of intervention for the six of us. This chapter concludes with a more detailed discussion about how our efforts as a group can be read as rhetorical intervention and the ways that this work has supported continuing rhetorical interventions in our work together.

First and foremost, our group created a concentration that represents and values the work that we do as teachers, writers, and researchers and that invites undergraduates into this work. This curriculum intervenes by positioning composition and rhetoric as a primary space for undergraduate study rather than simply a prerequisite for an English major as defined by traditionally literary fields. Although the current concentration may not be the dream plan for any of the six of us, we generally agree that it provides a starting point for conceptualizing what writing and rhetoric might make possible for students.

Second, the energy and spirit that went into constructing this concentration can be read as an intervention into commonplace attitudes toward the role of curricular work as "just service" within department culture. Although our group negotiations were rocky at times, we chose to work together as a group, while many faculty working on the other nine concentrations did not. The administrative procedures for this curricular reform were designed to keep the process streamlined, efficient, and to minimize divisive conflict and reduce workload. The procedures, perhaps unintentionally, marked this work as "service" and as an extra burden. The fact that our group met frequently and spent so much time conceptualizing and talking through issues related to the development of this concentration suggests that we viewed this work as more than burdensome service. While the resulting concentration might be read simply as a conservative response to administrative directives (because we followed the mandate to organize existing courses rather than create a whole new set of courses, for instance), the six of us did subvert these assumptions by meeting regularly, negotiating language, developing dream plans, and working to articulate the terms of this first consensus. Perhaps one reason we never chose to resist the administrative directives wholesale—to explore any radically subversive enterprise—is because we needed to learn more about each other. Our dream plans, for instance, functioned as opportunities for self-representation and positioning our commitments more than they functioned to build a group consensus about what a concentration in writing and rhetoric might mean for undergraduates. We needed to build a collective group identity through such work before we could begin imagining how to represent the value of such work for others.

Perhaps the most visible benefit of going through the process of constructing the concentration is group members' current commitments to continue such curricular reform at both the graduate and undergraduate level. In the past year, the six of us have met several times to discuss how we might revise mission statements, develop rationales for new courses, and reconsider the entire first-year writing program. We have begun to turn our eyes to the daily documents that figure our intellectual work and to consider how we might reframe them to better represent who we are. And beyond curricular development, we have begun to consider how we might rhetorically intervene in other institutional spaces to articulate and make public the work of composition and rhetoric. For instance, we have begun to develop a Web page that describes our program in rhetoric and composition—a process that has invited us, again, to think hard about how we want to represent ourselves and our collective interests while, at the same time, representing our individual differences and approaches. We have also begun discussions about how to better represent our intellectual work collectively in more nationally visible ways. We've brainstormed ideas for a regional center for the study of literacy, for instance, and discussed ways that we, as a group, might become more active in shaping public discussions of K through 12 educational issues such as standards and assessment in Nebraska.

Finally, and perhaps most important, we've become more conscious about how we need to put on the table our assumptions about the nature of our work, not only in terms of preserving and maintaining a collective identity to get our work done but also in terms of imagining our future faculty lives. As one group member said:

> Our whole cycle of talks about the concentration...have helped me see where I can be helpful on down the road....They've also given me ideas about how to reconnect, like with those writing courses....Those talks have helped me to see that there is going to be a moment where I can see myself in those courses in ways that are more manifest than they are now.

Ultimately, creating the concentration meant that we needed to forge, for ourselves, a group identity, a way of being together that would enable us to speak across our experiences in a "unified" voice while also seeking to name and preserve the valuable differences in our beliefs, philosophies, generational perspectives, and disciplinary identities. While corporate pressures to shape curricular reform inevitably inflect our discussions, through the process of constructing the concentration we've come to realize the power we do have to intervene in conversations and spaces that are important to us. This curricular work has meant concentrating our different disciplinary affiliations, institutional histories, generational perspectives, and social and political commitments into a flexible and provisional vision.

Note

1. We appreciate all our colleagues' goodwill in their generous support of our research and in their multiple readings of and responses to this manuscript.

Works Cited

Commission for Development of Criteria for Evaluation and Prioritization of Academic Programs. *Final Report* (13 September 2000), *www.uneb.edu/planreport/planreport.html.*

Cordes, Henry J., and Michael O'Connor. "UNL: Confronting Mediocrity" Series. *Omaha World Herald* (7–10 January 2001): A1+.

Currie, Jan, and Lesley Vidovich. "The Ascent Toward Corporate Managerialism in American and Australian Universities." *Chalk Lines: The Politics of Work in the Managed University.* Ed. Randy Martin. Durham, NC: Duke UP, 1998. 112–44.

Griess, Karen. "Third UNL English Professor Leaving for Greener Pastures." *Lincoln Journal Star* (30 April 1999): 1B.

Morris, Adalaide, J. Lawrence Mitchell, and Philip Smith. "External Review Team Report." Lincoln: University of Nebraska English Department, 1997.

North, Stephen, et al. *Refiguring the PhD in English Studies: Writing, Doctoral Education, and the Fusion-Based Curriculum.* Urbana, IL: NCTE, 2000.

Porter, James E., Patricia Sullivan, Stuart Blythe, Jeffrey T. Grabill, and Libby Miles. "Institutional Critique: A Rhetorical Methodology for Change." *CCC* 51 (2000): 610–41.

Ramage, John. "The Writing Certificate at Arizona State University." *Coming of Age: The Advanced Writing Curriculum.* Eds. Linda K. Shamoon, et al. Portsmouth: Boynton/Cook, 2001. 135–48.

Chapter Eleven

Changing the Program(s)
English Department Curricula in the Contemporary Research University
James E. Seitz

I teach in a sizable English department at an urban, state-related research university in southwestern Pennsylvania. That may seem a simple statement with which to begin this chapter on curriculum reform in the postmodern, globalized, corporatized university, but in recent years I've become increasingly aware of how my work (and thus, much of my life) is conditioned by each set of terms—"sizable English department," "urban, state-related research university," "southwestern Pennsylvania"—marking its institutional and geopolitical location. These particulars are not merely a group of "factors" that mildly influence my otherwise independent actions as a teacher and scholar. Rather, they are crucial determinants in my habitation of a social, professional, and disciplinary space that implicitly bespeaks certain possibilities for and constraints on my working life not just at the present moment but also in the years to come, regardless of whatever curricular reconfigurations my colleagues and I may imagine, pursue, or even attain.

This academic year, this English department has 52 tenured or tenure-stream faculty, 18 full-time nontenure-stream faculty (most of whom are on one-year contracts), 55 part-time faculty, 4 visiting instructors (who are actually graduate students completing their dissertations), and 76 teaching fellows and assistants. The department has almost 800 undergraduate majors—a rise of nearly 300 students in the past three years—and there are usually several hundred applications each year to M.A, M.F.A, and Ph.D. programs. In short, this is a large operation requiring a good deal of administrative oversight just to keep the system running, much less to instigate change. A colleague who directs one of our programs recently observed:

This department is like a huge, rudderless tanker plowing through the sea; you can't simply command it to stop or turn around. My job is to persuade as many people as I can to stand on a certain side of the tanker and lean hard into the railing, with the hope that, in several years' time, we will have managed to change its course by a few degrees, so that ultimately the department ends up in a different place than it would have otherwise.

I find this a useful metaphor, one that reminds me (as one who co-directs another of the department's programs) to avoid grand visions of rapid trans- formation that can produce frustration and early burn-out. It reminds me that institutional change, however slow, is nevertheless possible, and that seemingly minor shifts in direction can have significant consequences over the long run. But as with all metaphors, this figure has its limits: If the English department is a tanker, what is the "urban, state-related research university" in which my department is housed? I suppose it might be considered the sea, or perhaps the wind, but such formulations would forget that the university is itself a kind of tanker subject to various forms of weather—a tanker even more vast and difficult to turn than the department. As the largest employer in the surrounding metropolitan area, this university is both enriched and circumscribed by its ur- ban setting; and its state-related status presents a hurdle when soliciting funding from the legislature. "State-related" in this case means that the university is more expensive for students than fully state-funded institutions, but that its faculty salaries are considerably worse. And its location in southwestern Pennsylvania affects—sometimes positively, sometimes negatively—the university's ability to attract and retain faculty, students, and staff.

As at many other large research universities, the board of trustees and upper administration have responded to these challenges by concentrating on enhancing the university's public image. Revealingly, our chancellor opened last year's report on the state of the university by referring to Clark Kerr, who argued that a university's reputation, once established was its greatest asset. Thus the administration carefully monitors external rankings compared to other institutions and regularly crows about improved SAT scores among entering students (even though SAT scores do not predict relative success in college). "Star" faculty in various disciplines are wooed or retained with lavish offers that far exceed their colleagues' salaries so that the university may maintain its image as a major research institution. In addition, state-of-the-art sports and recreation facilities are under construction in order to attract students and athletes within and beyond the region. Meanwhile, upper-level administrators who carry out the board's wishes are rewarded with exorbitant "performance incentive bonuses" added to their six-figure incomes.[1]

I won't belabor the point. Many other scholars have already noted the ways in which these increasingly prevalent practices conceive of the university as a company (complete with CEO, board, and administrative executives who run the business) seeking investors (patrons who contribute to capital campaigns) and consumers (students who take courses) on the higher education market, wherein other universities are competitors rather than partners in the search for knowledge and understanding. As Paul Delaney comments:

> Universities now position themselves within a purely differential system where each institution, and each department within it, seeks to raise its status by meeting the expectations of its peers. What universities now "produce" are . . . indicators and ratings that place them within well-publicized hierarchies and that in turn generate research funding, popularity with would-be students and faculty members, larger endowments, and the like. (93)

Within such a system, knowledge has become, even more explicitly than in the past, a commodity to manufacture and advertise: The more knowledge a university can claim to possess, the more "value" that university accrues.

What interests me about these oft-cited features of the contemporary research university are their effects not only on the curricular structure of English departments but on the specific measures by which those of·us working within English departments envision altering that structure. Faculty in English tend to see ourselves as antagonistic to the corporate conception of university, and we consequently imagine that our ideas for curriculum reform are untainted by the corporate desires evident in the discourse of university trustees and presidents. In what follows, I suggest that the market-oriented approach to higher education plays a larger role in English studies curricula than we may suspect—even our best efforts to revise these curricula are shaped by the very forces we presume to oppose.

The Great Divides

Like most departments of its size, the English department in which I teach divides its curriculum into separate programs—in our case, literature, children's literature, creative writing, film, and composition—that are responsible for courses in their subdiscipline.[2] The literature and creative writing programs offer separate tracks through the English major; the film program offers its own major (not technically "in" English but nonetheless housed administratively in the department); the composition program provides a wide sweep of introductory and advanced writing courses; and both the composition and the children's literature programs offer courses for students seeking to become schoolteachers. All programs contribute courses to the department's graduate curriculum, which, in addition to M.F.A. and M.A. degrees, offers a Ph.D. in Critical and Cultural Studies.

At first glance, this may seem a reasonable—even potentially fruitful—way to arrange the resources of a large English department. After all, professors have been trained to perform research and publish in the subdisciplines that have come to constitute English, so it would appear logical to set up curricular entities that identify these subdisciplines and give students the opportunity to work within them. It would also appear fair to grant these programmatic entities something approaching equality in the department's self-presentation and curricular offerings—hence, the move to parallel tracks through the major or, in the case of children's literature, a special certificate. In short, subdisciplinary programs allow faculty to teach what they know best and students to take a range of courses within a single realm of an expansive discipline, thereby engaging in a curriculum—so goes the argument—that is deep and broad.

Dividing the English department into programs and tracks sounds sensible in part because of how thoroughly we are immersed in the corporate model of the university. One feature of this model is its notion of the "target audience"—consumers to whom a particular product is designed to appeal. By creating programs in literature, composition, creative writing, and so on, we faculty imagine "reaching" students who might not necessarily be attracted to the study of English in general but who may be attracted to a distinct sector of the field. Accordingly, the major can be marketed as a set of package tours, wherein students choose from several different routes, each of which departs from the same point of origin (freshman composition) but moves to its own unique set of destinations. The buses that carry students along these routes are run by the same company, but the company does considerable subcontracting (with part-time faculty) in order to cut labor expenses. Hoping to compete more effectively with companies in other disciplines, our department recently added a new tour—the honors English major, designed to appeal to the "best" students on campus.

I recognize the cynicism of my metaphor, but I think it is important that we come to terms with the relationship between our curricular structures and market-driven concerns. Separate programs within an English department lead faculty to identify themselves all the more forcefully with their areas of specialization—and with their own marketability within those areas. After all, the most prevalent way to increase one's market value is to publish heavily inside one's subdiscipline, not to investigate a broad sweep of interests across the discipline as a whole (which can lead to the charge of dilettantism). Working in a subdisciplinary program—wherein we say of ourselves, "I'm *in* the creative writing program" or "I'm *in* the literature program"—reinforces this habit of mind. In part, this is because others within one's program tend to "keep up" with and discuss publications in that specialized field, and in part because one's reputation beyond one's institution is largely a matter of influencing other programs in that field, not other English departments, which are themselves similarly balkanized.

As a member of one such subdisciplinary program (in my case, a composition program), I am encouraged, subtly and not-so-subtly, to bond with my colleagues in the program and, when necessary, engage in political battles against colleagues from other programs. Loyalty to one's program earns respect from other members of that program, even if it may earn scorn from members of other programs. The resulting *turf war,* in which departmental programs struggle for power and resources, leads faculty to approach the curriculum as a competitive battle for students. Note, for instance, that an unstated, but not unhidden, responsibility of any program director is to retain or increase the strength of that program's presence in the curriculum, and that faculty within a program often assess a director on her ability to do so. As David Damrosch observes, "a patterned isolation of disciplines, and then . . . of specialized fields within disciplines" leads to "a heady mix of scholarly alienation and disciplinary nationalism that shape the questions we ask and the ways in which we ask them. These scholarly values in turn foster . . . alienation and aggression at all levels of academic life" (6).

While it can be argued that improving a specific program contributes to the general improvement of the department, I question how a gain by one program actually contributes to the welfare of other programs. An English department split into programs is less like a house of shared rooms where cohabitants congregate than like an apartment building composed of "units," where each group of inhabitants leads separate lives: We faculty may enter our living spaces from the same corridor, but we'd never mistake the corridor for home.

What complicates this picture is the fact that some of us teach on more than one track, in more than one program. Among these faculty, for whom loyalty to a single program is called into question by their interest in multiple realms of the departmental curriculum, programmatic divisions are recognized as problematic. (Or perhaps I should say *experienced* as problematic, since most will pay lip service to the notion that programs create arbitrary borders.) The trouble is that, even if certain faculty would like to address the larger English studies curriculum within which various programmatic curricula are housed—to consider, for instance, relationships among programs and possible collaborations—there is little in the structure of the department to enable or motivate such work. Each program has its own standing curriculum committee, but there is no departmental curriculum committee—no body of faculty that convenes to review, discuss, or make proposals regarding the overall curricular arrangement.[3]

None of which is meant to contend that programmatic entities are useless or that academic specialization is without value. But I am concerned that the programmatic model makes it difficult, even well-nigh impossible, for English departments in research universities to accomplish more than superficial curriculum reform. As Gerald Graff indicates, disciplinary changes in English have typically been adopted by merely expanding rather than transforming existent curricula; new courses (in critical theory, African American literature, creative nonfiction, and so on) are added to the catalogue, and new programs and tracks through the major (in composition studies, film studies, and so on) are added to the departmental organization. The result of this process of accretion is an impressive variety coupled with what Graff calls "the incoherence of a curriculum that is content to go on endlessly multiplying courses and subjects like boutiques at the mall" (10). Accordingly, in their self-presentation, English departments tend to emphasize the variety and ignore the incoherence—or, when faculty do respond to the problem of incoherence, programmatic allegiances often lead them to seek coherence *within their particular program,* not within the English studies curriculum as a whole.

This tendency is presently in evidence in my department. A common reading of the department by its faculty is that the film and creative writing programs are currently in good condition, with a solid base of students, improved funding, and a well-articulated mission. At the same time, the literature and composition programs are perceived to have gradually lost some of their sense of purpose, and in response have been energetically endeavoring to shore up their foundations through faculty rejuvenation, reappraisal of curricula, and earnest discussion in each program's set of committees and subcommittees. As a participant in these efforts, I do not mean to underestimate their potential. But I do think it significant that all such ventures have occurred within programmatic boundaries. Faculty who teach literature are at work on their program, and faculty who teach composition are at work on theirs—but the idea that faculty from various programs might work together on the departmental curriculum seems little more than the nostalgia of a hopeless idealist. In some ways, that's all it *can* be, for the departmental curriculum ceases to exist as a common concern.

Again, I say this not to condemn the attitudes of others but as an observation on practices of which I am very much a part. In recent years, I have fully endorsed the composition program's efforts to improve its image through developing a graduate program, adding undergraduate courses designed for prospective teachers, and re-imagining our website to attract more students to our upper-division and graduate courses. This is the kind of mentality a department composed of programs cultivates—a mentality in which we think of curriculum as a realm of programmatic, not departmental or university, possibilities. And this is exactly the mentality that the corporatized research university would have us retain.

Curriculum Reform and Student Choice

To illustrate how departmental programs can contribute to the corporate vision of higher education, I turn to an ongoing attempt at curriculum reform in the composition program that I co-direct. Although the history informing this move to alter the current curriculum is much more complex than I present here, I hope this description gives a sense of how even our best intentions are increasingly conditioned by the conception of students as consumers in the higher education marketplace.

Like numerous other composition programs at large universities, our program is in many respects overwhelmed by the obligation to offer first-year writing to thousands of incoming students who are required to take it. The fact that composition programs are so burdened by this obligation is one reason why Sharon Crowley and others have called for the first-year writing requirement to be abolished. Struck by Crowley's argument that, in the absence of the requirement, composition programs would be "in control of course enrollments, offering only the number of sections that can be responsibly staffed and supported" (245), faculty in our program recently attempted to persuade an associate dean in charge of curriculum review to consider revising the first-year writing requirement so that students could choose from a variety of courses to fulfill it. As it stands, the first-year requirement is almost always fulfilled by taking General Writing, a course offered by the composition program. We recommended the requirement be fulfilled not only by this course but also through other introductory writing-intensive courses offered by other programs in the English department (the literature program, for instance) and by other departments in the university.

Our proposal was rejected. The reason given? Advanced undergraduates had recently completed a survey in which the administration asked them to rank how well courses in the core curriculum had contributed to their college education—and the first-year writing course had received the highest scores. Understandably, the associate dean had little desire to change the requirement regarding what students taking the survey had claimed was the core curriculum's most effective course; and the composition program found itself in the ironic position of having its proposal defeated by the program's own pedagogical success. (Yet note how success was measured—through a multiple-choice survey much like the customer satisfaction forms common at restaurants and other businesses.)

Undeterred, composition faculty were so determined to challenge the hegemony of the anonymous first-year writing course that we embarked immediately on another route to the same end. Even if General Writing were to be required for all entering students, we decided that we could nevertheless make progress on both of our central goals: (1) improve the working conditions of those teaching the course (particularly part-time faculty), and (2) diversify first-year course offerings within our program. We approached the former by refusing to hire more part-time faculty to staff additional courses needed for an expanding first-year class, instead managing to convince the administration to convert several existing part-time lines to full-time lines that, though nontenure-stream, consist of three-courses-per-semester teaching loads, service expectations (one committee assignment), and compensation.[4] Because of this change, part-time faculty who had for years felt discouraged and isolated are participating in the program with striking energy, helping to shape our discussions of policy, curriculum, and pedagogy.

I don't want to make grand claims on behalf of full-time nontenure-stream staffing, which appears to be the compromise toward which English departments are moving with the corporatized university.[5] What I wish to focus on here is the second major goal currently pursued by the composition program—to diversify the courses by which students may satisfy the first-year writing requirement. When the administration rejected our plan to have the requirement met by writing-intensive courses in departments across the curriculum, we decided there was no reason why a good deal of variety could not be created by our own program; in fact, such variety was *already* present in the many different versions of General Writing offered by the faculty and teaching assistants who taught the course. The problem, as we had long known, was that students had no way of recognizing this variety—or acting on it, through their choices at registration—because most sections were simply labeled General Writing (GW) in the catalogue, and all teachers (except for tenured or tenure-stream faculty) were named "Staff." But why not name different versions of the course through subheadings that identify either the subject matter of a particular section (e.g., GW: Popular Culture, GW: Race in America, and so on) or the form of writing the section will emphasize (GW: Academic Writing, GW: The Personal Essay, etc.)? We could even design a program booklet with course descriptions and instructors' names, thereby helping students locate a section of GW best suited to their interests.

These plans are still under debate, so it is difficult to say how the curriculum will develop. What strikes me about our desire to "diversify" the first-year course—and then publicize its diversity—is its similarity to product diversification in the world of corporate business and advertising. Much like companies suddenly happy to claim diversity as both a goal and an attribute, those of us in the composition program, myself included, have been attracted to a wide range of first-year writing courses that would meet the needs and interests of multiple students, whom we would enable to make informed decisions at registration. Perceiving that our product, General Writing, is no longer fit for the contemporary curricular market, we've imagined "tailoring" the course in ways that better suit today's student consumers, granting them those all-important choices that buttress the individual's sense of power and significance on a campus at which they might otherwise feel (with good reason) powerless and ignored. General Writing would be produced in a variety of shapes for a variety of students, just as General Motors produces a variety automobiles for a variety of customers. Students will be able to glance through an advertising booklet in the advising office that displays different versions of the course and determine, based on subject matter, teacher, and (let's not forget) time of day, the closest match to what they're shopping for that semester. Register early to get the best bargain!

Obviously this parallel with the world of business was not a conscious part of our planning. But that is precisely my point: We presume, as members of the Left-leaning culture of English departments, that our curriculum challenges the corporate ethos of the major research university, when in fact the *structure* of that curriculum—even the structure of our proposals for reform—supports rather than subverts such an ethos. Working within a system that approaches students as consumers, we may unwittingly reform the curriculum in ways that derive from that system, even when we imagine ourselves to be acting in the interest of our students. After all, transnational corporations also speak of providing services for their clients, who are supposedly the ones empowered by what they purchase.

Strangely enough, I now find myself brought full circle to an understanding of the potential value of a first-year writing course that does *not* identify different versions or instructors in the course catalogue. While General Writing is a wrongheaded name for this course, the notion of a course in the core curriculum whose multiple sections have sufficient commonality in their purposes, goals, and methods that individual differences need not be disclosed or promoted in advance seems to me a worthy alternative to that which would turn all parts of the curriculum into an elaborate menu of specialized choices. Moreover, that this course would be taught by a "staff"—teachers who together articulate the aims of the course and organize its materials—strikes me as a potentially forceful response to a curriculum in which faculty largely design courses on their own, apart from their colleagues. The result of individualistic course design is a woefully fragmented and incoherent curriculum, where we find long lists of courses but little or no imagined connections among them.

The dozens of sections of first-year writing in my department are not, for the most part, taught by a collaborative staff. The term "staff" in the course catalogue signals the low status of those categorized as such more than a principle of cooperation guiding their work. The extent to which this group—composed of full-time and part-time nontenure-stream faculty and graduate teaching assistants—will, along with tenured and tenure-stream faculty in the program, collaborate as a staff remains to be seen. Now *that* would be a goal worth pursuing.

An Alternative: Cross-Programmatic Collaboration

I have argued that by dividing the English department into curricular programs—complete with directors, office staff, budgets, faculty lines, and courses, along with undergraduate and graduate students who choose a particular program as their area of concentration—we assist rather than resist corporate models of higher education that define the curriculum as a set of discrete products targeted toward various student markets, not as a reflexive process committed to the integration of knowledge. Curricular programs encourage us to identify and work closely with faculty within our subdisciplinary fields, which makes it all the more difficult for intra- or interdepartmental alliances to develop. The persuasive power of such an approach to the curriculum derives, in part, from its appeal to the ideology of individualism. Students are taught to regard themselves as individuals who need to purchase the right set of courses to "get ahead" both within and beyond the university. As Jeffrey Williams remarks: "Students have been unabashedly reinvented as consumers, as shoppers at the education store, buying a career-enhancing service" (747). Given that our society makes fewer and fewer promises of assistance if things don't work out as planned, it is understandable that most students would adopt this attitude. And faculty at research universities are often themselves shopping for the best deal—that is, the highest salary, least teaching, most research assistance, and so on. This, too, is understandable; the right package can provide a comfortable life. Moreover, if one desires community, there is always the community of those who publish and attend conferences in one's area of specialization.

What is easy to call for but terribly difficult to bring about is a collectivist curricular practice, one in which faculty from different programs in the English department articulate a curriculum whose vision is larger than that of any single program. In such a curriculum, courses among various programs would be integrated rather than segregated so that the relationships between one course and another could be explored by faculty and students alike. As Graff has observed, some of these relationships are antagonistic (hence his call for "teaching the conflicts"), but I think an equal amount of attention should be given to the interdependent relationships (between courses or areas of study) that implicitly structure inquiry in the broad discipline of English. After all, literature, creative writing, and composition might conceivably have something to do with one another.

Yet English departments at research universities are generally too large and divided to achieve complete curricular integration of different programs. The best hope for change lies in initially modest endeavors that model, on a small scale, integrative curriculum reform and give faculty and students the opportunity to engage in alternative forms of teaching and learning. For example, next year faculty teaching what we call "core" courses in our department's M.A. program—that is, required introductory graduate courses in literary theory, composition pedagogy, film history, and textual practices—will plan and teach these courses in tandem rather than in isolation. Working as a group, these faculty members will identify goals for the core curriculum and articulate ways in which their courses, not each identically but together as a whole, will pursue such goals. While the methods for integrating these courses may vary (faculty have thus far discussed establishing a common theme for the year, or perhaps a common text, though other possibilities exist, including team-taught sessions and multicourse colloquia), the point is that, for the first time since the core curriculum replaced our M.A. exam several years ago, faculty teaching the core will work collaboratively to make explicit the relationships between courses offered by different programs.

As one designing this curricular plan with our department chair, I think it imperative to emphasize one of its most crucial elements: the budgetary funds that will be given to faculty who teach in the core. The problem with collaboration is that it takes additional time, and few faculty are willing to pour extra time into departmental affairs. I say this not as a criticism but simply to acknowledge a significant reality: faculty are busy and time is short.[6] Recognizing that faculty often need more than mere verbal encouragement to collaborate, our chair converted a fund for an annual small conference into a fund for the M.A. core courses so that faculty teaching these courses can invite guest speakers to address students, take students to cultural events related to the core's theme, or arrange whatever intellectual/social occasions will assist in their teaching. By providing resources they wouldn't normally have, the chair has attracted an enthusiastic group of faculty to address the fragmentation of our graduate curriculum. Although it could certainly be claimed that the need to provide faculty with additional funding to promote curricular collaboration is another sign of the corporate climate of the contemporary university, wherein all incentives are monetary, the funding in this case provides a collective rather than individual resource. By supporting collaborative curriculum development, the fund will serve as a benefit to the students who will participate in the collaboration.

What is ultimately significant is not the fund but the revised structural obligation that accompanies teaching in the core: To participate in this part of the curriculum, faculty must agree to work with colleagues who are also teaching in the core. Thus, what was once a set of courses that encouraged teachers to represent their particular subdisciplinary program is now a set of courses that encourages faculty to represent the English department and its mission as a whole. Given that there is currently little sense of a shared mission among faculty in the department, the articulation of commonalities will no doubt be a challenge—one confronted annually by core course faculty. Indeed, the collaborative feature of the core will force a new group of faculty each year (for these courses are rotated among a fairly wide range of tenured and tenure-stream faculty) to rearticulate the objectives of the core and the ways their courses can help achieve them. Yet however ad hoc this work may sound, our hope is that the initial year will establish a thoughtful precedent to guide future discussion of graduate courses. You have to start somewhere—and that place in the curriculum designated as the core seems a potentially fruitful location for defining common purposes. Moreover, curriculum reform in this instance does not mean providing students with more consumer choice within ever-expanding programs; rather, it means bringing together faculty across programs to integrate their perspectives on what constitutes study in their shared discipline.

I recognize that this faculty collaboration affects only part of my department's graduate curriculum and has no effect on the undergraduate curriculum. It represents no more than a beginning—a small beginning. Yet under the current curricular model, in which English departments at research universities are divided into large, competitive programs, successful reform is more likely to endure by starting with modest ambitions. The proof will lie in the "pudding": If collaboration across programs creates a viable alternative (or supplement) to programmatic tracks, both for faculty and for students, then its influence may spread throughout the department or even beyond the department's borders. I have suggested that such an alternative will require the commitment of faculty who must not only devote time and energy but also learn to work closely with those outside their subdisciplinary programs, and of departmental leaders such as the chair, who must help design collaborative curricular spaces and provide resources for the faculty and students who will inhabit them. From the outset, we need to recognize that a collaborative curriculum demands more of its participants than an individualist curriculum; but, over time, it potentially gives more back.

Working together, faculty have the opportunity to make their courses more meaningful and more influential—part of a collectively articulated project, not an isolated shot in the dark. The resulting curriculum might offer students what the current one does not: an education whose different pieces constitute a dialogue rather than a disconnected set of monologues. It is through just such dialogue that curricular programs in English departments could forge a whole greater than the sum of its parts.

Notes

1. In 1999 to 2000, for example, the chancellor received a $35,000 bonus from the Board of Trustees beyond his $265,000 salary. Salaries for top officials at major research institutions are often considerably higher than this, but well over 10 percent of the chancellor's income was tied to the board's satisfaction with his performance.

2. I use "subdiscipline" and "subdisciplinary" to describe the fields of literary studies, composition, creative writing, and film studies. Given each of these fields could be said to constitute its own discipline, I recognize that my terminology is problematic. I find these terms useful for indicating a pervasive institutional arrangement—namely, the collection of a broad array of fields under the name of "English."

3. For an essay exploring the difficulties of English department curricular reform at a "large state university," see Dorman, Liggett, and Nardo.

4. The "MLA Survey of Staffing in English and Foreign Language Departments, Fall 1999" lists an average salary for full-time, nontenure-stream faculty in doctoral-granting English departments of $33,874. The $29,000 salary in my department is well below this, but the three/three teaching load is an improvement over four/four loads that are common elsewhere.

5. For an argument on behalf of this compromise, see Murphy.

6. Holt and Anderson note the irony that, even though the working hours per week of faculty rose sharply in the 1990s, public and political demands for increased faculty workloads continue (132).

Works Cited

Crowley, Sharon. *Composition in the University: Historical and Polemical Essays.* Pittsburgh: U of Pittsburgh P, 1998.

Damrosch, David. *We Scholars: Changing the Culture of the University.* Cambridge: Harvard UP, 1995.

Delany, Paul. "The University in Pieces: Bill Readings and the Fate of the Humanities." *Profession* (2000): 89–96.

Dorman, Wade, Sarah Liggett, and Anna Nardo. "Changing Institutions, Changing Teachers: A Conversation About Curriculum Revision." *ADE Bulletin* 114 (1996): 30–38.

Graff, Gerald. *Beyond the Culture Wars: How Teaching the Conflicts Can Revitalize American Education.* New York: Norton, 1992.

Holt, Mara, and Leon Anderson. "The Way We Work Now." *Profession* (1998): 131–42.

Kerr, Clark. *The Uses of the University.* Cambridge: Harvard UP, 1963.

"MLA Survey of Staffing in English and Foreign Language Departments, Fall 1999." Modern Language Association. (2001) *www.mla.org.*

Murphy, Michael. "New Faculty for a New University: Toward a Full-Time Teaching-Intensive Faculty Track in Composition." *College Composition and Communication* 52 (2000): 14–42.

Williams, Jeffrey. "Brave New University." *College English* 61 (1999): 742–51.

Chapter Twelve

Composition and Rhetoric, Inc.
Life After the English Department
at Syracuse University
James Thomas Zebroski

Rather than occasional criticism by amateurs, I should think that the whole enterprise might be seriously taken in hand by professionals. Perhaps I use a distasteful figure, but I have the idea that what we need is Criticism Inc., or Criticism Ltd.

—John Crowe Ransom (329)

[T]he much-discussed Syracuse University program, for all its difficulties—rhetoric and composition now function outside the confines of the English department—still has much to teach us about the whole process of refiguring the discipline.

—James Berlin (162)

Professionalizing Composition and Rhetoric

In 1987, I came to Syracuse University (SU) as a faculty person appointed in both the Writing Program and the English department. The Writing Program had the year before, under the impetus of a new director, a new English chair, and a new dean of the College of Arts and Sciences, begun to pull away from being part of the English department. All concerned believed there were advantages in what might be termed the professionalization of writing instruction and scholarship. And that professionalization, it was thought, might best be accomplished in a freestanding, independent writing department positioned within the college but with ties across the university. Over the next decade, the tenure-line faculty in Writing, by 1994 a total of ten, had contracts that distributed salary and commitments between Writing (60 percent) and English (40 percent). As I write this, I am the only faculty person who has retained contractual ties with English. We have added another faculty line so there are now eleven of us. The ten others have placed their contracts fully within the Writing Program. In some respects, I feel like the vestigial limb—the appendix of body English. In this chapter, I want to use this odd perspective to look back on the process of departmental separation and independence to analyze the losses and the gains. More important, I track two external forces that have had a huge impact on writing and English over the past fifteen years.

I allude to these forces in the epigrams that begin this chapter. One is the long-running trend toward *professionalization*—that is, the creation of a specialized, formal knowledge in institutional spaces and the establishment of certified professionals who use this formal knowledge for the purpose of "treating" a clientele. In *The World's Body,* John Crowe Ransom proposed that college English departments should make their object of study the literary work of art, not its history. Ransom proposed that college English departments should produce both criticism of that art and the critics who do such work. Ransom, reviewing the state of criticism in the first three decades of the century, argues that criticism has been left to the amateurs. He says that the English department's business in a literal sense, indicated by his figure of the corporation in his essay's title, should be to produce *professional* critics and a *professional,* sophisticated criticism. He explicitly ties this goal to the very existence of a department of English and to scholarly identity and affiliation:

> It is really atrocious policy for a department to abdicate its own self-respecting identity. The department of English is charged with the understanding and communication of literature, an art, yet it has usually forgotten to inquire into the peculiar constitution and structure of its product. English might almost as well announce that it does not regard itself as entirely autonomous, but as a branch of the department of history, with the option of declaring itself occasionally a branch of the department of ethics. (335)

Ransom connects the object of study with the institution of departments—and disciplines—to carry on that work. Academic units are tied to professionalization. If a collective of scholars agrees that their study is central to professional identity construction, in capitalism it is logical to "incorporate"—that is, to form an officially recognized institutional structure that pursues as a collective that common goal. Disciplinarity, in some respects, calls for further professionalization. We are interpellated as subjects into a call to professionalize.

Thus, in some respects, the program with which I have been affiliated since 1987, as well as composition and rhetoric as a whole ever since doctoral programs in composition and rhetoric have been established separately from literary studies, is simply carrying out the imperative that Ransom argues for: to be fruitful and multiply, in capitalism, to professionalize.[1] Professionalization, then, follows both the internal logic of knowledge creation in capitalist society—to

specialize and formalize knowledge, and to create classes of people who manage and produce such knowledge—and the ever-present external logic of the
free market, where, if there is a profit to be made then there will be strong encouragement, even an irresistible economic incentive, for academics to pursue
that knowledge and create specialists in that knowledge. The Syracuse Writing
Program simply extended the same logic of the professions in establishing itself
as a quasi-department to pursue this objective.

The second force at work in the formation of the Syracuse program and
composition and rhetoric as a whole, is relatively new. James Berlin's *Rhetorics,
Poetics, and Cultures* argues that we live in a new emerging form of capitalism,
what he and others call post-Fordist regimes of capital, which has risen only
in the past thirty years; and that these new social conditions are not unrelated
to the emergence of new theories for analyzing the world (postmodern theory)
and new needs to refigure the English curriculum, English studies, and college
English departments.

Berlin, in the epigraph of this chapter, sees the separateness of rhetoric
and composition from English at Syracuse to be a "difficulty," implying that
English threw composition and rhetoric out of the department. This is not really accurate. The English faculty at Syracuse were, to an extent, probably
happy to see writing go, but so were the composition and rhetoric faculty.
There was not much disagreement on that, only on the specifics of the divorce
decree. There was then an acceptance of the reality of professionalization.
What is surprising is that Berlin seems to want to hold back what is a nearly
unstoppable trend in the capitalist production of knowledge: increasing professionalization. The same process of professionalization that has driven English
departments at least since Ransom's invocation of the enterprise in his "Criticism Inc." finds its logical end in a separate unit devoted to composition and
rhetoric.

What was less visible at the time the Writing Program was formed were
the ways that the shift in work to post-Fordist regimes of capital was to have
profound effects on the evolution of the program. This is indicated by the
persistence of that word *program*. The Writing Program at Syracuse, from its
inception, has been something other than a department. That the unit has retained
the appellation *program,* through all the changes of the past fifteen years, points
to the immense impact of post-Fordist forces. Although there are an increasing
number of studies that examine the corporatization of the university, very few
of these analyses are specific to composition or English studies at the local,
departmental level.[2] In the following section, I examine the forces of post-
Fordism and how they have overdetermined the Writing Program's evolution.
Such a study of how these macro-forces have become embedded at the micro-
level of our everyday life, I hope, will help workers in other departments spot
similar tendencies, perhaps offering some idea of how to intervene.

My controlling idea is that, while there have been many advantages gained
by going with the forces of professionalization and post-Fordism, there have

also been serious drawbacks and increasing dangers. This chapter's title, then, signifies what I take to be the inevitable end of this logic, if we do not collectively intervene. That end is nothing less than the complete corporatization of both composition and rhetoric, but also English studies. And such a potential corporatization is both undemocratic, in that the people involved are not part of governance and decision making, and elitist, in that many people and groups, of necessity, are left behind.

Post-Fordism in the Groves of Academe: The Case of Syracuse

The Writing Program at Syracuse has been shaped into a post-Fordist quasi-department since 1986—sufficient time to get the distance needed to begin to evaluate the achievements and the failures of the institution without personalizing the issues. Six different administrations (directors and co-directors) have run the program. The following examples and observations, then, are *not* about any single person or about the institution per se, but rather the forces at work that have constructed that institution from 1986 to 2001. Those forces are at work in all composition and rhetoric and English departments, regardless of whether they follow the same path as Syracuse. This description is not meant to forward a model, but rather to understand in a deeper way the forces now constructing the new workplace.

Let me start by simply describing, briefly, some of the Writing Program's accomplishments and shortcomings. Among its accomplishments are the following:

- Creating and implementing a fully developed *undergraduate curriculum in composition and rhetoric*. This curriculum is theory-based, premised on a notion of development in both the discipline of composition and in student writing. It includes a freshman writing studio that focuses on process and theory, and a sophomore writing studio that focuses on rhetoric. Both of these courses are university requirements. The old introduction to advanced writing course was replaced by a range of upper-division electives geared mostly to writing requirements in majors.

- Creating and implementing a *doctoral curriculum in composition and cultural rhetoric* (CCR). A core of required courses starts off the CCR curriculum, which includes the introduction to doctoral study in CCR, a history course (development of modern composition studies), twentieth-century rhetorical studies, interdisciplinary studies of language and literacy, and a research processes and premises course. The track (i.e., major) courses—one majors in either composition or rhetoric—includes advanced theory in composition, advanced theory in rhetoric, ancient rhetoric, curriculum, discourse analysis, and social history of rhetoric.

- Constructing, for the first seven years of the program, a collaborative and mutually supportive *teaching community* that advanced understandings of writing both at Syracuse and nationally through teacher talk and research on the undergraduate curriculum.

- This teaching community was *diverse and fairly egalitarian,* including faculty in composition and rhetoric, teaching assistants who were graduate students in English and composition and rhetoric, and instructors.

- *Professionalizing writing instructors,* which included supporting their attendance at national conferences in composition and rhetoric, and then later, financially supporting numerous presentations on the work done on the curriculum at national conferences. It also included consolidating teaching assignments; support for 3:2 loads or less; class sizes of twenty or fewer; reducing the number of instructors in the program accompanied by increasing pay and benefits; regularized, renewable contracts; an evaluation committee made up of only instructors to do regular reviews; and for a sizable number of instructors, release time for administrative activities.

- *High scholarly productivity.* The Writing Program created a site where full-time faculty frequently wrote for each other and the program and often published versions of these texts in national forums. In 1987, one faculty wag said that this was the most "writingest" faculty they knew of. The publication rate of the faculty as a whole has been and remains extremely high.

- A departmental culture or ethos that stresses a sense of collective mission in exploring, learning about, and sharing with others on and off campus what was seen by the full-time faculty as the *cutting-edge of knowledge about writing.*

The shortfalls of the Writing Program include the following:

- *A near-elimination of full faculty say in curriculum and shared governance.* There have been no full faculty, shared governance committees. Instead, the program arranged all service and administrative work either through year-to-year, direct appointments at the discretion of the director, or through large task forces (teams) in which full faculty were always outnumbered and often disregarded. The task forces were sometimes run by instructors who were appointed by the director as leaders. Instructors, whose contracts were renewed frequently, the longest being every three years, always played a crucial role in task-force work. In 2000, the program moved toward a committee system of governance, but at the time of this writing, that committee system has taken on many of the traits of the task-force system.

- *High full-faculty turnover.* While typical departments find their biggest personnel problem to be veteran faculty who may not contribute much but have high salaries or resist change, the Writing Program had the opposite problem: a faculty workforce that had a turnover rate comparable to a fast-food restaurant. From 1986 to 2002, the full-time, tenure-line faculty lost two faculty back to English (one permanently, one for seven years), and brought in and lost eight other faculty. In this period, the Writing Program lost a total of ten full-time, tenure-line faculty who ranged from untenured to full professor. Male and gay faculty have left in large numbers.

- *Nonfaculty administrators.* A nonfaculty staff, appointed and answerable annually to the director alone, after 1991 or so, ran program administration, including writing across the curriculum (WAC) and writing in the disciplines (WID) connections across campus, the Writing Center, instructor development, new TA training and orientation, undergraduate student complaints, and teacher disciplinary action.

- *A director position that has never been open to any review.* Although the program has been reviewed internally and externally, the director was never reviewed as part of this or any other process. The director was accountable only to the dean of the College of Arts and Sciences.

- A department culture that stressed *entrepreneurialism* over academic freedom. The program, indirectly and implicitly, has discouraged work on poststructural theory and politics of writing. Scholarship from the left of the political spectrum has faced departmental resistance and a few faculty believe that sanctions have been taken by program administrators to discourage such scholarship. In contrast, any sort of scholarship that has emphasized workplace or professional writing or other practices favored by university administration, including computers and composition, service-learning distance-learning, WAC and WID, have received unquestioned moral and financial backing. Full faculty have critiqued such projects at their own risk knowing that, in the past, other kinds of support were threatened if politically left positions were taken.

- *A growth in the percent of full-time, tenure-line faculty devoted to Writing Program Administration.* We have now eleven full-time, tenure-line faculty. Nearly half of these positions are filled by people who either have Writing Program administration (WPA) as their scholarly specialization, have served as administrators often, or are in full-time administrative appointments which come with release time and financial stipend.

- *The use of release time to create a two-tier instructor cadre as well as a two-tier faculty.* The program is clearly divided into two classes—one class that "produces" in the traditional sense of teaching large numbers of students at both the undergraduate and graduate level and the other class that gets released from teaching every term and manages the value produced. Adding together instructor and faculty populations, the program probably has at any given moment 35 percent to 40 percent of all teachers in the program in some way committed to administration.

So that's the good, the bad, and the ugly of the past decade and a half. The more important question is in what ways has post-Fordism constructed these effects, these results?[3] David Harvey equates post-Fordism to a flexible regime of accumulation:

> *Flexible accumulation,* as I tentatively call it, is marked by a direct confrontation with the rigidities of Fordism. It rests on flexibility with respect to labor processes, labor markets, products, and patterns of consumption. It is characterized by the emergence of entirely new sectors of production, new ways of providing financial services, new markets, and above all, greatly intensified rates of commercial, technological, and organizational innovation. (147)

The Writing Program corresponds to every point Harvey makes, to a lesser or greater degree. First, the *program* was explicitly constructed and publicly touted (at least in program meetings) as the opposite of traditional—Fordist—English departments, both in content and structure. That is one reason why the name has remained, since *program* marks a break with Fordism. Changing all assignments nearly every year—even the locations of mailboxes and office assignments—shows the post-Fordist quality of everyday life in the Writing Program and speaks to Harvey's description of post-Fordism's flexibility of labor processes. The full-time, tenure-line faculty rarely know more than one or two terms ahead of time what they are teaching or when. In fact, it was not unusual in many years to change these assignments within weeks of the start of the semester. Task forces change their members every year, sometimes several times during the year. All administrative assignments also change frequently at the director's discretion. Faculty meetings are called frequently—the first five years of the program we met nearly every week for two to three hours—without an announced agenda. Often meetings became places where additional work was assigned to faculty or where the WPA faculty announced what they had done for us and the program. Faculty were expected to be on-call and available long after the term was over and well before school began for unofficial weeks of meetings. Personal research agendas were ignored or even discouraged.

The flexibility of post-Fordist labor market fits nicely with the WP's "professionalization" and "empowering" of instructors. The need for flexibility in products is reflected in the development of in-house documents and in-house publishing outlets, run by instructors given release time and cited as research and scholarship. The need for flexibility in consumption practices can be seen in the WP's acceptance of the university chancellor's view that students are customers and by the WP's desire to put forward designer or "linked" versions of standard freshman and sophomore writing courses that appeal to specific disciplines. Such designer, customized freshman and sophomore composition courses—and a whole array of such upper-division writing courses—it was hoped would bring in income from well-off departments and schools for such services. Finally, the nearly immediate acceptance of service learning in all writing courses on the part of most of the WPA faculty signals as unquestioned acceptance of the value of service for freshmen who are new to the university and have a hard enough time at first even finding the building and room of the class on campus. This increase in what students must do to get through their writing courses, as well as the potential such learning has for the complete outsourcing of teaching to the charity and corporate "sponsors," fits with what Harvey outlines as post-Fordism. This doesn't even consider the possibilities of online, virtual courses that promise even further, deeper cuts of labor costs and other expenses. All of these changes were accompanied by an almost frenzied piloting of new courses and teaching practices, as well as constant innovation in research, scholarship, administration, service, and even the terms and vocabulary that we used.

Post-Fordism of this sort, then, has impacted the Syracuse University Writing Program in a big way. But it is rarely a direct, cause–effect kind of influence; rather it is more usually an overdetermination of factors, the gradual elimination of things that don't fit, and the increase in the number of those things that do fit in a post-Fordist environment. Let us briefly focus on four specific sites of this post-Fordist overdetermination—the WP curriculum, the WP social structure, the WP departmental culture or professional ethos, and the WP arrangement and execution of power.

WP Curriculum

The substance of the curriculum at both the undergraduate and graduate level has increasingly been made to relate to the marketplace, whether that marketplace is mediated through other disciplines on campus and their construction of the "professional," as is the case in WAC and WID and the designer writing courses described previously, or whether that relation is rather direct as is the case of the doctoral program. In fact, the full-time, tenure-line faculty have met to "adjust" the approved Ph.D. curriculum several times in its three-year existence because of annual shifts in the MLA job list. When there was a rise in the number of positions in technical communication, we were asked to consider adding courses and faculty for that. The rise in the jobs asking for computers and composition knowledge led the dean to approve an additional tenure-line appointment for a digital rhetoric faculty person.

As I mentioned before, the new upper-division, undergraduate writing courses were generated by the WPA faculty in conjunction with the faculty in specific disciplines which would feed majors into these courses. It should not be surprising that a large number of the courses deal with public policy and civic writing (SU has the renowned Maxwell School for Citizenship), technology (SU houses the Newhouse School of Communications), and professional writing (the School of Management is large and various business majors are popular among SU undergraduates). There never was any faculty vote on whether these courses would be the best. The faculty who did not agree simply had to

accept the categories for these courses fait accompli. The Writing studio that
was offered as a meeting place of these and other students in the past—as one
of the few oases in a desert of hyperprofessionalism—was eliminated (the word
used is "inactivated") in fall of 2001.

Social Structure

One of the most important shifts in flexible accumulation has been the change
in the way work is structured—that is, the social structure of the workplace.
Replacing the Fordist hierarchy in which supervisors with forepersons manage full-time workers is a small core of a few overworked full-time workers
paired with peripheral labor, increasingly managed by WPA faculty. The WP is
classic post-Fordist in this design. Eleven full-time faculty work in a program
that processes five thousand undergraduates and twenty doctoral students each
year. Normally, a department of twenty or thirty full-time, tenure-line faculty
would do comparable work, so there is a large savings on faculty salaries. This
is achieved by fully using instructor and TA workers (this is in part why so
many managers are needed, at least early in the process), and by outsourcing
as much work as possible through linked courses with the disciplines, service
learning, writing-intensive courses in the disciplines, and through writing consultants. The working conditions of the peripheral labor, especially instructors,
are improved enough to offer them choices and a say in the program. Work
is increasingly done on task forces populated and run by instructors or staff
workers, always under the direction of the director.

"Leadership" positions for over a dozen instructors exist in WP to run
quality groups (locally called coordinating groups) that monitor other teachers,
TAs as well as less favored instructors. Such leadership positions provide release
time for the coordinator–instructor, quality control for a large and notoriously
complex curriculum, and monthly reports to the assistant directors and the
program director on any problems or issues that arise. Through such a social
structure explicitly geared to manage labor and control product quality, there is a
real opportunity to monitor faculty political and theoretical positions especially
in the quality-control groups used to monitor new TAs, committees on which
faculty must serve. This mechanism of forced inclusion and collaboration in
task forces as well as TA training records the knowledge produced by faculty
and teachers into written forms—reports by leaders, position papers by the
participants—which are sent to the top, sometimes to be appropriated in the
research of the program leaders. All of this is accomplished through a task force,
a "flattened hierarchy," and release time for those at the top of the pyramid.

Program Culture and Ethos

The WP has always followed and privileged an entrepreneurial ethos that
encourages faculty workers to invent something that will bring in money or

some equivalent. Students are customers to be kept happy. Any sort of negative student-written evaluation is regarded in faculty reviews with suspicion, even if such negative comments might well signify that students were challenged to learn something. What ultimately matters is that students leave the course with what administrators take to be a good experience. Student evaluations are examined closely and no faculty advances take place if there are minor student objections. Students know this, of course, and use this knowledge to put pressure on faculty during the term to reduce or change their requirements. Not surprisingly, a recent review found that in the required freshman and sophomore writing courses, 50 percent of the students enrolled get As, the rest receive Bs.

Beyond the classroom, the WP buys into the university system of short-term, soft-money grants. Faculty and instructors are encouraged to apply for such grants and are rewarded for getting them. Often such grants provide, in some form or other, release time. This privileging of entrepreneurialism and competition reached a kind of apogee during recent discussions about assigning emerging upper-division courses. That task force, made over into a committee, bandied about an idea that, since there were few slots for these courses that were desired by many faculty and instructors, those who wanted to teach the course would submit a fully worked out syllabus as a proposal. The "best" syllabus would win the competition and the person who wrote the syllabus would be given the opportunity to teach the course. It remained unclear exactly who would judge the syllabi—the faculty chair, the WPA of undergraduate writing, the director of the program or the task force, where staff, TAs, and part-time faculty outnumber full faculty by four.

Power Relations

Richard Sennett says that one characteristic of the post-Fordist regime of capital is that power is ever *more concentrated, but not centralized:*

> One of the claims made for the new organization of work is that it decentralizes power, that is, it gives people in the lower ranks of organizations, more control over their own activities. Certainly this claim is false in terms of techniques employed for taking apart the old bureaucratic behemoths.... The managerial overburdening of small work groups with many diverse tasks is a frequent feature of corporate reorganization.... To make such experiments with tens or hundreds of thousands of employees requires immense powers of command. To the economics of inequality the new order thus adds new forms of unequal, arbitrary power within the organization. (55)

For all the talk about flattened hierarchies and empowering workers to come into the conversation, power in the WP, like the new corporation, is still concentrated in a few positions flowing out of the director's office. Teams have little say about what it is they are to do, but rather are free to develop the means, as long as they produce.

Since 1987, workloads of all workers have increased not decreased. Everyone works both out of their homes and on campus, and weekends see large numbers of workers on campus and often in required meetings, usually called conferences or retreats. Full-time faculty have been taken increasingly out of the decision-making process. The faculty have been told that the traditional committee system of shared governance is antiquated and "dysfunctional." The American Association of University Professors (AAUP) has heard the same argument elsewhere, as Martin Snyder notes:

> Boards and administrations have justified their intrusion into areas of primary faculty responsibilities by citing the need for greater flexibility and nimbleness in responding to rapidly changing conditions in the social, technological, economic, and political environments. They see faculty governance structures as dinosaurs ill suited to the corporate norms they would impose for managing higher-education institutions. In so doing, they fail to observe the fundamental difference between the academic and corporate communities. Not only are their goals different—making a profit as opposed to providing an essential service to the community—but they are also constituted in radically different ways. (1)

By diffusing some power to the task forces and teams, by including peripheral labor into the decision-making processes, by "empowering" and grooming peripheral labor always on short-term contract for leadership positions usually reserved for faculty with Ph.D.s, and by doing away with as much faculty shared governance in curricular and hiring decisions as possible, the new workplace makes it easy to replace any worker at any time. The overall organization is less dependent on any single individual and his or her expertise, in fact, making the individual increasingly reliant on the organization. If the individual feels able to get a better deal elsewhere, the organization is flexible enough and has absorbed enough knowledge and work to go on quite well without that person. In fact, it is better off if such individuals leave and are replaced by newer, more docile, and far less-expensive workers. The high turnover rate of full-time faculty is not the exception but the rule in a post-Fordist quasi-department.

All of this raises the question of whether there is a new case to be made for reconceptualizing composition and English as cultural critique, for seeing composition and rhetoric less as the enculturation of writing skills and writing abilities, less as the formation of authors and reinvention of authorship, and more as a critique of the ways that subjectivities are formed in post-Fordist regimes of capital. Until recently, I have resisted this move in composition and rhetoric. Such a conception has often been put forward in a theoretical form that I find objectionable both in terms of its acceptance of a post-Saussurean view of language, and in its hermeneutic focus on textual critique rather than a rhetorical focus on action. But it may be that cultural critique offers the only resistance now possible to the likely emergence of Composition and Rhetoric, Inc. and English, Inc.

Reconceptualizing Composition, Rhetoric, and English Studies

So where does this analysis leave us? What actions, if any, does such understanding of post-Fordism in our midst, in our departments, and in our curricula suggest? In particular, how does work on curriculum respond to what in retrospect sometimes seems like the inevitable working out of economic laws beyond anyone's ability to resist? Is there space left in the academy, English, or composition and rhetoric that will not soon be corporatized? Can English and composition and rhetoric be *de*-corporatized?

I would not be writing this chapter if I were not somewhat optimistic about social change and about socializing English and composition and rhetoric. In fact, despite the fact that publishing is a capitalist enterprise, anyone who knows the history of this book, knows that the editors, out of principle, resisted that impulse in the very selection of publishers. The easy way, the profitable way, would have been to include "pragmatic" administrative, WPA-centered material. Such a move would have recommended the book to a wider set of consumers but would have compromised it as a whole. The editors decided not to go that way and, in taking that stand, made a chapter like this possible. We need to always keep in mind that no institutional structure is singular, that it makes far more sense to view institutional structures as Swiss cheese, rather than as *2001: A Space Odyssey* monoliths.[4] The increased number of such books and articles critical of the corporate university, taken with a view of recent uprisings—for instance, the worldwide protests against free trade, the IMF and the World Trade Organization, or a few years before, the populist support for the mostly part-time workers striking UPS—seem reason to hope. It is, of course, true that any action or understanding, any theory, any text, or any subject position can be co-opted by capitalism. But that is reason to construct flexible concepts of institutional structures rather than to give up hope. I have argued elsewhere that focusing on the construction of value rather than the simple transmission of unchanging meaning in pedagogy is one step forward (Zebroski, *Thinking*).

Perhaps one way to resist post-Fordist forces is to produce a wide array of language concepts and practices from which we and our students can choose, and to vary our choice according to the rhetoric and the hegemony of the situation. For the moment, it might be helpful to reconceptualize English, composition, and rhetoric. Let us go back to John Crowe Ransom in the sense of viewing our task as the teaching of criticism and the production of critics. But this time around, let us see that criticism and those critics not in a formalistic way, but in a *social* way. Perhaps we can see English studies as the site in the new university where we do *social criticism of language use.* Composition then might be viewed as *social criticism of language productivity,* while rhetoric could be conceived as *social criticism of language effects.* Our goal would be to develop knowledge with students who become *social critics of language use, including their own.* If we began with such a reconceptualization, what does that do for us? I think it can open up at least four spaces.

First, I think such a concept and practice opens a space for *organizing.* Although I do not want to offend people, I think that to counter post-Fordist forces, we must begin to identify not with "the professional"—Richard Miller and Kurt Spellmeyer, among many others have shown us that we are living through the twilight of the professions, after all—but, as Jim Berlin showed, we need to identify and affiliate as workers. Berlin always carefully uses the phrase, "workers in English." Others have argued we share more with workers than management, including James Sledd and Sharon Crowley. This logic leads us to dismantle our professional ethos and replace it with worker conscious-ness. The logic of that is unionization. We need to join unions. If that is not possible at our workplace at this time, we need to join nationwide working asso-ciations that see themselves as resisting post-Fordist distortions of work in the academy.

Workers who are professors need to support workers in academe who are not—adjunct faculty, TAs, and service employees. We need to join with them and support them in their attempts to organize unions and when they are organized, we need to support work actions. The local service workers at Syracuse University (SEIU Local 200A) went on strike in the fall of 1998. The discussions that occurred among faculty in support of these workers did more for faculty organizing and faculty morale than anything I observed in all my time at Syracuse. We need to critique the notion that professors are somehow not workers; the administration certainly has. We need to dismantle our professional ethos in English and writing studies. This may well be more difficult to achieve than any other change.

Second, we need to *expand* the kinds of knowledge our curriculum pro-duces. We need to go beyond the instrumental, the vocational. In Ralph Tyler's 1949 book, *Basic Principles of Curriculum and Instruction,* we have some sug-gestions. To be sure, Tyler's book is deeply flawed and is the source of many problems that have beset curriculum workers in the past fifty years. But given Tyler's modernist and Fordist conception of the curriculum specialist as a sort of technician or social engineer, it is revealing that even Tyler does not accept as limited a notion of knowledge as many specialists in composition and rhetoric currently do.[5] Tyler lists four kinds of learning experiences: (1) those to develop skill in thinking, (2) those helpful in acquiring information, (3) those helpful in developing social attitudes, and (4) those helpful in developing interests.

These are fairly carefully worded, but I would associate a certain kind of knowledge with each. The first kind of knowledge is *knowing-how to or procedural knowledge,* and composition and rhetoric overemphasizes this almost to the exclusion of any other sort of knowledge. We tell ourselves we teach process, or rhetoric, or business writing, or computers, or program administration; what this almost always means is that we show students *how to* do these practices. The danger of putting all our eggs into this basket is that we overcommit on what we can deliver and leave critique out. The outcomes assessment movement loves this sort of knowledge because it can be fairly easily evaluated and because students never quite perform sufficiently well unless the curriculum is reduced to training students to perform in a testing situation. Procedural knowledge can also be separated from ethics and politics. Composition and rhetoric workers must resist accepting procedural knowledge as their only claim in the university, just as literary workers need to resist making propositional knowledge their primary claim in a university.

The second sort of learning experience is associated with *knowing-that or propositional knowledge.* Composition and rhetoric has mostly ignored this sort of knowledge, associating it with large lecture classes and multiple-choice testing. Literature workers have been drawn more to propositional knowledge about canonized literary texts and theories. But the most procedural knowledge course has a propositional knowledge dimension, since the goal is not only to develop practices but also to develop concepts from those practices and from other forms of instruction. So we need to put procedural knowledge into a dialectic with propositional knowledge.

Yet beyond both of these sorts of knowledge, composition and rhetoric rarely go, even though Tyler himself suggests that there are far more important and far different kinds of knowledge and learning experiences in this ranking. The last two learning experiences are where most of our attention and labor should be. The experiences that develop social attitudes deal with *tendencies or proclivities,* especially in the long run—what might be termed *knowing to.* Here can be a site in the curriculum that resists post-Fordism. Such tendencies may not be overt and visible, and they certainly are difficult, if not impossible, to measure in the short run.

Tyler's last sort of experience might, when we come to English and composition and rhetoric, be termed *knowledge about lifelong language use.* The English language does not provide a ready label for this kind of knowledge. Perhaps it is a *knowing of* the possibilities inherent in any moment. I believe that if composition, rhetoric, and English studies would focus less on procedural and propositional knowledge and more on knowledge focused on attitudes and life-long interests, what we do in the curriculum would be more resistant to post-Fordist forces.

Third, scholars in English studies need to look beyond our current boom, beyond the current interest in developing more courses for undergraduates and graduate students, beyond developing more degrees and specializations, beyond

seeing curricular work as synonymous with curriculum development. For we
can be sure of one thing, that with every capitalist boom, comes a bust. We need
to move from curriculum development to understanding curriculum. Workers in
colleges of education faced this dilemma nearly thirty years ago. As one of the
leaders of an antideveloper's movement tagged the Reconceptualists, William
Pinar distinguished between curriculum development and understanding curriculum. He notes that "the era of 'curriculum development' is past"; Pinar says:

> The main concepts today are quite different from those which grew out
> of an era in which school buildings and populations were growing ex-
> ponentially, and when keeping the curriculum ordered and organized
> were the main motives of professional activity. Curriculum develop-
> ment: Born 1918. Died 1969.... We live in a different time.... the
> general field of curriculum, ... that field is no longer preoccupied with
> development. As we shall see, the field today is preoccupied with *un-
> derstanding*. To understand curriculum does not mean that many of
> us do not want to change curriculum, both theoretically and institu-
> tionally.... However, many degrees of complexity have entered our
> conceptions of what it means to do curriculum work, to be a curricu-
> lum specialist, to work for curriculum change. In general, we are no
> longer technicians, that is, people who accept unquestioningly others'
> priorities. (6)

English studies, especially composition and rhetoric, have yet to begin
this transition from curriculum development to understanding curriculum. One
of the ways post-Fordist forces might be resisted is for workers in English to
consider making this transition. It is not an easy task to escape the "developer's"
mentality when the forces are going your way. English studies, nonetheless,
needs to plan for the day that will come, when such seeming advances will
come under attack from the same forces that support them now.

Fourth, this shift logically leads to what might be termed a more ecological
understanding of curriculum. Recycling courses and opening up spaces within
existing structures can be as important as creating wholly new structures that
simply reproduce the status quo. Instead of a land developer's ideology of
curriculum—slash-and-burn empire-building in the most superficial sense—
we need to think of curriculum and courses in literature, composition, and
rhetoric as preserves, as opening spaces for difference to exist and thrive.

These four strategies of containment begin the process of constructing livable and sustainable environments within literary studies, composition studies,
and rhetoric. Thirty years ago at the end of a federal grant that supported a
Project English Curriculum Center, one of the primary investigators, Donald
Bateman, warned us about the "developer-trap" in that project's final report:

> Without question this process must proceed if advance is to take place,
> but if advance is to be educationally significant in any universal sense,

new programs must not be frozen for public consumption, but invented out of the stream of new knowledge by particular teachers and classes. (2)

What I have been trying to aim for in this chapter, and what I believe this book is trying to work toward, is an alternative to the developer's trap.

Notes

1. I mostly agree with Nystrand, Greene, and Wiemelt in their argument of the "late" formation of the discipline of composition studies in the late 1970s, when doctoral programs and large numbers of journals specific to composition came into being, although other disciplinary practices must be considered.

2. See Martin and White and Hauck. In a broad sense, Berlin initiated this project for English. Within composition and rhetoric, Mazurek begins a more "micro" study and from another theoretical perspective, Parks begins this work at the national level.

3. I parallel this discussion with the work of Gee, Hull, and Lankshear. These scholars provide an incisive critique of how cutting-edge research gets co-opted by post-Fordist capitalism.

4. This Swiss-cheese metaphor comes from Bill Readings when he was at Syracuse, though he applied it to discourse and language.

5. For an example of a limited notion of knowledge in composition and rhetoric, see the recent vetted document from the Writing Program Administrators Steering Committee of Outcomes Group ("WPA").

Works Cited

Bateman, Donald, and Frank Zidonis. *A Grammatico-Semantic Exploration of the Problems of Sentence Formation and Interpretation in the Classroom. Volume I*. Project Final Report No. 2133. Columbus: Ohio State University Research Foundation (May), 1970.

Berlin, James A. *Rhetorics, Poetics, and Cultures*. Urbana, IL: NCTE, 1996.

Crowley, Sharon. *Composition in the University: Historical and Polemical Essays*. Pittsburgh: U of Pittsburgh P, 1998.

Gee, James Paul, Glynda Hull, and Colin Lankshear. *New Work Order: Behind the Language of the New Capitalism*. Boulder: Westview P, 1997.

Harvey, David. *The Condition of Postmodernity*. Oxford: Blackwell, 1990.

Martin, Randy, ed. *Chalk Lines: The Politics of Work in the Managed University*. Durham, NC: Duke UP, 1998.

Mazurek, Raymond. "Class, Composition, and Reform in Departments of English: A Personal Account." *This Fine Place So Far From Home*. Eds. Dews and Law. Philadelphia: Temple UP, 1995. 249–62.

Nystrand, M., S. Greene, and J. Wiemelt. "Where Did Composition Studies Come From? An Intellectual History." *Written Communication* 110 (1993): 267–333.

Parks, Stephen. *Class Politics: The Movement for the Students' Right to Their Own Language*. Urbana, IL: NCTE, 2000.

Pinar, William, William Reynolds, Patrick Slattery, and Peter Taubman. *Understanding Curriculum: An Introduction to the Study of Historical and Contemporary Curriculum Discourses*. New York: Peter Lang, 1995.

Ransom, John Crowe. *The World's Body*. New York: Scribner's, 1938.

Sennett, Richard. *The Corrosion of Character: Personal Consequences of Work in the New Capitalism*. New York: Norton, 1998.

Sledd, James. "Return to Service." *Composition Studies* 28.2 (Fall 2000): 11–32.

Snyder, Martin. "New Issues, Old Problems Define Governance Today." *Footnotes: The American Association of University Professors* (Fall 2000): 1.

Tyler, Ralph. *Basic Principles of Curriculum and Instruction*. Chicago: U of Chicago P, 1949.

White, Geoffrey, and Flannery Hauck, eds. *Campus Inc.: Corporate Power in the Ivory Tower*. Amherst, NY: Prometheus Books, 2000.

"WPA Outcomes Statement for First-Year Composition." *College English* 63.3 (January 2001): 321–25.

Zebroski, James Thomas. *Thinking Through Theory*. Portsmouth, NH: Boynton-Cook, Heinemann, 1994, 131–36 and 142–44.

Chapter Thirteen

Technological Imbalances
The English Curriculum and Distance Education

Joyce Magnotto Neff and Juanita Rodgers Comfort

When Chalmers McGeagh Roberts reached his eightieth birthday, he wrote a book entitled *How Did I Get Here So Fast?* With some revision, that question can be posed to English studies: How did IT get here so fast? Whether "IT" refers to information technology, instructional technology, interactive television, or all of the above, English studies is being profoundly affected by IT. Distance education is a case in point.

English faculty who enter the world of distance education immediately face the administrative and curricular implications of technology. Frequently, composition and rhetoric faculty make the initial forays into distance education because our courses are desirable components of the professional degree programs marketed to off-campus students, or because economic forces pressure faculty to use the latest technology. However, views of curriculum held by administrators designing professional degree programs may clash with those of faculty who develop writing and rhetoric courses for liberal arts curricula. Universities invest heavily in instructional technologies that faculty might not have chosen, yet we are constrained to teach in the environment created by these investments. While many English faculty are relative newcomers to IT, we believe it is our place to determine why, and to what extent, we will incorporate technology into our courses, based on the pedagogical goals of our discipline. Hence, the central question guiding our discussion: What are English faculty *doing* about IT?

Between us, we have more than ten years of experience teaching on various distance systems in community college, university, and government settings. In addition to the intercampus remote delivery system[1] that we both have taught in, Joyce has used the Internet and video-streaming as delivery methods. Our comments in this chapter are drawn from research done by us and our colleagues[2] who have studied various aspects of the Teletechnet system of distance education at Old Dominion University, one of the largest providers in the country. We have analyzed the impact of distance education on composition and rhetoric curricula by interviewing students, faculty, administrators, site directors, technicians, and instructional designers, and by studying course videotapes and student texts. This long-term research has made us aware of the complexity of teaching English courses from a distance.

We begin by examining the dissonance between "progressive" and "professional" views of literacy education that can complicate curricular issues in distance education. Against this backdrop, we identify three sets of troubling imbalances that composition and rhetoric instructors confront when they teach in distance settings: (1) administrative versus faculty ownership of curricula, (2) the teacherly stances of content-provider versus facilitator, and (3) delivery systems versus instructional practices. These balancing acts condition faculty responses to administrative decisions that affect our courses. However, these balancing acts also suggest ways to increase our input in those decisions. After reviewing the curricular implications of our experiences, we propose some strategies that may help instructors in similar situations to critically engage their own distance-education curricula.

Perspectives From Progressive Versus Professional Education

Distance education responds to the legitimate needs of people who cannot travel to a university to obtain what is fast becoming a basic credential for employment in many fields. Over the past decade, Old Dominion, a comprehensive state university with 19,000 on-campus students, has become a major player in distance education. Teletechnet recorded 21,000 course registrations by more than 7,000 students in the 2000–01 school year. Classes are transmitted by interactive television and video-streaming to thirty-nine sites in five states. Students receive the classes at community colleges, corporate offices, military bases, ships at sea, and their own homes.

English faculty teach primarily in the Professional Communication (Prof-Comm) degree program, one of nineteen undergraduate distance programs offered. The catalog description of the Prof-Comm program clearly announces its intention to meet students' needs:

> The Professional Communication degree is designed for (a) returning students already working in a position of authority who are interested in expanding their *management skills* and/or increasing their *eligibility for promotion* or (b) students interested in communication-related

occupations. The degree will develop *skills* in the areas of interpersonal and organizational communication, professional writing, marketing, management, and public relations. (Teletechnet [emphasis added])

The words highlighted in this passage suggest that the Prof-Comm curriculum emphasizes *professional training* that essentially transfers to students a set of discrete tools, resources, and skills. The degree is viewed pragmatically, both by the program administrators who wrote the description and by prospective students who see it as a certificate of proficiency. Conversely, many of us who teach within the humanities engage the Prof-Comm curriculum in the spirit of *progressive education.* We might have written a different program description, stressing that courses will stimulate students' critical consciousness of the cultural codes, historical precedents, political exigencies, and ethical considerations that underpin a given skill. Beyond certifying proficiency, the Prof-Comm degree should, but often does not, signify a level of sophistication that distinguishes the degree-holder as an insightful, responsible communicator.

It would be a mistake, however, for those of us in the humanities to assume that our contribution to a professional curriculum is simply to add a liberal-studies dimension, without regard for whether the program administration or students find that dimension relevant. In the classroom, we need to help students build conceptual frameworks for communicative acts, while simultaneously devoting more attention to the pragmatic details of human discourse. This means reevaluating course objectives, teaching strategies, and assessment methods to encourage students to develop critical perspectives that connect meaningfully to practical applications, as those students rightly expect. Since technology is being theorized by scholars in composition, literacy, rhetoric, and cultural studies,[3] our contribution can indeed strengthen the curriculum.

The interactive televised (ITV) course, supported by a range of computer-based applications, is the mainstay of the distance-education program we discuss in this chapter. We characterize the ITV course in terms articulated by John Hartley, as a kind of *media discourse* in which "socially established sense is encountered and contested" (quoted in O'Sullivan 94). The effectiveness of an ITV course as media discourse depends on content and mode of delivery (the broadcast, with its supporting online tools). The concept of delivery that prevails in distance education (i.e., delivery as a function of a "seamless" technology, easy to use and intuitive in nature) suggests a troubling disjunction of content and medium. According to one source, seamless technology "should *merely* be a means to deliver course content, facilitating the learning process" (Illinois Online [emphasis added]).

We propose an alternate view: Just as rhetoricians have come to think generally of language as conditioning meaning, we consider that delivery systems function as a kind of "language" that conditions what a course "means." That is, we note that delivery systems influence the way course content is constructed by the instructional "team" (instructor, technician, IT support staff, program administration) and ultimately construed by the students. In short, technology elements of distance learning constitute *ways of knowing.* Delivery systems, thus, can be thought of as rhetorical constructs replete with strategy and style, projecting both an academic and a popular-culture *ethos,* capitalizing on students' own sensibilities regarding education and professional success.

Ideally, faculty who teach and conduct research from this vantage point should be able to collaborate with the rest of the instructional "team" to achieve a shared understanding of learning outcomes and to devise appropriate technology strategies. But in many instances, these parties act at cross-purposes with each other, making curriculum-related decisions according to their competing liberal or professional visions of literacy education. Nevertheless, we must not allow the challenges that arise from this situation to keep us from losing sight of IT's potential to help us engage in productive, critical inquiry with our students within an exciting, new, media-centered culture.

Imbalancing Acts: Technology and Curriculum

One approach to the complexity of IT and curriculum development is to tease out sets of simultaneous balancing acts that English faculty negotiate when their institutions move into distance learning.

Administrative Versus Faculty Ownership of Curricula

Distance-education initiatives, which create new spaces on university organizational charts, have a curricular impact. Whether they branch off academic affairs, feather the cap of an innovative president, or grow alongside a weekend college or experiential-learning program, distance initiatives are funded and managed outside of departmental boundaries because of high start-up costs for the technology and because of complicated administrative needs at receiving sites. These "complicated" needs often arise when the university functions as a corporation hoping to maximize profit by seeking new markets in which to "sell" their product. For example, the Teletechnet distance program was initiated by the State Council for Higher Education, funded by the Virginia General Assembly, after Old Dominion prepared a proposal identifying three main objectives for distance education: to increase access, to be cost-effective, and to stimulate economic development efforts.

The Teletechnet program is marketed to students who have already earned associates degrees. In early 1994, university administrators and distance-education specialists selected a B.S. in Professional Communication as one among several degree programs well suited to this audience. Prof-Comm is housed in the Interdisciplinary Studies program with neither the English department nor the Communication department having sole control over its requirements. What is disturbing in this scenario is that marketing studies were used to determine curriculum and eventually to decide the number and types of English courses included in the Prof-Comm program; however, faculty were not always informed about curricular decisions that affected their teaching.

Juanita's first experience in Teletechnet illustrates the unfortunate consequences of such miscommunications. A few semesters ago, she developed Introduction to Rhetorical Studies as a requirement for English majors. In this course, students would learn how to use methods of rhetorical criticism both to interpret artifacts of popular culture and to appreciate academic texts as expressions of particular discourse communities. Choosing textbooks that foregrounded rhetorical theory, cultural criticism, and the construction of academic texts, she designed a course that relied heavily on small-group discussions based on frequent individual writings (expecting an on-campus enrollment of no more than thirty-five students). Without her knowledge, and before the course was ever taught in *any* setting, Rhetorical Studies was designated as a core course in the Prof-Comm curriculum.

No one advised Juanita ahead of time that she would have a much larger enrollment with significantly different needs; she had no time to rethink her teaching focus, textbooks, and/or assignments. When she walked into the broadcast studio on the first day of class, she noticed on the introductory slide showing on the TV monitors that someone had changed the title of her course to read "Introduction to *Rhetoric and Communication.*" She encountered fifty-eight students, not thirty-five, most of whom had little interest in rhetorical theory, popular culture, or academic discourse.

Neither tradition nor disciplinary expertise has had much influence on curricular decisions about English studies and distance education at our university. Neither has current staffing in the English department where ITV courses in management writing and rhetorical studies must be assigned to already over-scheduled composition and rhetoric specialists.[4] This reverse method of devising curriculum—starting with market analysis rather than with tradition or with disciplinary expertise or with the fact that process-driven writing courses might be less successfully delivered on ITV than lecture-driven courses—increases tension between faculty and administrators over curricular control.

None of the writing and rhetoric classes taught on Teletechnet has had fewer than 35 students; some have had 60 students (on-campus writing classes continue to be capped at 23 students). A writing-intensive course taught in fall 2000 had 180 students. The English faculty we interviewed professed strong support for increasing student access to higher education although that goal conflicts with maintaining reasonable class size. For faculty, the writing-intensive nature of the Professional Communication degree is better suited to small, highly interactive classes. For administrators, economies of scale (enrolling more students at more locations) and distribution of the product (reaching geographic areas underserved by higher education) have the highest priority (Kline).

Teacher as Content Provider Versus Teacher as Facilitator

Charlotte Gunawardena and others (Neff, Berge) encourage distance faculty to become facilitators in learner-centered classrooms and to explore the possibility of an open, contingent ethos. On the surface, this advice fits in with current composition pedagogy that advocates learner-centered classrooms and a mix of independent, interactive, and interdependent activities.

Unfortunately, it is not easy to enact a facilitator role in distance settings in which technology constructs the teacher as a dispenser of information and invites students to "time their own learning." Distance systems that require faculty to post syllabi, lecture notes, and handouts to a website before a course begins or a roster is available undermine the notion of teacher as facilitator. No doubt, a presentational mode of delivery serves the pedagogical goals of many disciplines, but it works against contemporary composition and rhetoric theory and pedagogy.

Students too often see their participation in the ITV course primarily in terms of taking "good" notes (i.e., recording whatever appears on the monitor in preparation for a standardized examination on that material). At the same time, composition and rhetoric faculty see their participation primarily in terms of directing students to challenging readings, designing stimulating writing prompts, creating opportunities for students to interact with each other across sites, monitoring the timing and pacing of classroom activities, ensuring that a range of viewpoints emerges in discussions—all of which create a learning space in which students build on what they already know. Evaluation in this context ranges well beyond standardized exams; it requires demonstrations of increased critical abilities in discussions, activities, and writings.

The tension arises when composition faculty bring a social constructionist pedagogy and a facilitative ethos into a system that promotes portable, self-contained units of instruction and independent rather than interdependent learning. In Teletechnet, the tension is exacerbated in three ways. First, because of administrative pressure to increase enrollments and legislative pressure to graduate students within short time frames, distance classes have some students who have not met prerequisites and may not be ready to participate as self-regulated learners. Students who are used to a high level of direction and structure expect the teacher to give them definitive answers. Second, being a facilitator is riskier than delivering a prepared lecture. In televised or video-streamed classes, instructors cannot close the door (as is possible in a traditional classroom), experiment with facilitating versus lecturing, and learn from their mistakes. Technicians, instructional designers, administrators, and site directors are free to watch, intervene, and judge the instructor's performance. Third, distance-education systems that develop from an economic impetus to serve more students in the least-costly manner tend toward a Fordist model with its focus on central administration, mass marketing, and a division of labor in the production process (Simonson et al.).

When instructors teach face-to-face (f2f) classes in mediated rooms or computer labs, they can rely on the more adept students to work with the novices at their workstations, and classmates are usually happy to help out. This kind of collaboration supports a social constructionist pedagogy and lifts some of the pressure to "know it all" from the instructor's shoulders. But because distance-education students are usually physically isolated, it is much more difficult for them to provide each other with hands-on help. Their technical support begins and ends with the instructor.

Tension is especially high in distance education when students expect the instructor to present them with an already-constructed course while faculty expect to co-construct the course with the class. When an instructor cannot enact a pedagogy that she believes best supports curricular and course goals, there may be further disconnections between her intentions and student perceptions. As a result, lower teaching evaluations are a fact of life in Teletechnet courses (Dare). An immediate consequence concerns what counts as work and whose labor is rewarded. At Old Dominion, teaching evaluations determine 40 percent of a faculty member's merit raise and are part of the documentation used for promotion and tenure. When we first taught on Teletechnet, we were new, untenured hires as has been the case for many English faculty assigned to distance education. Joyce's more recent experience on tenure and promotion committees suggests that lower evaluations and hours spent to prepare distance courses (sometimes at the expense of research) do not improve a candidate's chances for tenure.

Delivery Systems Versus Instructional Practices

Curriculum designers and faculty must share an understanding of what happens in writing and rhetoric classes that are taught as media discourse, not simply delivered via "transparent" technology. This shift in focus is suggested in a statement by the Penn State Office of Distance Education: "Distance education is not simply the addition of technology to instruction; instead it uses technology to make possible new approaches to the teaching/learning process" (Distance Education). To be effective teachers of writing and rhetoric in the distance setting, faculty must consider both the merits and drawbacks of their technology options.

Teaching a televised course forces faculty to become aware of their very presence as teachers, both physical and rhetorical. Broadcast delivery pushes a teacher-fronted classroom. The technology in each studio requires instructors to spend time at a console so that they can manipulate the Internet connection, PowerPoint slides, a white board, and an overhead camera. When a class has video-streamed students as part of the enrollment, the pull to stay at the front of the room is even stronger because movement produces choppy video transmission. Instructors are also continually within students' view in f2f classrooms, and they can be just as bound to the front of the room by constraints such as tethered overhead projectors or classrooms too small to accommodate alternate configurations. But there is a profound psychological difference between these two situations. In a televised course, even students in the broadcast studio are pulled into a curious relationship with the visual image on the TV screen, which can negate the instructor's physical presence. Juanita remembers vividly the first time she looked out at the ten students in her studio "audience," expecting to meet their eyes, and discovering they were all watching her on the monitors around the studio. Students relate to the televised course in light of their prior conditioning to the broadcast medium, or what Barry Brummett calls *media logic*. Faculty become "edu-tainers"—analogs to the talk-show host or the evening news anchor. They are expected to perform engagingly, yet they are regarded passively, responded to privately, or not talked back to at all. Further, instructors cannot respond to the nonverbal rhetoric of students they cannot see. When eye contact, head nods, and other gestures cannot be attended to, the dynamic of class discussion is diminished.

Instructors who hope to shift the focus away from this "solo performance" mode employ a range of computer-based tools that promise to increase student ownership of their learning: resource-laden course websites, email for writing conferences and other correspondence, synchronous chat programs and asynchronous Internet discussion forums to facilitate discussion groups outside of broadcast time, and MOO-based writing tutorial services. These tools enable more meaningful interaction among distant students, between students and teachers, and between students and the "virtual" world around them—something that cannot be effectively managed via the broadcast medium alone. Nevertheless, faculty have to spend hours learning how to manipulate new tools, and so do the students. As Gunawardena says, "Although I was trained as an instructional designer, it was a significant challenge to plan and design a learner-controlled instructional system for the distance class, and I spent much more time designing this class than I had ever spent designing a traditional class" (61). One of our interviewees concurred: "[Teletechnet] course preparation is more involved and detailed than that for f2f classes, but it prepared me less for actual teaching" (Brooke).

Before we can direct students' attention to substantive issues related to mediated discourse in the workplace, we have to spend valuable class time helping the most skittish students learn the basic functions of the tools they must use to complete their assignments. We explain . . . and explain again; we demonstrate . . . and demonstrate again. The time that this kind of learning demands can be enormous, and we test the patience of those who already know the technology as we try to serve those who don't have a clue. The good news is that software designers are working on more user-friendly systems. The bad news is that every time we teach a course, instructional designers want us to use the latest system. The worst news is that students must learn the latest system too. Imagine that almost every semester, students must deal with a different way of getting assignments, communicating with the instructor, submitting work, completing group projects, and checking out library materials. Students spend the time learning this array of technology because they must in order to pass their courses, but their resentment often shows up on teacher evaluations.

Faculty are further challenged to work against the potentially negative impact of computer-mediation on today's approaches to writing pedagogy. Because "electronic spaces, like other spaces, are constructed within contextual and political frameworks of cultural values," Gail Hawisher and Cynthia Selfe warn us that "the use of technology can exacerbate problems characteristic of American classrooms" (137, 129). Instructional technology then *jeopardizes* the more interactive, student-centered approach to writing instruction that composition specialists have worked for years to establish. For instance, new technology will not prevent instructors who are uninformed by today's theories of composition from creating overly directive Internet discussion prompts that force students to consider only the "answers" that those instructors have in mind. They can still use e-conferences to deliver one-way directives on error correction instead of promoting two-way or group exchanges about more global concerns. And they can still rely on generic "drill-and-practice" (handbook-based) software that bears little relationship to the actual texts students are producing.

Strategies for Coping in a Technological Setting

When curricula are unilaterally developed, when classes are too large, when students and faculty are not given choices about delivery media, or when training is inadequate, everyone loses (e.g., Dallas, Dessommes, and Hendrix; Jones and O'Brien). Instead, we must develop strategies and take actions that lead to sound curricular and technological choices. The following sections contain some suggestions.

Be Informed About Best Practices and Guidelines

Faculty can use materials from many professional organizations to lobby for technology that enhances best practices in their disciplines. For example, eight regional higher education accrediting commissions are developing "Best Practices for Electronically Offered Degree and Certificate Programs." These guidelines (and accompanying questions to ask about an institution's distance program) can be downloaded from the website for the North Central Association of Colleges and Schools Commission on Institutions of Higher Education. In the section on curriculum and instruction, one guideline deemed "essential to quality distance education programs" insists that "[a]cademically qualified persons participate fully in the decisions concerning program curricula and program oversight."

The Modern Language Association (MLA) has issued both the MLA "Guidelines for Institutional Support and Access to IT for Faculty Members and Students" and the MLA "Guidelines for Evaluating Work with Digital Media in the Modern Languages." The Guidelines for Institutional Support state: "Departments and institutions should . . . provide access and support for all faculty members and students" (60). The MLA guidelines also state: "Departments and institutions should . . . appoint technical support staff knowledgeable about research and teaching in the modern languages" (60). At Old Dominion, when the assistant vice-president for Academic Technology insisted that two computers per distance site were sufficient regardless of the number of students registered at that site, faculty began lobbying to change the policy. In another instance, the instructional aide assigned to Joyce's management writing course had little knowledge of the course content, yet he was the interface with the streaming students and made judgments about which of their questions to forward to Joyce. Using MLA guidelines, Joyce has made the case that instructional assistants be knowledgeable in the subject area being taught.

Adopt a Collaborative, Interdisciplinary, Politically Aware Approach to Curriculum

In distance education, because instructional designers, engineers, computer scientists, and administrators/managers are inextricably involved in curricular decisions, curricular revision itself becomes interdisciplinary. Faculty can benefit from alternative viewpoints proposed by these stakeholders, just as they often suffer from them. Likewise, the diverse levels and kinds of knowledge that distance students bring to the classroom make alternative curricula worth investigating; for example, a "methods" curriculum such as that proposed by Scholes (theory, history, production, consumption) or a "types of knowledge" curriculum advocated by Zebroski in this book (procedural knowledge, propositional knowledge, knowledge of the social uses of language, and knowledge about life-long language use). The distinction between education and training discussed earlier can enrich distance curricula when it is openly debated by students and others who live in both worlds. We have found that professional writing programs create an excellent opportunity for English faculty to educate current and future managers about writing and rhetoric. In Joyce's management writing class, for example, students were vocal about curriculum and delivery choices available to them, and one group developed a proposal directed to the distance-education vice president at the university.

As faculty, we can inform others about the value of writing and rhetoric and their place in the curriculum. We can explain the contexts that support best practices, and we can strengthen the link between pedagogy and technology. Perhaps we can convince others of the value of hiring faculty with both pedagogical and technological credentials, faculty who can be rewarded at tenure time for such expertise.

Participate in Technology Development

To ensure that hard-won knowledge about writing pedagogy informs curricular decisions and software purchases we need to participate in IT development. Technology that supports current writing pedagogy is now available or under development. Faculty who wish to emphasize group authorship and intertextuality can investigate software such as CentraNow and InterWise, which use multiple audio to enable students to talk in a synchronous format about a text as they view that text on their individual screens.[5] J. Barrow in the Department of Computer Science at the University of South Africa has developed SuperText to help distance students organize expository writing. Barrow's goal was to design software supporting both classical and romantic models of writing and provide process support so that the software "reverses the accent on the final product typical of word processors" (19). A caveat: We must ask students about their needs, account for the time it takes students to master new technology, and reward that investment if we require it. Just as the balance between work and reward is important to us, so it is to students.

The implementation of distance education often conflicts with values traditionally associated with English studies. Going from a f2f class to a distance class is not a simple transition or adaptation of what we currently do for a different delivery system. In distance-delivery systems, many individuals in addition to the instructor have authority over curriculum and pedagogy. As we have tried to show in this chapter, what faculty advocate as an informed pedagogical and curricular stance must be counter-posed against what others advocate as an informed technological and economic stance.

Notes

1. *Intercampus remote delivery* is a term used by Alan McMeekin to identify a lecture/tutorial delivery to remote campuses using one- or two-way video and two-way audio. The Teletechnet system at Old Dominion uses such a system, which it refers to as ITV (interactive television), along with video-streaming.

2. Joel English, Collin Brooke, Lane Dare, and Dawn Hayden have taught on and studied Teletechnet.

3. For example, see Handa; Hawisher and Selfe; Hawisher, LeBlanc, Moran, and Selfe; and Lanham.

4. Literature faculty are now asked to teach required literature courses in a new B.S. program in teacher education (Pre-K–6); their commitment to that program, while trying to meet coverage needs in the English department, further constrains them from participating in Prof-Comm.

5. To preview CentraNow go to *www.centranow.com*. To preview InterWise go to *www.interwise.com*.

Works Cited

Barrow, J. "A Writing Support Tool with Multiple Views." *Computers and the Humanities* 31 (1997): 13–30.

Berge, Zane. "Changing Roles of Teachers and Learners Are Transforming the On-line Classroom." Baltimore: University of Maryland—*www.edfac.unimelb.edu.au/online-ed/mailouts/1998/aug30.html#Anchor-CHANGING*.

Brooke, Collin. Personal interview (22 September 2000).

Brummett, Barry. *Rhetoric in Popular Culture*. New York: St. Martin's P, 1994.

Dallas, Phyllis Surrency, Nancy Bishop Dessommes, and Ellen H. Hendrix. "The Distance-Learning Composition Classroom: Pedagogical and Administrative Concerns." *ADE Bulletin* 127 (Winter 2001): 55–59.

Dare, Lane. "The Cost of Technological Tensions: Is the Tail Wagging the Dog?" Conference on College Composition and Communication. Denver, 16 March 2001.

Distance Education Clearinghouse. "Some Definitions of Distance Education"—*www.uwex.edu/disted/definition.html*.

Gunawardena, Charlotte N. "Changing Faculty Roles for Audiographics and Online Teaching." *The American Journal of Distance Education* 6 (1992): 58–71.

Handa, Carolyn, ed. *Computers and Community: Teaching Composition in the Twenty-First Century*. Portsmouth, NH: Boynton/Cook, 1990.

Hawisher, Gail E., and Cynthia L. Selfe, eds. *Passions, Pedagogies, and Twenty-First Century Technologies*. Logan: Utah State UP and NCTE, 1999.

Hawisher, Gail E., Paul LeBlanc, Charles Moran, and Cynthia L. Selfe. *Computers and the Teaching of Writing in American Higher Education, 1979–1994: A History*. Norwood, NJ: Ablex, 1996.

Illinois Online Network. "Glossary of Terms"—*http://illinois.online. uillinois.edu/IONresources/glossary2.html*.

Jones, Colin, and Teresa O'Brien. "The Long and Bumpy Road to Multi-Media: Hi-Tech Experiments in Teaching a Professional Genre at Distance." *System: An International Journal of Educational Technology and Applied Linguistics* 25 (June 1997): 157–67.

Kline, Jeanie. Telephone interview (1 March 2001).

Lanham, Richard. *The Electronic Word: Democracy, Technology, and the Arts*. Chicago: U of Chicago P, 1993.

McMeekin, Alan. "Flexible Learning and Teaching and IT." Monash University Flexible Learning and Technology Conference (1 October 1988). Available online at *www.its.monash.edu.au/aboutits/its-papers/flt.shtml*.

MLA. Committee on Computers and Emerging Technologies in Teaching and Research. "Guidelines for Evaluating Work with Digital Media in the Modern Languages." *ADE Bulletin* 127 (Winter 2001): 61–62.

———. "Guidelines for Institutional Support of and Access to IT for Faculty Members and Students." *ADE Bulletin* 127 (Winter 2001): 60.

Neff, Joyce Magnotto. "From a Distance: Teaching Writing on Interactive Television." *Research in the Teaching of English* 33 (1998): 136–57.

North Central Association of Colleges and Schools, Commission on Institutions of Higher Education. "Best Practices for Electronically Offered Degree and Certificate Programs"—*www.ncahigherlearningcommission.org*.

O'Sullivan, Tim, et al. *Key Concepts in Communication and Cultural Studies, Second ed.* London: Routledge, 1994.

Roberts, Chalmers McGeagh. *How Did I Get Here So Fast?: Rhetorical Questions and Available Answers from a Long and Happy Life*. New York: Warner, 1991.

Scholes, Robert. *The Rise and Fall of English*. New Haven: Yale UP, 1998.

Simonson, Michael, Sharon Smaldino, Michael Albright, and Susan Zvacek. *Teaching and Learning at a Distance: Foundations of Distance Education*. Upper Saddle River, NJ: Merrill/Prentice Hall, 2000.

Teletechnet Distance Learning Program. Old Dominion University, Bachelor of Science in Interdisciplinary Studies, Professional Communication, 2000–2002—*http://web.odu.edu/webroot/orgs/ao/dl/teletechnet.nsf/pages/undergraduate*.

Chapter Fourteen

The Great Work
Recomposing Vocationalism and the Community College English Curriculum
Daniel Collins

Fall 1995—I am part of a committee pairing instructors from Cape Fear Community College (CFCC) in Wilmington, NC, where I teach, with representatives from the local General Electric (GE) plant. The purpose is to compare how what gets taught at CFCC coinsides with job skills necessary for successful GE plant operations in order to uncover ways in which school culture could better replicate work culture, at least with regard to GE. I am skeptical, wondering why I should turn my classes over to GE. Do they have my students' best interests in mind? Are they going to employ them satisfactorily and meaningfully for the remainder of their working days (or at least as long as my students want to work there), making sure that their later years are comfortable and, at least monetarily, worry free? If not, why bother? Why not instead teach students how the language of corporate efficiency generally works against them and how they might intervene in such discussions on their own behalf?

Reading the Mission Statement of CFCC's English department, I am struck by how it speaks to more than our students' employment status: "The English Department provides for the empowerment of students as more effective and efficient listeners, speakers, readers, writers, and critical thinkers; the enhancement of student success in other courses, in jobs and careers; and the facilitation of students' connectedness of self and others for the appreciation and understanding of diversity." This statement suggests a curriculum responsive to the lives of students. It treats students as beings enrolled in educational programs designed to make them lifelong learners through an enriched understanding of themselves in a world of others.

The cornerstone of the community college is its *rootedness* in the community of which it is a part (Brint and Karabel vi). Corporations like GE know this. They also know they can exploit ideals of community rootedness, and commercial motives partly explain their interest in CFCC in the first place. The challenge for community college English teachers is to acknowledge their investment in an institution with intimate ties to business without allowing these ties to dictate their pedagogy. Such ties can align writing and reading to business practices, imparting skills according to corporate need. English classes are vital to helping students make sense of their worlds: to see that the composition of our environments impacts who we are and how we live; to see that experience is mediated through language and that through language we can voice concerns, construct identities, and create spaces from which to struggle for what we believe to be good and possible.

Thomas Berry offers an important conceptual framework to reinforce this rootedness: *The Great Work,* roughly, the question of what it means to live productively in a world with others. Berry, a cultural historian perhaps best known for his 1988 book, *The Dream of the Earth,* believes all epochs have their challenges that become the impetus for Great Work. The Great Work of our epoch is the stewardship of our planet. Unlike the Great Books curriculum that focuses on reading canonical works of Western literature, a Great Work curriculum refers to nothing less than the revising of our lives: "The historical mission of our times is to reinvent the human—at the species level, with critical reflection, within the community of life-systems, in a time-developmental context, by means of story and shared dream experiences" (159). According to Berry, "story" refers to the ongoing narrative of human development. "Dream experience" is our collective dreaming toward a better world, "something radiant with meaning that draws us on to a further clarification of our understanding and our activity" (164). Both notions, story and dream experience, reflect an insistence on the importance of human knowledge. Often in direct conflict with profit motives, to know is to compose a world equally beneficial to all life-forms.

We do not usually talk about a community college education in terms of "story" or "dream experience." "Training," "efficiency," "excellence": this is the current, commodified discourse of school. Much of the debate surrounding the community college stems from the contested nature of the term "vocational." What vocational means determines how and what students learn. Shirley Brice Heath defines *vocational* in terms of "responding to personal, spiritual, and civic needs, as well as business changes" (231). This contextualization expands the notion of *vocation* to include more than job skills, and it provides a context with which to consider curricular change toward Great Work. A vocational education builds community and creates outlets for creative expression to produce shared understandings about our relationship with each other, with nature, and how we experience and know the world.

But such curricular redevelopment challenges institutional power alignments. Addressing curricular change, Stanley Aronowitz writes, "On what basis should this effort proceed? To specify a 'wish' list of curricular suggestions
without addressing the burning issue of governance condemns any effort to
mere abstraction" (164). Referring to community college governance, Kevin
Dougherty isolates the influence of a wide range of groups with competing
interests: local and state officials, students, school board members, community college presidents, private interest groups, local businesses and industry,
and articulation agreements with four-year institutions (8, 27, 240). Dougherty
argues:

> Most policymakers firmly believe that what is good for business is
> on the whole good for the entire community, for business constitutes
> the core of our economy and entire community. Insofar as business's
> training costs are lowered through publicly subsidized vocational edu-
> cation, business clearly benefits, but so does the community at large in
> the form of increased employment, a larger tax base, and so on. And
> even if policymakers are dubious about business, they believe that
> vocational education helps disadvantaged students by making them
> more employable. Hence, policymakers need little prompting from
> business to provide programs that very directly benefit business. (29)

Policymakers dominate the ways in which the community college is marketed as an alternative to four-year schools. Coupled with a loosely aligned
faculty with minimal power, the end result is a historically fragmented curriculum (McGrath and Spear 35). The traditional community college English
curriculum is generally comprised of a series of disjointed writing and literature
courses. What is lacking is a sense of cohesion across courses. With each course
perceived separate unto itself, teachers become isolated from each other and
their respective disciplines, and students lack a common referent to begin to
understand the nuances of academic culture (Commission 18). In lieu of such
incoherence, I advocate community college English education as Great Work.
The intent is to place education into larger social and natural contexts and orient
learning toward planetary stewardship. Students are still equipped with work-
based skills and knowledge, but also with an understanding of work in relation
to place and planet, moving toward a mutually beneficial relationship with earth
and its inhabitants, and reproducing this relationship into new cultural forms
that can be passed on to succeeding generations.

Ecological thinking calls for curricular and institutional integration. Reading and writing are not artificially separated; distinctions among composition,
literature, and creative writing do not exist. Instead, introducing students to signifying practices broadly conceived, each individual course is reading- and
writing-intensive, drawing from works of fiction and nonfiction alike. Students write and read to identify and understand personal and communal re-
sponsibilities to an emerging world, one that is working and alive. Students

engage questions of place and culture, even the exploitative forces of corporate profit.

The Great Work curriculum is comprised of four courses, one per semester over the typical two-year period for an Associate's degree. The order reflects one's local environment as the starting "place" to consider our connections to each other and to our surroundings, moving toward more universe-oriented designs. Hence, different locales will prompt specific kinds of investigations, and different texts will be more appropriate to certain geographical areas. The Great Work provides a common orientation regardless of locale and texts: It asks students to engage education in relation to their desired futures and their desired future for the planet.

A Sense of Place

Toni Haas and Paul Nachtigal write: "Public schools should shoulder the responsibility as public institutions to help young people claim their identities as inhabitants of a particular place" (10). In order to provide students opportunities to discover their interconnection with their environments, community college teachers ask students to document places of interest, of value. Students narrate a sense of place according to their attachments, experiences, and so on. They illuminate "unwritten" truths nestled in potentially taken-for-granted local landscapes. Some of these illuminations will be unsettling, as when they uncover ecological disturbances or previously unnoticed forms of racism, sexism, and homophobia.

To further their research, students document oral histories, examine public records (e.g., deeds of ownership), track histories of buildings, neighborhoods, and communities—tasks designed to engender a rich understanding of the complexities of experiencing place across sometimes competing perspectives. The environmental expense of inhabiting place—the ways in which natural resources reinforce habits, agendas, and the cultural costs (identity, history, meaning) of living and working—is also explored. From mansions to shacks, monuments to speakeasies, public parades to porn shops, the coherence (Hayden 27) of place is examined.

Classes explore local bioregions (e.g., lore, custom, and knowledge that capture the nuances of specific places). Looking at landscape and cityscape descriptions within localized texts and comparing those descriptions with the state of current geophysical realities offers students a powerful sense of ongoing geographically and ecologically localized histories. Printed histories of place and projected plans for growth also provide further information to structure understanding. Locality, as such, no longer remains static.

Locality determines the teacher's choice of texts; however, certain texts might be used as theoretical frameworks or as case studies for possible emulation. These include Janisse Ray's *Ecology of a Cracker Childhood,* in which Ray tells her story along with the story of the Georgia longleaf pines;

Wallace Stenger's *Wolf Willow,* a mixture of fiction and nonfiction, history and narrative focusing on southern Saskatchewan; Eliot Wigginton's classic, *Sometimes a Shining Moment,* an account of the inception and development of the Foxfire program; Tony Hiss' *The Experience of Place,* a book that examines our sense of connection to place through examples; and John Stilgoe's *Outside Lies Magic,* a guide to understanding the history of place via a sharpened observation of mundane objects.

Students also read various creation myths and folklore to examine how cultures conceive the inception of the universe and the relationship among all forms of life. From folklore published by local presses to canonized works, students examine contested meanings of place and see themselves in their communities so that they can more insightfully question what is expected of their presence.

Composing Community

The Commission on the Future of Community Colleges, a collection of community college teachers and administrators who met in the mid-1980s to redefine the mission of community colleges into the twenty-first century, writes: "The building of community, in its broadest and best sense, encompasses a concern for the whole, for integration and collaboration, for openness and integrity, for inclusiveness and self-renewal" (7). In contrast to the corporate community of "excellence" measured by profit, the Commission envisioned the community as "not only a region to be served, but also a climate to be created" (7). Paul Theobald and Bill McKibben offer two useful definitions of community in this context. Theobald advocates for a place-conscious pedagogy that "enhance[s] the quality and feel of the relationships between people" and forwards this definition of community: "Community is a place where people who may not like each other nevertheless work together to advance the welfare of that which they hold in common" (121). McKibben agrees, positing community as "this twining of lives, this intense though not always friendly communion" (171).

To begin, students describe their sense of their community. They question place and culture: Where do you live? What is community? Do you feel a part of local communities? Which ones? How should humans organize their lives together? How can communities retain their local particularities against franchised universals? What problems exist and what remedies are available? What else should be done to make your community more responsive to the needs of its constituents? Local texts, newspaper articles, oral histories and personal interviews, contemporary scholarship, and any other visions of community provide a rhetorical framework for further discussion and analysis.

As Haas and Nachtigal describe, "Community is how we collectively create a story about our place" (21). With this definition, Haas and Nachtigal place writing and reading in line with an examination of the composition of community and the lives of our students. Character sketches designed around local citizens, short stories and poems prompted by local histories and current events, descriptive passages inspired by local landscapes—all of these will not only help students gain a deeper appreciation of local knowledges, but they will also sharpen their analytical skills as they discover the often distressingly fragmented forces that disrupt many ideals of community and ecological well-being.

Further, students are asked to identify and project the kinds of alternative communities required for doing a better job at the custodial task of Great Work. As Gerald Graff, Bill Readings, and others have argued, education engages deeply dissensual, conflictual work. There are many resources to aid these tasks. Prospective readings could include calls to action, such as Paul Loeb's *Soul of a Citizen,* or Sam Smith's *Great American Political Repair Manual,* Wendell Berry's *What Are People For,* and Daniel Kemmis' *Community and the Politics of Place.* Efforts to compose community provide students with the conceptual tools to examine the basic premises of what it means to live in a community so that the issues of the "community" in community college is used as a starting point for serious introspection into personal and collective life. In this way, students grow in their understanding of themselves and begin to comprehend both the interdependencies of public life and the disturbing imbalances reinforced by transnational global capitalism.

The Meaning of Work

As Richard M. Freeland reminds us, work, properly understood, can be a realm of "personal growth, intellectual adventure, social purpose, and moral development" (B11). *Work,* occupations and preoccupations that constitute daily actions, can and should be discussed in the context of the community college English curriculum, but under expanded perspectives, as Mark Jury explains:

> Such a curriculum should ask students to wonder about the nature of work, and about the rewards, the trials, the tribulations, the power and politics of work. It should ask them to develop a sense of the history of work in their communities. It should encourage them to ask questions about the necessity of work, of being of use, and of being used, encourage them to wonder about the impact of certain work on the land, and on the spirit. It should ask them to ask questions of their community, of their teachers, of their parents, and of themselves. In short, it should prompt them to use language to look at the world—including the world of work—critically. (236)

To investigate work, students examine local economies. What companies exist? According to what kind of hierarchies? How has this economic landscape changed over time, and what predictions are being made about the future? As the Super Wal-Mart is being built, what kind of impact—economic, social, environmental—will it have on the community? As another

Food Lion/Subway/Pizza Hut/Blockbuster stripmall is developed, what positive and negative effects rip and ripple through the community? As work creates
standards (visions of the good life) based on material gratification distant and
separate from local culture or allegiance to place (Korten 131), how are communities affected and what can we do to provide a better way?

For David Korten, *livelihood* refers to "a means of living or of supporting life" (Korten 289). Furthermore, *livelihood* "evokes images of people and
communities meeting individual and collective needs in environmentally responsible ways—a vision of a localized system of self-managing communities"
(289). Discussing careers and occupations provides a conduit to understanding
planetary systems: What materials are used in their field of work? What are
the geographical origins of their materials? Can they be produced/purchased
locally? If natural, what is the impact of their "harvest"? Are there more environmentally friendly alternatives to these resources, and if so, why aren't they used?
What sorts of recycling practices exist? What can and should be done to minimize the impact of industry on natural environs? Who is exploiting whom?
Why? What can be done about injustice? What is the demographic of workers
in their expected field of employment? What are the prospects for employment
locally and elsewhere? What quality of life exists within the field?

To answer these questions, students might explore the histories of companies, the influence of zoning laws and other land use policies, and the ecological
and economic impact of certain businesses and industries. Students might read
Bob Black's tirade against meaningless work, "The Abolition of Work." Studs
Terkel's *Working* would prove invaluable, as would Jeremy Rifkin's *The End
of Work*, John McPhee's *The Second John McPhee Reader*, and Wes Jackson's
Altars of Unhewn Stone. With work as the focus, students question how occupations can be fulfilling and enriching to the planet.

Language and Work

The study of work can meaningfully include the contextualized rhetorical practices used at their places of employment. These rhetorical practices can be
identified and critiqued for the social relations they enact in the workplace.
What communicative capacities are needed to conduct business, given predominant social relations? Is their community college education adequately
preparing them for such demands? Students analyze standard company communicative practices (memos, letters, meetings, and so on) to identify how
practices and social relations operate. Their findings can be used to critique
organizational patterns and communicative practices. Against the complexity
of their findings, students can examine how textbooks generally paint communicative practices in misleadingly broad strokes. They might also be challenged
to produce alternatives to traditional business communication practices.

Work as symbolic activity is the focus here, the effects of language on workers, environments, economies, and bioregions. Korten argues that local cultural

symbols are outdone and done in by "universal" corporate symbols: "The architects of the corporate global vision seek a world in which universalized symbols created and owned by the world's most powerful corporations replace the distinctive cultural symbols that link people to particular places, values, and human communities" (158). Korten cites Akio Morita, founder and chairman of Sony, who believes local cultures and icons should give way to those of the larger market economy. Morita, according to Korten, deems "distinctive local cultures as a trade barrier" (153). This transposition comes at high cost:

> Our cultural symbols provide an important source of identity and meaning; they affirm our worth, our place in society. They arouse our loyalty to and sense of responsibility for the health and well-being of our community and its distinctive ecosystem. When control of our cultural symbols passes to corporations, we are essentially yielding to them the power to define who we are. (158)

Given Korten's description, students catalogue their local symbolic order according to indigenous and transplanted symbols and the relative power and merit of each in their communities. What's out there? What was out there five, ten, twenty years ago? What do these changes suggest about the environmental, cultural, and economic landscape of our communities? Is this the direction the community wants and should take? If not, who is making the decisions? How can better choices be made for our security and the well-being of the planet?

The bulk of the work for this course stems from student analysis of site-specific communicative practices. Helpful supplemental materials could include Robert Bellah's *The Good Society*. Two recent texts that articulate symbolic machinations within the larger economic order are Kalle Lasn's *Culture Jam* and *No Logo* by Naomi Klein.

Conclusion

The Great Work curriculum uses the rootedness of the community college, its students, and local businesses to help students cultivate a critical sense of their respective fields, local communities, and the evolving universe. As Kurt Spellmeyer reminds us, "[O]bjects, images, ideas, and human beings, all of these become commodities when they no longer remind us of our connection to the world and to our fellow human beings—not the world and humanity in some general sense but this place where I live and the people to whom I am bound by concern, love, mutual dependence, and the power of memory" (287). The Great Work curriculum equips students with work skills while also helping them to critically engage life in their community and beyond. In terms of their respective technical fields, students acquire more developed understandings of production practices and deepened appreciation for communicative practices. Students gain understanding of day-to-day technologies (making them highly competent technicians and artisans), but they also begin to identify and understand the exploitive forces that disrupt individual and community well-being in specific settings.

With regard to their communities, students define themselves and their occupations according to the particularities of place, not merely with regard to present conditions, but in relation to prospective futures. In short, students become activist workers and citizens trained according to a very broad sense of work.

Works Cited

Aronowitz, Stanley. *The Knowledge Factory: Dismantling the Corporate University and Creating True Higher Learning*. Boston: Beacon P, 2000.

Bellah, Robert, et al. *The Good Society*. New York: Vintage Books, 1992.

Berry, Thomas. *The Great Work: Our Way into the Future*. New York: Bell Tower, 1999.

Berry, Wendell. *What Are People For?* San Francisco: North Point P, 1990.

Black, Bob. "The Abolition of Work." *The Abolition of Work and Other Essays,* 17–33. Port Townsend, WA: Loompanics Unlimited, 1986.

Brint, Steven, and Jerome Karabel. *The Diverted Dream: Community Colleges and the Promise of Educational Opportunity in America, 1900–1985*. New York: Oxford UP, 1989.

Commission on the Future of Community Colleges. *Building Communities: A Vision for a New Century*. Washington, DC: American Association of Community and Junior Colleges, National Center for Higher Education, 1988.

Dougherty, Kevin J. *The Contradictory College: The Conflicting Origins, Impacts, and Futures of the Community College*. Albany: SUNY P, 1994.

Freeland, Richard M. "The Practical Path, Too, Can be High-Minded." *The Chronicle of Higher Education* (15 September 2000): B11.

Haas, Toni, and Paul Nachtigal. *Place Value: An Educator's Guide to Good Literature on Rural Lifeways, Environments, and Purposes of Education*. Charleston, WV: ERIC, 1998.

Hayden, Dolores. *The Power of Place: Urban Landscapes as Public History*. Cambridge: MIT P, 1995.

Heath, Shirley Brice. "Work, Class, and Categories: Dilemmas of Identity." *Composition in the Twenty-First Century: Crisis and Change*. Eds. Bloom, Lynn Z., Donald A. Daiker, and Edward M. White. Carbondale, IL: Southern Illinois UP, 1996. 226–42.

Hiss, Tony. *The Experience of Place*. New York: Vintage, 1991.

Jackson, Wes. *Altars of Unhewn Stone: Science and the Earth*. San Francisco: North Point P, 1987.

Jury, Mark. "Widening the Narrowed Paths of Applied Communication: Thinking a Curriculum Big Enough for Students." *Changing Work, Changing Workers: Critical Perspectives on Language, Literacy, and Skills*. Ed. Glynda Hull. Albany: SUNY P, 1997. 214–45.

Kemmis, Daniel. *Community and the Politics of Place*. Norman: U of Oklahoma P, 1992.

Klein, Naomi. *No Logo: Taking Aim at the Brand Bullies*. New York: Alfred A. Knopf, 2000.

Korten, David. *When Corporations Rule the World*. West Hartford: Kumarian, 1996.

Lasn, Kalle. *Culture Jam: How to Reverse America's Suicidal Consumer Binge—And Why We Must*. New York: Morrow/Avon, 2000.

Loeb, Paul. *Soul of a Citizen: Living with Conviction in a Cynical Time*. New York: St. Martin's P, 1999.

McGrath, Dennis, and Martin B. Spear. *The Academic Crisis of the Community College*. Albany: SUNY P, 1991.

McKibben, Bill. *The Age of Missing Information*. New York: Plume, 1992.

McPhee, John. *The Second John McPhee Reader*. New York: Noonday P, 1996.

Ray, Janisse. *Ecology of a Cracker Childhood*. Minneapolis: Milkweed, 1999.

Readings, Bill. *The University in Ruins*. Cambridge: Harvard UP, 1996.

Rifkin, Jeremy. *The End of Work: The Decline of the Global Labor Force and the Dawn of the Post-Market Era*. New York: Putnam, 1996.

Smith, Sam. *Sam Smith's Great American Political Repair manual: How to Rebuild Our Country So the Politics Aren't Broken and Politicians Aren't Fixed*. New York: Norton, 1997.

Spellmeyer, Kurt. " 'Too Little Care': Language, Politics, and Embodiment in the Life-World." *Rhetoric in an Antifoundational World: Language, Culture, and Pedagogy*. Eds. Michael Bernard-Donals and Richard R. Glejzer. New Haven: Yale UP, 1998. 254–91.

Stenger, Wallace. *Wolf Willow: A History, a Story, and a Memory of the Last Plains Frontier*. New York: Penguin, 1990.

Stilgoe, John. *Outside Lies Magic: Regaining History and Awareness in Everyday Places*. New York: Walker and Company, 1998.

Terkel, Studs. *Working: People Talk About What They Do and How They Feel About What They Do*. New York: New P, 1997.

Theobald, Paul. *Teaching the Commons: Place, Pride, and the Renewal of Community*. Boulder: Westview P, 1997.

Wigginton, Eliot. *Sometimes a Shining Moment: The Foxfire Experience (Twenty Years Teaching in a High School Classroom)*. New York: Doubleday, 1986.

Chapter Fifteen

Service Learning as the New English Studies

Ellen Cushman

In Spring 1998, Edward Zlotkowski, editor of the American Association of Higher Education's series on service learning, spoke to professors and graduate students at UC Berkeley about the rising popularity of community literacy projects in the university. He listed the many professional organizations and fields in the hard and soft sciences and the humanities that have adopted outreach initiatives in their efforts to revitalize intellectual work. When asked if English departments had developed these programs, Professor Zlotkowski noted that the National Council of Teachers of English had teamed with AAHE to produce *Writing the Community* (Adler-Kassner). However, when Professor Zlotkowski approached representatives from the Modern Language Association (MLA) to ask them to co-sponsor a proposal for a book in the service-learning series, the MLA representatives refused his offer. Their reasoning: They did not see enough scholarly interest in outreach among the professors they represented. This lack of interest in community literacy and service-learning programs among literary scholars occurs at a time when the field of English studies grapples to redefine itself in the face of employment cutbacks, overreliance on part-time labor, and pressure for accountability from students, administrators, and legislators. This lack of interest also occurs at a time when the MLA job market shifts away from tenure-track jobs for literature specialists toward tenure-line jobs for Ph.D. holders in rhetoric, composition, and professional writing. What values might contribute to this lack of interest in community literacy initiatives? What have revision models for English studies done to alter these values? How might service-learning initiatives present alternative revisions for English studies?

The Spring 2001 *MLA Newsletter* reveals trends that many in English studies find disturbing: "The three major subfields of English—British Literature,

American Literature, and Rhetoric and Composition—each claim roughly 20 percent shares of the job listings" (6). Since Ph.D. programs in rhetoric and composition often lead to more individuals having Ph.D.s in professional writing, jobs in technical and professional writing can be legitimately added to the number of jobs listed in rhetoric and composition. Thus, job listings that deal with the production of language have the largest share of the market— 23 percent in 1997, 28 percent in 1998, and 25.4 percent in 1999.

Some may be tempted to view these statistics as evidence for the growing vocationalization of English. Administrators have been more inclined in recent years to open tenure-track lines in English departments to new hires able to train students in the production of texts. Anyone who might make such a claim though has an incomplete understanding of the types and kinds of rhetoric and composition research taking place. Rather than simply imparting literacy skills that are indeed useful in the workplace, much research in rhetoric and composition engages students in the critique and appropriation of literacy practices necessary to influence and change workplaces and communities from within (Porter, Sullivan, Blythe, Grabill, and Miles; Sullivan and Porter; Flower, Long and Higgins; Prior; Geisler). In important ways, scholars in these fields have taken "the social turn" in the university as a serious call for redefining the role of the English scholar and the institution of English studies.

The Stakes of English Studies

In *Language and Symbolic Power*, Bourdieu uses economic terminology to describe cultural practices as complex exchanges of forms of capital (e.g., economic, cultural, and symbolic). Sustaining any field such as English studies, according to Bourdieu, demands that "all participants must believe in the game they are playing, and in the value of what is at stake in the struggles they are waging" (Thompson 14). When the field has overproduced individuals trained in a highly specialized cultural capital, the value of that cultural capital is reduced, leaving many players to question the value of the game played.

But the fields of English literary studies are also being questioned by those who back the game—legislators, taxpayers, alumni, and university administrators. "[O]ne forgets that authority comes to language from outside.... Language at most *represents* this authority, manifests and symbolizes it" (Bourdieu, *Language* 109). The authority of specialized academic discourses has been questioned by many of those who economically support the game. This in mind, Bourdieu's following statement takes on foreboding importance: "[C]ould rites of institution ... exercise their power if they were not capable of giving at least the appearance of meaning, a purpose, to those ... without a purpose ... quite simply, some importance ... ?" (126)

In valuing English studies, representatives of the field often weigh the *cultural currency* of some areas of English studies as more worthy than others.

The jobs available to new Ph.D. recipients indicate the growing schisms in English as subfields vie for and gain differing amounts of cultural capital. The schisms aren't simply represented in economic terms but also reflect the ability of any subfield of English to give at least the appearance of meaning, a purpose to those who engage in it, and to those who resource the game. When the cultural currency of a knowledge is reduced, a parallel reduction takes place in the symbolic power for the bearers of this knowledge. This downward spiral shakes the rites of the institution to exercise their power. The crisis of English studies as seen in the current job market is an identity crisis as much as an economic one.

Worthy Texts

The Spring 2001 *MLA Newsletter* lays open the lopsided discrepancies in the profession.

- In 1998, 47 percent of the listings sought candidates who studied the production of texts (45 percent of the listings sought candidates from literary studies).

- In 1999, 46.1 percent of the listings were in text-production related fields, as opposed to the 45.2 percent for literary studies.

- In 2000, 45 percent of the jobs listed were in text-production areas, while 46.3 percent were in literature (4).

At first blush, these statistics might give literary scholars some comfort. After all, almost half the jobs listed for the past three years were related to literary studies, and both British and American literature have seen increases in positions available. On the other hand, for roughly every two jobs that were created for the study of text consumption between 1997 and 2001, three jobs were created for the study of text production (media and communication, technical and professional writing, and rhetoric and composition).

The market for literature Ph.D.s has been oversaturated since before 1990 with the number of degree holders produced far outnumbering the number of available positions (see *MLA Newsletter,* Figure 4, p. 5). In 1997, for example, English departments produced roughly 1,175 Ph.D.s in English Language and Literature as reported by the National Center for Education Statistics ("Digest" 298). In 1997, only 694 *total* positions were available. Of those 694 positions, 271 were in British, American, and multiethnic literatures—271 jobs for 1,175 literary studies graduates. Rhetoric and composition continue to underproduce people with Ph.D.s for its demand. In 1997, 139 Ph.D.s were granted, but 161 of the job listings were in rhetoric and composition (298).

Although these statistics may not present a rationale for revising English studies in light of service-learning initiatives, they alert us to the lopsided emphasis of Ph.D. programs and signal the need for a more comprehensive study of English. Bérubé, Bérubé and Nelson, and James Berlin have proposed revising English studies toward cultural studies and social-epistemic rhetoric, respectively. While these proposals revise a notion of what counts as a text and context worth studying, they also replicate problematic epistemological values of traditional English scholars, especially in how they perceive students' critical abilities and replicate disciplinary boundaries (Cushman, "Beyond"). In other words, English departments continue to value the consumption of literary texts even though this kind of cultural capital leads to little symbolic or material capital for those who chose to interpret them.

Despite the need for more comprehensive English studies, and though some literature professors do question the value of interpreting literary texts, the MLA convention persistently offers the preponderance of program space to literary studies. Even though more than one-quarter of the MLA job listings in the past two years have been in areas that study the production of meaning, these areas were not included in relative proportion in the MLA's "calls for papers" for the 2000 MLA conference in Washington, D.C. Of 540 proposed sessions for the 2000 convention, 507 concerned the study of literary texts. Should one claim that the MLA convention need not represent other areas of English because the Conference on College Composition and Communication (CCCC) does, let me point out that the CCCC originated precisely because those interested in the study of text production could not and still cannot find space on the program at the MLA.

The inordinate value placed on literary texts in English departments has its roots, as Gerald Graff finds, in the period between 1875 to 1915, a burgeoning when "[t]he new professionalism could not have succeeded had it not accorded with a new national respect for progressive claims of science, specialization, and expertise" (64). During the 1900s when English departments established a canon of literary texts to be read as a prerequisite to college admission (Cain 99), the generalist professor of English begrudgingly gave way to experts who specialized in one specific area of the literary canon.

Although multiculturalism and postmodernism have challenged the value of the Dead White Male canon, MLA's call for papers for its 2001 convention illustrated how engrained the canons of literary studies are. The call was divided into areas of literary study—American, Comparative, English, French, German, Hispanic, and so on. These may better represent diverse literatures and perspectives, but they still index the value placed on the canons. The specialization still present in English studies works from two assumptions: One, English departments can afford to maintain the coverage model of literary studies even as this model garners departments few new positions. Carol Christ, vice chancellor and provost at UC Berkeley, states: "Departments must have a cogent, focused, long-range view of the field. It is no longer very convincing . . . to argue 'we just lost our Victorian Poetry person, we need to hire another faculty member in Victorian Poetry.' . . . It is no longer adequate to use a coverage model to argue for faculty positions" (56). The second assumption behind canons of literary study is that these specialists will value the consumption and interpretation of literary texts as opposed to the production of texts. James Berlin summarizes the work of Graff and Scholes in order to demonstrate "the invidious distinctions that privilege the study of literary texts over the study of other texts and text interpretation over text production" (85). Professors of literary studies have organized themselves around the canons of texts through a methodology based on interpretation and appreciation of these texts. This form of English studies has low market value when it comes time to find a stable position in English departments.

As I consider the market value of jobs in the field, I may be accused of being crassly materialist, or simply and wholeheartedly yielding to commercial values placed on working skills, or reducing the field of English studies to its least common denominator—vocationalism. Such claims not only ignore the very real ways that English studies is socially organized, and a socializing organization, but also ignore the precarious and compromised positions into which degree holders have been and continue to be placed.

Consuming Worthy Texts from a Discreet Distance

In the nineteenth century, Mathew Arnold helped to articulate a set of dispositions that to some degree still influence the work of many literary scholars. According to Thomas Miller, "Arnold turned writing literature to presenting it as 'a criticism of life,' a criticism that is essentially characterized by its *disinterestedness*. ... Arnold stressed that the critic 'must keep out of the region of immediate practice in the political, social humanitarian sphere ... because criticism requires the perspective of a 'spectator' who is 'disinterested'" ([emphasis his], 269). If disinterest in the practical and political earmark the critical stance of many literary scholars in the past century, few have the luxury to adopt this unengaged position today. In the case of Arnold, he occupied the unenviable position of an English school inspector when England was revising the structures of funding for schools. Arnold opposed the Revised Code but failed to influence the decision makers. This "revised code" significantly altered Arnold's job, which was originally one of advocacy for schools, into a job that placed him in the role of judging schools that were required to administer tests to determine school funding levels (R. Miller 69–72).

> Ultimately, then, Arnold's turn to criticism ... —coming, as it does, in the wake of his failure to influence the shape of the country's education policy—must be seen both as an act of despair and as evidence of how overwhelmingly seductive it can be to believe that in a better world, criticism alone would have the power to bring about cultural change. (75)

Arnold's argument for a disinterested scholar came when he despaired that a scholar could make a difference in education policy. Such an argument provided him with a coping mechanism against the political impotence he faced, a way to rationalize his withdrawal from daily politics into the comfort of high-minded criticism, and "a dream of inverted social relations that Arnold was in no position to bring about" (75). His critical position, thus, removed him from "the arts of engaged response, of compromise, of multivocal persuasion" that rhetoricians practice as a matter of course (75).

For too long, many literary scholars have produced literary criticism for the sake of advancing their narrow specializations. The problem now is that English professors have not been accountable to public spheres—few have attempted to make this knowledge relevant, accessible, or responsive to public concerns. Some scholars in English studies, particularly from multiculturalism and cultural studies, have helped redefine what counts as a text and context worthy of study, and thus have tried to make English studies more relevant to larger publics. Yet, fundamentally, Arnoldian assumptions remain entrenched even in these lines of work. For example, multiculturalism opened up American literary canons to African American, Latino/a American, and Native American writers, but canons or subcanons of ultraspecialized selections of writers have replicated the values of traditional literary canons. The canons of literary study may be more inclusive as a result of multiculturalism, an impressive accomplishment, but canon reproduction remains intact around the core values of consuming texts, maintaining a disinterested critical stance, and the interpretation of a select, though more inclusive, set of authors.

Although there are a handful of scholars who are noteworthy exceptions, according to Aronowitz:

> [I]n general, multiculturalism as both a slogan and an intellectual practice has signified integration and subordination into the prevailing disciplinary construction of American academic knowledge. On the whole, the movement no longer constitutes an alternative perspective on Western civilization and its history. It may thus be argued that by mainstreaming themselves, women's, ethnic, and African-American studies have become ordinary academic departments and programs. (132)

The multiculturalism movement has relegated much of its intellectual vitality and political power by too closely replicating the traditional forms of knowledge making. Many subaltern theorists have developed and argued for a jargon-laden publication style that reaches only select audiences initiated in the "correct" political theory. Some multicultural scholars have adopted all the trappings of the "star system," which further removes them from the daily political issues and social classes they claim to represent.

The values of narrow expertise, privileging particular texts for consumption as opposed to production, disinterestedness, and canon formation around literary criticism still permeate English literary and cultural studies. The calls for new English studies disappoint because they often replace only one arm of the discipline for an equally flawed alternative.

The "New" English Studies

In *Teaching the Conflicts* (Cain), Gerald Graff calls for a curricular shift in English studies that would engage students in the disciplinary debates and conflicts over culture (22). By Teaching the Conflicts that focus on the critical debates about the text, Graff attempts to make academe a more "legible institution" that will reduce students' alienation from academic discourse and knowledge-making practices. The work of literary critics will be demystified, less esoteric, as students engage in it.

Graff takes important strides in revising English studies in proposing this model: First he sidesteps the canon debates by proposing that, whatever the text, the "intellectual vocabularies in which . . . these texts are discussed in academic environments" should be the focus of class discussion. He bolsters the cultural currency of literary criticism by making the undergraduate classroom a market for its consumption, whereas previously that market was sustained with graduate students. Second, he shifts the focus of English studies away from the study of texts to how differing social perspectives and theoretical frameworks allow a text to be interpreted. The shift, in other words, is away from the text, to the academic interaction around the text. Finally, by asking students to become participant–observers in academic culture, Graff brings a distinctively social science methodology to the humanities.

For all the strides that are taken in Graff's proposal, limitations remain, some of which are linked back to traditional English studies' values. John Schilb has pointed out that the study of academic discursive debates over topics in many fields has been the focus of Writing Across the Curriculum (WAC) scholarship and teaching in rhetoric and composition. In this light, Graff's proposal can be critiqued in the same ways that WAC has been, namely, that students are seen as outsiders whose own discourse is devalued as they are initiated into the privileged discourse of academe. Other problems are embedded in Teaching the Conflicts model, and these center around the assumption that academic culture, texts, and literary debates are more important to study than community cultures, texts, and debates. Students are asked to become participant–observers—to adopt a methodology for study that the professors themselves are not willing to adopt in relation to students' cultures. That is, in Teaching the Conflicts, the literary professor can still remain aloof from the politics, issues, and debates taking place in students' communities.

Literature itself can be powerfully instructive when it comes time to understand the conflicts taking place in students' and community residents' daily lives. Literary works themselves still hold significant cultural currency because they illustrate how characters and players negotiate the social world. When Oprah Winfrey endorses a literary work, that piece catapults to the best-seller list not for what literary critics have said about it, but because the work, in Oprah's estimation, artfully illustrates and exemplifies life's complexity, a nuance of action, and/or a subtlety of perception. Rather than making literary works into vehicles for self-help, Winfrey's endorsements manifest the cultural worth that literary works have long held in the broader public for their ability to represent conflict resolution for communities of readers.

Imagine the possibilities that Graff's model of Teaching the Conflicts might have when fused with outreach initiatives. Conflicts could be locally situated and illustrated through literature. The interpretations and criticisms produced could help solve or lend perspective to these conflicts. The community members, students and professors could work together using various readings and produce various writings to address what all deem as the conflict under study. All participants could be exposed to and practice with various discourses, an activity that literacy scholars have suggested can facilitate crossing cultural and class borders. Various knowledges could be brought to bear in problem-solving activities without the privileging of academic knowledge above the others (see Flower).

Moving to another revision of English studies, Robert Scholes' *The Rise and Fall of English* presents a comprehensive and evenly balanced sense of a new English studies that offers students training in theory in order to understand the history, production, and consumption of texts (147). Theory would offer students "a canon of methods to be used in studying the other three aspects of textuality: how to situate a text (history), how to compose one (production), and how to read one (consumption)" (147). In this revision of English studies, the consumption of texts has been balanced with other intellectual activities now found in English departments. He includes a methodology that would allow students to understand and engage the social uses of texts. Like Graff, Scholes sidesteps the canon debates by including not only a broader conception of texts (from bumper stickers to epic poems) but also a sense of the breadth of English studies.

Despite Scholes' careful attempts to eschew indoctrination into English studies, his reconstruction of English as a discipline assumes that students haven't yet gained a textual power of their own. Critical savvy exists in communities where some would least expect to find it (Cushman, "Critical" and *The Struggle*). While English scholars can augment students' rhetorical sophistication, students do come to universities with forms of textual power. A larger issue with Scholes' model, though, rests in a presumption that textual power is anything more than ultimately an academic exercise, something that engages students in only the knowledge making and inquiry peculiar to English departments. The professor still remains disinterested in daily politics and social uses of text because the methodology of gaining textual power never asks the professor to move beyond, or outside of the discipline, to understand how textual power manifests itself in workplace and community settings.

But what if the textual-power model of English studies were to incorporate a community outreach component? One of the greatest strengths of Scholes' model—the idea that "textuality, rather than literature, [is] its principal object"—would work well with community members and students who themselves engage in many forms of textual power in their efforts to solve real-life problems. When the value of the literary is balanced with the value of literacy, the possibility of well-informed problem solving emerges, where all stakeholders are versed in multiple discourses. If theory offers common methods to be used in studying the other aspects of textuality, then again community members, students, and professors could work together to gain a flexibility in understanding and solving a problem from multiple perspectives while using the tools of text production and consumption, all with a nuanced understanding of the situation that history and theory might provide.

Graff's and Scholes' reconstructions of English studies might work well to help literary scholars reform their work in light of service learning. First, the purpose of studying the conflicts and textual power would be made abundantly clear in a community setting. Second, students, professors, and community members could share knowledges without necessarily privileging one over another. Third, various texts could be valued for both their consumption and production during problem-solving activities. And finally, the cultural currency of the knowledges produced in English studies could perhaps increase in light of its real-world relevance in new markets.

Service Learning and Literary Studies

From the perspective of many literary scholars, Scholes' and Graff's models for reforming English studies probably seem radical, but from the margin of English studies, their models can be seen as more conservative in that they avoid questions of utilitarianism and public service. These "radical" models of change for English departments still ultimately allow English professors to remain beyond secular concerns. These models for reform never ask the hard questions that students, legislators, and administrators ask of the work done in English departments: What is the purpose of English studies in society? How can the knowledge produced in English studies apply to institutional and community settings? What are we doing here? Why? And for whom?

ᵣ These questions assume that the knowledge made in English can be of service to the public, "service" of course being another dirty word in English departments (Hessler). Yet, one of the most important attacks on English studies comes from the public sector—administrators, students, and legislators. "The research mission is being de-emphasized"—Thomas Miller's polite way of saying underfunded, downsized, and harshly criticized—"because it is not seen to yield knowledge of the utilitarian value and liberal education is being held accountable to the practical needs of the world of work" (280).

To be held accountable to the practical needs of workplaces and communities, does not necessarily mean that English studies' scholars must forsake interpretative theories, history, and the consumption of texts. English studies *must* avoid simple vocational training: the uncritical, unexamined acquisition of skills that apply mechanically to workplace production and distribution of information, products, and services. However, vocationalism should be differentiated from utilitarianism and pragmatism. Utilitarian knowledge can be made and put to use by well-rounded, knowledgeable, socially conscientious students, citizens, and professors who together try to better the public and private institutions they are both critical of and reliant on. *Pragmatism* in this sense challenges the myth that disinterested, ironic, critically distant scholars can opt out of their reliance on the social economy. The most self-defeating stance that English studies' scholars can adopt is the one that ignores considerations of the economic and social worth of the cultural capital that universities produce. Any reform of English studies must consider how ultimately the knowledge made in English can be of economic and social value, can accrue cultural capital, and can help its bearers accrue symbolic capital.

Community literacy programs, often termed service-learning initiatives, provide one economically and socially viable alternative for knowledge-making practices in English studies. These initiatives have been taken up by composition and rhetoric scholars because of the ethical and civic promise that service learning holds (see Adler-Kassner, Crooks, and Watters; Flower, Long, and Higgins; Deans; Underwood et al.; Flower and Heath; Cushman "Beyond"; and the Campus Compact mission statement at *http://www.compact.org/about*). In these initiatives both the professors and students, in collaboration with nonprofit organizations and local communities, produce knowledge. In service-learning programs, students and professors spend part of class time as researchers—observers, interviewers, tutors, and participant–observers—at sites outside the university. The knowledge of all collaborators is marshaled in order to address social tensions, to inform decision makers of local problems and needs, and to bridge long-standing social and class-based schisms between universities and communities (Cushman and Emmons).

In these programs, academic knowledge and debates have equal value to other knowledges, and all knowledges play important roles in problem solving. The knowledge and skills students gain has a social and pragmatic function; while it helps students gain a foothold in the workplace upon graduation, this knowledge has been imbued with a socially just application. The students often come away from these applied learning situations with an understanding of how to change institutions from working within and against them. Most service-learning initiatives have developed in light of John Dewey's goal of facilitating the development of informed citizens (Deans). The courses' contents include readings, theories, or debates that facilitate students' understanding of local problems and needs.

Service learning not only alters the ways students gain and use knowledge, but the ways professors do as well. Because service learning works best when real social problems or issues have been targeted, service learning demands an interdisciplinary, broad range of theories, texts, history, and means of producing meaning. These initiatives cannot rely solely on highly specialized knowledge production because of the nature of the problem-solving tasks at hand (Cushman, "Critical"). Professors in service-learning initiatives must command and flexibly apply multiple forms of academic knowledge if they hope to establish a sustainable program. The knowledge production in these initiatives thus appeals to multiple audiences and fields, both inside and outside of academe. The actual day-to-day work and institutional roles of professors align more with public intellectuals who serve various publics.

The research, teaching, and service roles of professors potentially dovetail together well with service learning, thus leveling the traditional hierarchy among professional duties (Cushman "The Public"). Although these roles can become mutually sustaining, Underwood et al. find that engaging in research is the most difficult aspect of service learning to achieve because the teaching and service administration demand so much of the scholar's time. The research and methodology arms of community literacy have yet to be well integrated into many community literacy programs begun in composition and rhetoric. Without such an integration of the research and methods, the institutional sustainability of these initiatives, the stability of the professor's position, and the quality of students' experiences can be compromised.

Even though few guidelines exist for evaluating service-learning initiatives, a 1996 Michigan State University committee of college deans, professors, and administrators from the Office of the Provost developed *Points of Distinction: A Guidebook for Planning and Evaluating Quality Outreach,* which defined four areas of assessment for community literacy programs: significance, context, scholarship, and impact. *Scholarship* is defined as a major indicator of an outreach program's sustainability and includes a survey of the stakeholders' knowledge resources, applications, generation, and utilization (22–23). *Context* includes the appropriateness of methodological approach, among other indicators (20–21). *Impact* assesses the depth of relations developed by stakeholders, the extent of the collaboration, and the scope of learning and service. Thus, scholarship is the key component for administrative assessment of community literacy initiatives, with teaching and service seen as necessary, though tertiary, aspects of the program. Unfortunately, many of the outreach initiatives developed by composition and rhetoric scholars, with a few notable exceptions, have not yet integrated research and methods into the teaching and service components of the work.

While there are few examples of service learning in literary studies, Professors Teresa Tavormina and Jenny Banks at Michigan State University have developed a new initiative called the Life Reading Project, which presents interesting possibilities for outreach and literary studies:

> The Life Reading Project is an academic service-learning opportunity in which participating MSU students will discuss the human issues raised by literature with off-campus community groups, and share the insights gained from these discussions with other MSU students at the end of the term. The readings will be chosen from syllabi of selected MSU English literature courses each semester.

Students read books chosen from the professors' course syllabi in small discussion groups formed with community members in retirement and community centers in the area of Okemos and East Lansing. The professors often choose not to be present at these meetings, not because of Arnoldian disinterestedness but sensitivity to the nature of the group's work. Banks and Tavormina "try not to be present for the actual discussions of the literary works (so that the groups become real book groups, not miniature 'classes')" [her aside, personal communication]. When attending a meeting, they stay in the background, as one student observed in his reflective journal:

> It was felt that should a professor be present . . . the community members and students [might defer] to the knowledge and experience of the professors in the subject matter, and thus creat[e] an 'expert' among the group members and undermin[e] the feeling of equality within the group. It was decided, however, to forego this worry and have Professor Tavormina present anyway, though she expressed the desire to stay in the background for the meeting." *(www.msu.edu /~tavrmina/LRPjnls 1FS00.htm)*

Rather than making the expert professor the center of the collaboration, Banks and Tavormina opted to facilitate the interactions without directing them. In this sense, their work is in line with many of the community literacy initiatives in composition and rhetoric.

The question remains though: How would literature-based community literacy initiatives contribute to the knowledge-making processes of literary scholars? Literary interpretation in the community literacy projects would also need to be a decentered, collaborative process in which the expert isn't the center or broker of the interpretative process. The products that emerge from such a process would likely shift the critical lens away from scholars' interpretations of a text, and recenter it on, perhaps, the multiple and competing interpretations produced by collaborators. Another shift in knowledge production might involve accounting for the roles that literature played in ameliorating a current social problem. Although Tavorima finds, in her position, that she need not link her research to the Life Reading Project, "it may be that not tying a service-learning project to one's research and eventual publication is a luxury more easily engaged in by tenured faculty" (personal communication). This would seem to be the case at present for full professors, but if these projects are to obtain sustainability and garner appropriate rewards by the university, research will eventually need to be added to community literacy projects, especially as more and more assessment measures of these programs that emphasize research are developed. In any event, literary scholarship that was centered around community literacy projects would call for an understanding of literature not solely as object, but as central to experience: literature as read and lived.

Service-learning and community literacy initiatives represent one kind of scholarly endeavor in rhetoric and composition that revises English departments from within their institutional structures by allowing professors and students to: (1) Make knowledge in what John Schilb calls "socially responsible ways"; (2) collaborate with community members and nonprofit organizations to create knowledge together in order to address social issues; and (3) engage in the methods, history, theory, and literacy practices needed to earn a living as socially responsible, knowledgeable, and active citizens. Although service learning may well present one means of revising the discipline of English studies, few debates about the new English studies consider how community literacy initiatives might contribute to the cause.

It may well be that service learning continues to remain at the margins of English studies because these initiatives fly in the face of so many traditional social values and dispositions of English studies' scholars. The knowledge in community literacy is self-reflexively applied; it's of service to communities and students; it's self-consciously aware of its cultural and economic value. Scholars maintaining community literacy projects are involved in the common lives of community members; they're simultaneously researchers, teachers, and servants who work across disciplines. Even in the brightest manifestos for the reform of English studies, few imagine the kinds of radical shifts in knowledge-making practices encompassed in community literacy projects.

Service learning demands that English professors adapt their previous dispositions, which is no easy task. It is no coincidence that service learning in English studies is developing in rhetoric and composition, a field that has been and continues to be marginalized in English studies. Thomas Miller, in tracing the history of the marginalization of rhetoric and composition argues that "the borders of the educated culture have been its most dynamic area of development" (280). Judging from both the marginalization and popularity of service-learning initiatives, it might be high time for English studies scholars to look to the borders of the field for change. In the meantime, those of us who occupy this marginalized position have redirected our energies away from "challenging the marginalization of rhetoric and composition within English departments" to "exploiting that position to broaden the base of the humanities" (Thomas Miller 281). For many on the border, service learning as the new English studies enacts our hopes for civic-minded scholarship, teaching, and service.

Works Cited

Adler-Kassner, Linda, Robert Crooks, and Ann Watters, eds. *Writing the Community.* Urbana, IL: NCTE, 1997.

Aronowitz, Stanley. *The Knowledge Factory.* Boston: Beacon P, 2000.

Berlin, James A. *Rhetorics, Poetics, and Cultures.* Urbana, IL: NCTE, 1996.

Bérubé, Michael. *The Employment of English.* New York: New York UP, 1998

Bérubé, Michael, and Cary Nelson. *Higher Education Under Fire: Politics, Economics, and the Crisis of the Humanities.* New York: Routledge, 1995.

Bourdieu, Pierre. *Language and Symbolic Power.* Cambridge: Harvard UP, 1991.

———. *The Logic of Practice.* Stanford, CA: Stanford UP, 1990.

Cain, William E., ed. *Teaching the Conflicts: Gerald Graff, Curricular Reform and the Culture Wars.* New York: Garland Publishing, 1994.

Christ, Carol. "Retaining Faculty Lines." In *Profession 1997,* 54–60. New York: MLA, 1997.

Cushman, Ellen. "Beyond Specialization: The Public Intellectual, Outreach, and Rhetoric Education." *Rhetoric Education in the Twenty-First Century University.* Ed. Joseph Petraglia. Albany: SUNY P, in press.

———. "Critical Literacy and Institutional Language." *Research in the Teaching of English* 33.3 (1999): 245–74.

———. "The Public Intellectual, Activist Research, and Service-Learning." *College English* 61.1 (1999): 68–76.

———. *The Struggle and the Tools: Oral and Literate Strategies in an Inner City Community.* Albany: SUNY P, 1998.

Cushman, Ellen, and Chalon Emmons. "Contact Zones Made Real." *Literacy in the Community and Workplace.* Eds. Glynda Hull and Katherine Shultz. New York: Teachers College, in press.

Deans, Tom. *Writing Partnerships: Service-Learning in Rhetoric and Composition.* Urbana, IL: NCTE, 2000.

Digest of Education Statistics. "Table 258: Degrees Conferred by Institutions of Higher Education, by Sex of Student and Field of Study: 1996–1997." *National Center for Education Statistics* (30 Oct. 2000)—*http://nces.ed.gov/pubsearch.*

Flower, Linda. "Partners in Inquiry: A Logic for Community Outreach" In Adler-Kassner et al., 95–118.

Flower, Linda, Eleanor Long, and Lorraine Higgins. *Learning to Rival: A Literate Practice for Intercultural Inquiry.* Mahwah, NJ: Erlbaum, 2000.

Flower, Linda, and Shirley Brice-Heath. "Drawing on the Local: Collaboration and Community Expertise." *Language and Learning Across the Disciplines* 4:3 (October 2000): 43–56.

Geisler, Cheryl. *Academic Literacy and the Nature of Expertise: Reading, Writing, and Knowing in Academic Philosophy.* Mahwah, NJ: Erlbaum, 1994.

Graff, Gerald. *Professing Literature.* Chicago: University of Chicago P, 1987.

———. *Teaching the Conflicts.* New York: Garland, 1994.

Hessler, Brooke. "Composing and Institutional Identity: The Terms of Community Service in Higher Education." *Language and Learning Across the Disciplines* 4.3 (October 2000): 27–43.

Miller, Richard. *As If Learning Mattered.* Ithaca, NY: Cornell UP, 1998.

Miller, Thomas. *The Formation of College English.* Pittsburgh: U of Pittsburgh P, 1997.

MLA Newsletter. Phyllis Franklin, ed. 33.1 (Spring 2001): 4–5.

Points of Distinction: A Guidebook for Planning and Evaluating Quality Outreach. Michigan State University: Office of the Provost, 1996.

Porter, James, Patricia Sullivan, Stuart Blythe, Jeffrey Grabill, and Libby Miles. "Institutional Critique: A Rhetorical Methodology for Change." *College Composition and Communication* 51.4 (June 2000): 610–43.

Prior, Paul. *Writing/Disciplinarity.* Mahwah, NJ: Erlbaum, 1998.

Scholes, Robert. *The Rise and Fall of English.* New Haven: Yale UP, 1998.

Sullivan, Patricia, and James Porter. *Opening Spaces: Writing Technologies and Critical Research Practices.* Norwood, NJ: Ablex, 1997.

Tavormina, Teresa, and Jenny Banks. "Life Reading Project." Michigan State University—*www.msu.edu/~tavrmina/LRP.htm.* 2/14/01.

Thompson, John. "Editor's Introduction." In Bourdieu, *Language and Symbolic Power.*

Underwood, Charles, Mara Welsh, Mary Gauvain, and Sharon Duffy. "Learning at the Edges: Challenges to the Sustainability of Service Learning in Higher Education." *Language and Learning Across the Disciplines* 4.3 (October 2000): 7–27.

Chapter Sixteen

Collaborative Learning Networks
A Curriculum for the Twenty-first Century

James J. Sosnoski, Patricia Harkin, and Ann Feldman

A Collaborative Learning Network (CLN) brings together a group of teachers–learners who pursue a specific inquiry and share their research expertise and resources through technology. In the curriculum, topics that would ordinarily be covered in a course are designed as projects in which students collaborate in the research. These projects move students out of the classroom into nearby neighborhoods and virtual environments.

Collaborative Learning Network curricula differ from typical curricula in two major respects. First, CLN courses go beyond the boundaries of the host department and the university. The traditional arrangement is that each department offers courses with syllabi, readings, and assignments that differ from overlapping courses in neighboring departments. In a CLN arrangement, departments work in concert with each other to design courses that count for credit in both programs and that can be taught by faculty in either one. Second, the curriclum addresses problems that concern various sectors of society.

We focus our descriptions of CLNs at the University of Illinois at Chicago (UIC), beginning with Jim Sosnoski's work on the Virtual Harlem project, which stands as a model for Collaborative Learning Networks using new learning technologies. Next, Patricia Harkin establishes a network that brings a (UIC) language, literacy, and rhetoric Program in touch with the changing circumstances of career outcomes. We then describe Ann Feldman's work to establish a partnership network in an introductory writing program.

Technology Networks: The Harlem Renaissance Project

Imagine a series of broadband, Internet II technology centers in Harlem, New York, giving access not only to the information highway at astonishing speeds but also to various cultural events. In those centers, imagine a room into which you enter into a virtual-reality scenario that is a historical replica of Harlem during the 1930s at the height of the Harlem Renaissance. Imagine courses at your university linked to these centers where students studying the poetry of Langston Hughes, the novels of Zora Neal Hurston, or the politics of Marcus Garvey can listen to their avatars talk about their work. Imagine students walking down the streets of Harlem in 1934, entering the Cotton Club to listen to Louis Armstrong's band.

What you have just imagined is a CLN focused on the Harlem Renaissance that links courses taught in schools at every level, including the Sorbonne in Paris, and universities in Amsterdam and Tokyo, to public cultural centers around the world. To date, twenty blocks of Harlem as it existed during the mid-1930s has been reconstructed in virtual reality. Bryan Carter, who conceived the Virtual Harlem project at the University of Missouri, writes:

> It is my dream to use virtual reality to enable students to become more than passive receptors of information, so common in many literature courses. . . . Currently, students are able to navigate the environment, examine storefronts, . . . and hear the sounds normally associated with a busy city. They can also hear some of the music written and pop-ularized during the period. In future phases, students will . . . be able to go inside various establishments, peer into windows, eavesdrop on conversations, interact with various historical characters by asking questions or having them recite a portion of a poem or speech, ex-plore Harlem at night and be exposed to . . . the musical culture that emanated from the Renaissance.
>
> While students are inside a particular establishment, we are now able to project videotaped images within the building so that we will be able to see a cabaret show, a choir singing or a street-corner debate. We have a motion platform that we will be able to incorporate into this environment so that students will be able to ride the trolley that circles "Virtual Harlem." And, finally, we are constructing a blue-screen set that will enable us to insert, within a virtual environment, anyone or anything we wish. Imagine being able to introduce students to his-torical figures personally within the virtual environment. I typically take my classes to the Virtual Environment Instructional Lab (VEIL) three to four times per semester in conjunction with a novel that we are reading at the time.

The Advanced Technology Center at the University of Missouri and the Electronic Visualization Lab at UIC are now jointly developing this project. It is, in part, collaborative research among groups at these two technology centers and others at the University of Arizona and Columbia University. At UIC, the Virtual Harlem team includes faculty and graduate students from the Electronic Visualization Lab, computer science, communication, fine arts, and, of course, the English as well as the African American studies departments. The other groups are similarly cross-departmental.

In 2001, Bryan Carter team-taught a course at Central Missouri on the Harlem Renaissance with Jennifer Brody, a professor in English and African-American studies at UIC. Their students supplied materials for incorporation in the virtual-reality scenario to a fine arts graduate student who is the main programmer for the project at UIC. Students from computer science and communication studied the pedagogical aspects of the course. They interviewed Bryan and his students using the video-conferencing equipment. These students took courses in the English department to learn about rhetorical analysis, narratology, and ethnography. Several creative writing students in Bryan's course at Central Missouri wrote narratives based on people living in Harlem during the twenties and thirties.

We are working with Chicago's Harlan High School to provide their students with access to Virtual Harlem because of their schoolwide theme—the "Harlan" Renaissance—which is based on various studies of the Harlem Renaissance. Similarly, we are working with Seaton Academy and the Duncan YMCA to provide similar access to Virtual Harlem. In addition, we are planning to hold a conference on the Harlem Renaissance at UIC, featuring work by students from Chicago high schools. Although these connections have been initiated, we are a long way from becoming a fully collaborative network. The long-range goal of Virtual Harlem–CLN is to establish a prototype for linking Chicago's various learning institutions together to share cultural resources.

The project is, however, not limited to Chicago institutions. Bruce Lincoln at Columbia University is planning to provide a Virtual Harlem hookup in technology centers to be built in Harlem. Soon classes in the English department at the University of Arizona, through collaboration with their Visualization Lab, will join the learning network. We plan to include Harlem Renaissance scholars from all over the world in the Virtual Harlem–CLN project.

This type of networked-learning environment, which conjures up the idea of McLuhan's global schoolhouse, can be accessed by students in schools and soon, perhaps, in some homes on virtual-reality theaters. If such global schoolhouses are the wave of the future, then we have to begin preparing faculty and students by designing curricula that take the following features of Collaborative Learning Networks into account: flexible spatial locations, flexible temporal parameters, reversible learner/teacher roles, modeling real problems in virtual states, on-the-job working circumstances, emphases on techniques of articulation and communication rather than on content, knowledge domain exchanges driven by problem solving, employment of technologies commonly used in business, and cost sharing between educational institutions and businesses.

These features of a technological educational environment have a number of implications for any curriculum. Curricula need no longer be designed on the assumption that a course will be taught by one person in a walled-in room on a campus at a fixed time for an invariant duration. Since the advent of electronic texts, curricula need no longer be designed on the assumption that its texts are limited to textbooks in campus bookstores or volumes in university libraries. Since computer modeling has become a standard mode of analysis, curricula need no longer be designed on the assumption that actual environments will be the only ones employed in research. Programs need no longer be designed on the assumption that persons who are not studying in that department will not have reasons to enroll in it.

Curricular experimentation like CLNs that involve distance education contrast sharply to the "professional"-ized curriculum described in this book by Joyce Neff and Juanita Comfort (see Chapter 13). They offer a critique of the exploitative ways that administrators sometimes use distance education to push conventional, content- and discipline-based courses out to more people at lower costs. In the distance-education curricula funded by UI-Online (the distance-education initiative of the University of Illinois), the emphasis is not on a shared learning experience but, rather, on delivery systems that provide accessible information for persons who wish to accredit themselves in a particular job-related area. For example, one will be able to learn about the current accounting or nursing techniques so that prospective employers will reward them with salaries at whatever level of the corporation they happen to be. If an employer wanted an employee who was acquainted with the latest version of Photoshop, then distance education is considered to be an ideal delivery system for the acquisition of that information. CLNs, on the other hand, although they often rely on the same technologies, invite the learners to contribute to ongoing research projects in various ways—as content providers, designers, programmers, artists, historians.

In contrast to both conventional classrooms and distance education, we have designed a networked curriculum at our university that takes into account three important phenomenon: (1) changes in the outcome of graduate programs required by changes in society, (2) changes in the ivory tower isolation and insulation of university learning required by changes in educational funding, and (3) changes in learning technologies required by changes in modes of communication.

We do not wish to suggest that collaborative learning units are some kind of panacea that will cure all contemporary educational needs. Like other technologies, what is programmed in by the designers is what is received by the users. If the programming does not allow for interaction, there will be no dialogue. If the programming is a-historical, there will be no diachronic dimension to the learning environment. An even more problematic aspect of electronic education environments is that they can easily be co-opted by commercial interests and turned into an industry. The browsers that make the popularity of the Internet possible have their prototype in Mosaic—a browser designed and implemented at the University of Illinois and taken over by software giants. As I write, commercial interests are watching the development of Virtual Harlem. It could happen that the Virtual Harlem project will end up as a room in Disney Quest whose links to Harlem Renaissance scholarship are severed with consequences similar to those that befell *The Scarlet Letter* in its most recent film version. We are far from evangelists for New Educational Media. We believe that strong criticism has to accompany every design, including CLNs.

The Preparing Future Faculty Project

The traditional outcome of a graduate degree in an English department is a tenurable position at a similar institution, but as the job market has changed, the Modern Language Association has begun to offer a series of sessions on "career management" at ADE summer meetings and at the MLA convention; these events were intended to get graduate students to change their idea of the "normal" outcome of their education and to begin considering positions in nonuniversity settings. This effort is also backed by Woodrow Wilson Foundation initiatives to foster internship programs, which place graduate students in a variety of local not-for-profit institutions. These changes in the expected outcome of programs housed in English departments also shift the objectives of the programs away from "fields" and "content areas" toward fostering abilities to collaborate on, articulate, and model problems that need to be addressed. UIC's Language, Literacy, and Rhetoric Program has been moving in this direction by revising graduate student preparation, especially in one of the core courses, English 501—"Introduction to Language, Literacy, and Rhetoric Methods."

The goals of these revisions are fourfold:

- *To establish partnerships* between UIC graduate students and faculty from a variety of postsecondary institutions.
- *To encourage UIC graduate students* to teach at community and local colleges.
- *To create an intellectual community* for English and writing teachers in the Chicago area.
- *To enable this community to serve as a means of counteracting the mythology* that naturalizes the value placed on earning faculty positions at research institutions.

The Preparing Future Faculty Collaborative Learning Network has the following five components:

1. *A partnership network of teaching exchanges* (called "the PFF Partners"). Three UIC graduate students, as part of their assistantships, teach at a local two- or four-year college rather than at UIC. The TA teaches courses, attends meetings at various levels of governance, and later presents a talk to the seminar (see item #2 below) on his or her experiences. In return, an administrator or faculty member from the beneficiary institutions helps

UIC prepare graduate students to teach in their choice of an environment. The TA also gets a written report from the mentor who evaluates strengths and areas to improve.

2. *A seminar on "Pedagogy and the Profession," whose members include graduate students from UIC and teachers from partner colleges.* It is a commonplace of narrative theory that a culture's "stories" teach that culture's members how to live their lives and establish their values. As many institutional historians and critics (e.g., Sosnoski, Shumway, Graff) have argued, the culture of North American graduate education in English tends to construct a romance narrative through which Ph.D. candidates learn to expect their training to culminate in positions like the ones occupied by their research professors. In that model, research is preferred to teaching so that faculty members should strive to spend as little time as possible in the classroom. This seminar will interrogate that narrative—with a view toward demonstrating that the values it embodies, while they may indeed be useful in research universities, are not universal. In Fall 2001, for example, we studied two or three "professional" narratives: a memoir, (e.g., Jane Tompkins's *A Life in School*), an institutional history (e.g., Gerald Graff's *Professing Literature,* Sharon Crowley's *Composition in the University,* Susan Miller's *Assuming the Positions,* James A. Berlin's *Rhetoric and Reality*), and an exercise in institutional critique (James Sosnoski's *Token Professionals and Master Critics,* Richard Miller's *As If Learning Mattered.*)

    Other sessions of this seminar will include a discussion by tenured or tenure-track faculty, from four-year and community colleges, who discuss their teaching and work in light of expectations to publish; a session devoted to University Governance and the placement of English departments within the college as a whole; a session exploring definitions of the "intellectual life" within and outside of local colleges; a session devoted to the effects of the publish-or-perish mandate on the lives of new assistant professors at the Research I universities; a session devoted to professionalism, focusing on conference presentation skills for both academic and nonacademic careers; and sessions devoted to syllabi and teaching philosophies.

3. *A series of mini-conferences on teaching in Chicago's diverse colleges.* Chairs and program directors at local colleges will describe recent staffing decisions. Whom have they hired and why? What kind of teaching experience do they look for? Guest speakers will include local and regional people whose careers are dedicated to discussions of teaching. Speakers would explore how perceptions about student differences translate into differing pedagogical practices. The UIC Graduate Student Organization will work with the PFF program to conduct an all-day symposium for doctoral students devoted to The Academic Career.

4. *An online PFF network unit will attempt to foster an intellectual partnership among English and writing teachers within the Chicago area.* This consortium will meet online to discuss issues of pedagogy as well as quality of life for professors who do not teach at Research I institutions.

5. *A writing PFF network unit: UIC is in the process of establishing computerlinked classes (especially in composition) with lecturers who hold appointments at both the research granting institution and one of the participating four-year colleges.* Lecturers and TAs would use their work to begin discussions about how distinctions between institutional missions and academic cultures affect pedagogical practices.

Redefining the Introductory Writing Program as a Partnership Network

At UIC, the first-year writing program has begun developing partnerships with neighboring agencies and institutions. These partnerships are structured as Collaborative Learning Network units. As in the case of the PFF initiative, Writing Program staff members are released from teaching first-year writing classes and funded to work instead at a community agency or school with whatever projects are appropriate—writing grants, reports, newsletters, or developing a literacy program. The composition staff member then returns to the writing classroom to design and teach "engaged" courses in which students learn, write about, and apply their knowledge in local, urban settings.

As a CLN, the Writing Partners Program is based on notions of partnership and engagement rather than the deficit relationship implied by the term service, which suggests that the community or society at large, has certain needs, and the university, as the home of experts, will fill these needs, often without any engagement with the community. In this earlier model, researchers used the community as a "laboratory, with more or less compliant 'guinea pigs'" (Wiewel and Broski 16). Within the Writing Partners Program–CLN, creating, applying, and disseminating knowledge depends as much on how community residents and agencies understand and analyze problems as it does on how academics understand them. This new emerging model for knowledge production, rather than being guided by the conventions of a particular discipline, is organized and carried out in response to a particular local problem. Whereas the quality of traditional research is typically determined by peer review, the productivity of a CLN project is judged by its success in ameliorating the problems it addresses as evaluated by the persons experiencing the problem.

As the role of the university changes in relation to social and economic developments, so the role of the writing course and the writing program must also change. It should no longer be seen as providing essential, basic services required for success in university life. The notion that the university

is capable of providing such services is, in fact, a myth. Instead, the teaching of writing should be seen in parallel to the work of the university, contributing to, encouraging, and sustaining inquiries that match the research endeavors of the faculty. One of the aims of the program is to give students a
strong sense that there is a dynamic connection between knowledge about writing and action-centered research. Mary Walshok argues that knowledge needs
to be "connected to sustaining civic culture" and requires "critical thinking
skills and familiarity with humanistic and intellectual knowledge sources as
well as opportunities to participate in communities of discourse that can facilitate insight and understanding" (79). This view of a writing program goes
beyond what is typically seen as the goal of an undergraduate curriculum—
learning how to compose standard documents. Writing programs should place
themselves squarely in the middle of this ongoing discussion, arguing for a
substantial role in preparing students to participate in sustaining civic culture. Writing needs to be understood as engaged work that is required to
respond to social problems, not as the imitation of some published author's
prose.

The Writing Partners Program brings to the writing scene (not necessarily
a classroom) a firsthand sense of the connection between urban issues and the
need to be articulate in order to respond to them. Seeing writing instruction as
central to the work of an engaged university changes its role from providing
an isolated skill to providing an intellectual lynchpin for the engaged academic
work that will follow in subsequent years.

In a reformed introductory writing program, students study writing as a
way to promote civic responsiveness and academic direction. Moreover, when
we conceptualize our relationships with others as partnerships rather than as
service, we move from a one-way relationship of disseminating knowledge and
charity to a two-way relationship in which knowledge and resources flow to
the community and back to the university. The Writing Partners Program links
community agencies, writing instructors, and first-year writing students into
a Collaborative Learning Network in which the flow of information, support,
and activity is reciprocal. The community agency forwards its own agenda; the
writing instructor broadens her professional and scholarly profile; and students
engage in writing activity in the context of social issues.

Ordinarily, when students participate in a community setting, what they
learn there is connected to the academic inquiry underway in a writing class
that examines the issues from a scholarly perspective. The notion of partnership suggests a more complex view of how civic engagement might find its way
into writing programs. Rather than focus on service activities to supplement a
curriculum, we focus on engaging students in a specific intellectual context that
will help them understand how writing might function as a means of production
in that context. Our concern mirrors that of Judith Shapiro, cultural anthropol-
ogist and president of Barnard College, who characterizes the challenge from
the perspective of a social scientist:

Many undergraduates today demonstrate impressive levels of civic engagement in the form of community service. They serve meals in soup kitchens, work in homeless shelters, and staff AIDS hot lines. They work as interns in a variety of social agencies. Too few of them, however, are able to raise their eyes to the level of policy and social structure. They need the sociological imagination to see how their on-the-ground activities fit into a bigger picture, so that more of them can cross the bridge from serious moral commitment to effective political participation. (B4)

When we teach writing in a CLN, the loop is not closed until knowledge from this project informs curriculum in the writing program at UIC. As described before, graduate students and lecturers design their own courses based on the conceptual framework and guidelines outlined here.

Needs Met by Collaborative Learning Network Curriculums

As English departments continue to evolve in the early decades of the twenty-first century, they face a number of institutional challenges. Collaborative Learning Network curriculums address some of our current needs. Many English departments have relatively large faculties by comparison with other departments in the university. English departments, however, typically run several distinctive programs and the size of the faculty associated with particular programs is likely to be very small. Often English department faculties are too small to staff a comprehensive graduate program. As a result, graduate students find themselves unable to take the courses they need to complete their programs. Independent study courses are little more than a stop-gap solution. Since a CLN-oriented curriculum draws on courses taught by faculty in other departments, it can help in such situations.

A correlative problem is that declining enrollments in graduate programs in English makes it difficult to keep undersubscribed courses afloat even when they may be required courses in a particular program. If only a handful of students enroll in a program and if some of those are M.A. students returning for a Ph.D., then it can easily happen that important program courses may be underenrolled. Again, a Collaborative Learning Network curriculum can help in such situations.

In most departments, subject area specialists rarely have colleagues who share the same intellectual interests in a specific topic. For many years, specialists participated in intellectual networks focused on their areas of expertise by joining national societies, attending conferences devoted to their subject, or traveling to the major conferences such as NCTE, CCCCs, and MLA. Prompted by advances in technology, many intellectual networks have migrated to the Internet. Collaborative Learning Networks, however, offer a much richer environment in which to work. A CLN typically uses an integrated set of technologies that range from the familiar listservs and websites to online forums, databases, publications, chat rooms, and video conferencing. The gains are considerable. Since Collaborative Learning Networks link departments like English, which traditionally are weak in technological skills, with departments like computer science or engineering, access to sophisticated modes of communication is much easier.

Collaborative Learning Networks are also cost efficient. By collaborating with other departments, needless duplication in staff and equipment is avoided—for example, several departments can share the costs of a technical support staff and equipment. Since it is not realistic to replace, retrain, or relocate faculty who have not been trained in the use of technology, CLNs linking several departments can provide opportunities for the faculty and students in those departments to learn how to use the new technologies.

Most departments do not have $1,000,000 Immersion virtual-reality caves to use as classrooms. Nor do they have Polycom plasma screens and broadband hookups to run video conferences. They rarely even have projectors that can flash images from computer screens to classroom screens. This list can easily be extended: VCR editing equipment, software like Macromedia's Director, digital cameras, and so on. It should be noted that the collaborators in the Virtual Harlem learning network have access to all of this equipment "on the job" and much more even though most of them are not members of the Electronic Visualization Lab where most of it is housed.

With respect to outreach needs, university professors, and English professors in particular, have public relations (PR) problems on several fronts. These problems are significant enough that the MLA has hired a full-time PR staff person to address them. Most difficulties stem from our intellectual isolationism and insularity. By treating nonuniversity personnel as co-workers, Collaborative Learning Networks can go a long way toward responding to this need. They also respond to the criticism of members of English departments as researchers whose work has nothing to do with anyone but themselves as students of arcane and useless arts.

The relationship between universities and their near neighbors is often a troubled one. Universities rarely contribute to adjacent neighborhoods and usually focus their research interests on governments and corporations who are at a distance. Although English department members usually do not think of themselves as research resources for their neighbors, the types of partnerships and CLNs we have discussed here obviously can respond to the needs of universities' neighbors and at the same time enliven faculty intellectual pursuits.

Increasingly, social service agencies feel the need to provide literacy activities that will offer clients opportunities for life skills and personal expressions that are otherwise unavailable. In addition, a UIC Writing Partners Program can offer immediate hands-on assistance to a busy development person or to a director who may have more writing projects than the agency can complete.

Similarly, people often are not able to take courses on campus even when they are offered in the evening. This has spawned a distance-education industry, and, in many areas, has produced very powerful delivery systems for the acquisition of information. CLNs provide quite a different model of learning even though it takes place at a distance. It seems obvious that not everyone will find the current versions of distance education viable learning environments, especially persons who need to have skills that cannot be learned as passive recipients of information. This is particularly true in the humanities. Information about Harlem in the thirties is not the same as a virtual experience of Harlem in the thirties nor is the passive reception of such information the same learning experience as the collaborative building of the virtual model of Harlem.

The virtues of such networked CLNs may have particular significance for public institutions because they usually have extremely limited resources and are understaffed. The Virtual Harlem project shows how a university research project can respond to the needs of public institutions. In the Chicago area, most high schools do not have sophisticated computer-assisted learning technologies. Yet, it is possible for them not only to share the materials created for Virtual Harlem on the low-end technologies they own, but also to visit university campuses, which provides occasions for sharing viewpoints, data, responses, and ideas. In projects, such as Virtual Harlem, it is possible for high school students to play significant roles.

What unites all these changes is that they respond to the changing needs of graduate students. We hope to make our program one that prepares future faculty for the future they are likely to encounter. The profile of the twenty-first-century researcher, even in the humanities, will include the practices that Collaborative Learning Networks foster—collaborating, boundary crossing, telecommunicating, networking, modeling, and designing.

We believe that Collaborative Learning Networks are the wave of the educational future—networks of schoolhouses in our global village. This wave brings with it both great promise and great peril.

Works Cited

Berlin, James A. *Rhetoric and Reality*. Urbana, IL: NCTE, 1987.

Crowley, Sharon. *Composition in the University*. Pittsburgh: U of Pittsburgh P, 1998.

Graff, Gerald. *Professing Literature*. Chicago: U of Chicago P, 1987.

McLuhan, Marshall. *The Global Village-Transformations in World Life and Media in the 21st Century*. New York: Oxford UP, 1992.

Miller, Susan. *Assuming the Positions: Cultural Pedagogy and the Politics of Commonplace Writing*. Pittsburgh: U of Pittsburgh P, 1997.

Miller, Richard E. *As If Learning Mattered: Reforming Higher Education*. Ithaca, NY: Cornell UP, 1998.

Shapiro, Judith. "From Sociological Illiteracy to Sociological Imagination." *The Chronicle of Higher Education* (30 March 2000): A68.

Shumway, David. *Creating American Civilization: A Genealogy of American Literature as an Academic Discipline.* Minneapolis: U of Minnesota P, 1994.

Sosnoski, James. *Token Professionals and Master Critics.* Binghamton, NY: SUNY P, 1990.

Tompkins, Jane. *A Life in School.* Reading, MA: Perseus Books, 1996.

Walshok, Mary Lindenstein. *Knowledge Without Boundaries: What America's Universities Can Do for the Economy, the Workplace, and the Community.* San Francisco: Jossey-Bass, 1995.

Wiewel, Wim, and David Broski. "University Involvement in the Community: Developing a Partnership Model." *Renaissance* 1 (1996): 16–23.

Afterword

Paula Mathieu and Claude Mark Hurlbert

"Our educational system is not a public service, but an instrument of special privilege; its purpose is not to further the welfare of mankind, but merely to keep America capitalist" (18). Upton Sinclair wrote these words in 1923 in *Goosestep: A Study of American Education*. This self-published 488-page work encompasses a detailed accounting of the influence of business on university education in 1920s' America. In researching the book, Sinclair traveled to twenty-five cities, interviewed thousands of people, and studied investment portfolios of dozens of universities to get a sense of the inner workings of their boards of trustees, presidencies, and curricular offerings. The resulting ninety-three chapters explore, in witty yet earnest detail, the shaping power of business on universities as well as the power of universities to act as businesses. He renames institutions like Columbia, Harvard, and the University of Chicago with telling titles, such as "The University of the House of Morgan," "The University of Lee-Higgison," and "The University of Standard Oil," as he details the holdings of their endowments and the occupations of their trustees. It is not through monopoly control, but through a system Sinclair names "interlocking directorates" that the interests of business exert control on higher education:

> There is a great university, of which Mr. Morgan was all his active life a trustee, also his son-in-law and one or two of his attorneys and several of his bankers. The president of the university is a director in one of Mr. Morgan's life insurance companies.... If the president of the university writes a book, this may be published by a concern in which Mr. Morgan (or a partner) is a director, and the paper may be bought from the International Paper Company, in which Mr. Morgan has a director through the Guaranty Trust Company. If you visit the town where the paper is made, you will find that the president of the local school board is a director in the local bank, which deposits its funds with the Guaranty Trust Company at a low rate of interest, to be reloaned by Mr. Morgan at a high rate of interest. The superintendent of schools will be a graduate of Mr. Morgan's university, and will have been recommended to the school board president by Mr. Morgan's dean of education.... (22–24)

We are far from the 1920s. The economic rules have changed since Sinclair's writing, but the game persists. Instead of a few well-known robber

barons spearheading control of university education, today's system of interlocking directorates includes a larger number of corporations with more highly
diversified investment portfolios. Even so, Sinclair's point that wealth's control
of education is not conspiratorial or unified persists. Moneyed interests inter-
lock and work together to make education cost-efficient, not from a base of
coordinated efforts, but out of generally shared interests and goals. Not all economic agendas are detrimental to education, but many of them are, especially
when economic priorities supplant educational ones.

Sinclair's analysis shows that universities are not only the objects of corporate interest; they are businesses themselves, with national and international
ties:

> Whoever you are, and wherever you live in America, you cannot spend
> a day, you can hardly spend an hour of your life, without paying tribute
> to Columbia University. I took a journey of seven thousand miles,
> and traveled on fourteen railroads. I observed that every one of these
> railroads is included in [Columbia's stock portfolio], so on every mile
> of my journey I was helping to build up the Columbia machine. I helped
> to build it up when I lit the gas in my lodging-house room in New York;
> for Columbia University owns $58,000 worth of New York Gas and
> Electric Light. . . . I helped to build it up when I telephoned my friends
> to make engagements, for Columbia University owns $50,000 worth
> of the New York Telephone Company. . . . I helped to build it up when
> I took a spoonful of sugar with my breakfast, for Columbia University
> owns some shares in the American Sugar Refining Company, and also
> in the Cuba Cane Sugar Corporation. . . . Crossing the desert on my
> way home, in the baking heat of summer I saw far out in the barren
> mountains a huge copper smelter, vomiting clouds of yellow smoke
> into the air. We in the Pullman sat in our shirt-sleeves, with electric
> fans playing and white-clad waiters bringing us cool drinks. Even so,
> we suffered from the heat; yet out there in those lonely wastes men
> toil in front of the furnace fires, and when they drop they are turned to
> mummies in the baking sand and their names are not recorded. Not a
> thought of them . . . troubles the minds of the thirty thousand seekers
> of higher learning who flock to Columbia University every year. With
> serene consciences these young people cultivate the graces of life,
> upon the income of $49,000 worth of stock in the American Smelters
> Securities Company. (24–25)

Sinclair's work represents a thorough example of institutional
storytelling—combining economic data with details about the people effect-
ing and being affected by university decisions. Every institution is both representative of larger economic trends and possesses unique local identities,
economic portfolios, and objectives forged in part by a nexus of interlocking interests. Even when English faculty face common obstacles, such as departmental

cutbacks and restructuring, the threats to our work take on unique characteristics at each institution. We would benefit from more work as thorough as Sinclair's research, at many institutions.[1]

Several writers in this collection tell hard truths about their local institutions—stories of initiatives gone wrong, mad desires to meet market demands, and the ways teachers and students lose out. One infrequently reads stories like these in a book collection. Since programs, departments, and universities are comprised of people fulfilling institutional roles, the playing out of institutional battles often takes on personal tones. Cutbacks and restructuring can occur as painful fights, even among colleagues. Discussing these experiences as institutional problems happens too infrequently. More often, institutional stories are circulated as gossip about personal bitterness or not told at all, because we mistakenly personalize economic issues and deem them unworthy of public discussion. This attitude of not wanting to "talk out of school" is an outdated notion of collegiality. When collegiality functions in this way, it is nothing more than a polite protocol that keeps us separate and silent rather than working together. As Hurlbert and Blitz argue, we need new forms of collegiality, ones that look toward humane ways of telling hard truths and communally assessing our own institutions.

"I really believe in truth, and in the power of truth to confute error," writes Sinclair, who continues:

> I take my stand on the sentence of Wendell Phillips: "If anything cannot stand the truth, let it crack." What I ask for is free discussion; what I want in the colleges is that both faculty and students should have opportunity to hear all sides of all questions, and especially those questions which lie at the heart of the great class struggle of our time. (474)

We recognize that making calls for truth-telling may seem hopelessly nostalgic in this age when the notion of truth has been rigorously attacked from theoretical, rhetorical, and political positions. But when we are talking about the lives of people—students, faculty, staff, and the public that is supposed to benefit from the presence of universities—it is necessary to determine whose needs are being met, what interests are being served, and who loses out in a given institution.

Truth-telling, however, is not an end in itself. We need institutional stories to understand our positions in order to imagine new and better ways of teaching English or organizing our work lives in relation to students and institutions. Two years ago, when we began this book with David Downing, we discussed Bill Readings' *The University in Ruins*. We tried to imagine teaching in light of Readings' proposal that we make questions of thought and social bonds the center of curricula: What is thought? What can and can't be thought? Who or what is served by our thinking? How does our teaching fulfill our obligations to others?

Several writers in this collection engage in visionary work, offering new ideas and justifications for English studies. "Ideas—technological, social, economic—are the basis for a better world; they must be learned, taught, and tested in the real world. Only when academics perform this function can they claim to be authentic professionals" (Smith 262). All plans conceive visions of utopia; proposed futures prompt critical examination of the present in ways that resist lapsing into cynicism. To teach to sustain our planet, to create networks of reciprocal engagement with community members, to rewrite vocationalism in order to place the acquisition of skills in a holistic view of life are just some ways to *re*think our work in English studies. We need these visions and others, to push English studies beyond English, Inc.

Note

1. This kind of work is being done by some activist groups and researchers. See, for example, note 1 in this book's Introduction, Smith, and Teachers for a Democratic Culture.

Works Cited

Hurlbert, C. Mark, and Michael Blitz. "Shadows of Collegiality." In Regina Paxton Foehr, ed., *Shadows in the University.* Portsmouth, NH: Boynton/Cook Heinemann (forthcoming).

Readings, Bill. *The University in Ruins.* Cambridge: Harvard UP, 1996.

Sinclair, Upton. *The Goose-Step: A Study of American Education.* Published by the author, 1923.

Smith, Jeremy. "Faculty, Students and Political Engagement." *Chalk Lines: The Politics of Working in the Managed University.* Ed. Randy Martin. Durham, NC: Duke UP, 1998. 249–63.

Contributors

DAVID B. DOWNING: Department of English, Indiana University of Pennsylvania

CLAUDE MARK HURLBERT: Department of English, Indiana University of Pennsylvania

PAULA MATHIEU: Department of English, Boston College

DAVID BLEICH: Department of English, University of Rochester

CHARLES BERNSTEIN: Department of English, State University of New York, Buffalo

DANIEL COLLINS: Department of English, Manhattan College

JUANITA RODGERS COMFORT: Department of English, West Chester University

ELLEN CUSHMAN: Department of English, Michigan State University

AMY GOODBURN: Department of English, University of Nebraska-Lincoln

ANN FELDMAN: Department of English, University of Illinois at Chicago

MAURICE KILWEIN GUEVARA: Department of English, Indiana University of Pennsylvania

PATRICIA HARKIN: Department of English, University of Illinois at Chicago

DEBORAH HOLDSTEIN: Department of English, Governor's State University

BRUCE HORNER: Department of English, University of Wisconsin, Milwaukee

KELLY LATCHAW: Department of English, Drake University

JOSEPH LENZ: Department of English, Drake University

DEBORAH MINTER: Department of English, University of Nebraska-Lincoln

JOYCE MAGNOTTO NEFF: Professional Communication Program, Old Dominion University

RICHARD OHMANN: Professor Emeritus, Department of English, Wesleyan University

DEREK OWENS: Department of English, St. John's University

ROB POPE: School of Humanities, Oxford Brookes University

PANCHO SAVERY: Department of English, Reed College

JAMES SEITZ: Department of English, University of Pittsburgh

JAMES SOSNOSKI: Department of Communications, University of Illinois at Chicago

DAVID STACEY: Department of English, Humboldt State University

JODY SWILKY: Department of English, Drake University

DAVID WOLF: Department of English, Drake University

CLAIRE WOODS: Centre for Professional and Public Communication, University of South
     Australia

JAMES ZEBROSKI: The Writing Program, Syracuse University